PR
4803 **REF** Critical essays on
.H44 Gerard Manley
C77 Hopkins.
1990

$40.00

DATE			

D1116212

Critical Essays on
Gerard Manley Hopkins

Critical Essays on Gerard Manley Hopkins

Alison G. Sulloway

G. K. Hall & Co. • Boston, Massachusetts

Library of Congress Cataloging in Publication Data

Critical essays on Gerard Manley Hopkins / [selected by] Alison G.
   Sulloway.
       p. cm. — (Critical essays on British literature)
       Includes index.
       ISBN 0-8161-8773-8
       1. Hopkins, Gerard Manley. 1844–1889 — Criticism and interpreta-
   tion.   I. Sulloway, Alison G.   II. Series.
    PR4803.H44C77 1990   89-15491
     821'.8 — dc20   CIP

This publication is printed on permanent/durable acid-free paper
MANUFACTURED IN THE UNITED STATES OF AMERICA

84702008

CRITICAL ESSAYS ON
BRITISH LITERATURE

The collection of essays Alison G. Sulloway chose as a centennial commemoration of Gerard Manley Hopkins's death represents an attempt both to suggest and to transcend the traditional critical conflict between the priest and the poet, the medieval scholar and the ardent and discerning commentator on the tumultuous Victorian age that shaped his poetry. Sulloway's selection indicates the force and stress of Hopkins's internal and environmental difficulties, and suggests that Hopkins achieved a far greater reconciliation with his kaleidoscopic and sometimes warring selves than much current and early Hopkins scholarship admits.

Two of these essays openly acknowledge the Jesuit or apocalyptic signatures upon the poet, the poems, and their readers, whether late Victorian or modern, lay or Jesuit. Three others describe different varieties of Victorian temperament, while five others, with widely varying attention to Hopkins the Jesuit, study the poet as poet. One essay significantly expands and alters the traditional assumptions about Hopkins's parents and what he might have inherited from each of them. But no matter how diverse these essays are in their purposes and treatment of the poet and the poetry, their collection in one place demonstrates why Hopkins's work enjoys an ever-growing international admiration among readers of every religious persuasion, as well as among those of none.

ZACK BOWEN, GENERAL EDITOR

University of Miami

CONTENTS

ABBREVIATIONS

Poems, or *P: The Poems of Gerard Manley Hopkins*, 4th ed., ed. W. H. Gardner and Norman Mackenzie (London: Oxford University Press, 1967). The numbers following the abbreviation refer either to the number of the poem, or when followed by a comma, to the page where the poem is to be found. Most scholars referring to poem numbers refer to this edition, and thereafter merely to the appropriate poem number.

Journals, or *J: The Journals and Papers of Gerard Manley Hopkins*, ed. Humphry House and Graham Story (London: Oxford University Press, 1959).

Sermons, or *S: The Sermons and Devotional Writings of Gerard Manley Hopkins*, ed. Christopher Devlin, S.J. (London: Oxford University Press, 1959).

Letters I, *Letters* 1, *B*, or *LB: The Letters of Gerard Manley Hopkins to Robert Bridges*, 2d impr., ed. Claude Colleer Abbott (London: Oxford University Press, 1955).

Letters II, *Letters* 2, *D*, or *CD: The Correspondence of Gerard Manley Hopkins and Richard Watson Dixon*, 2d impr., ed. Claude Colleer Abbott (London: Oxford University Press, 1956).

Letters III, *Letters* 3, or *FL: Further Letters of Gerard Manley Hopkins, Including His Correspondence with Coventry Patmore*, 2d ed., ed. Claude Colleer Abbott (London: Oxford University Press, 1956).

INTRODUCTION

Literary scholarship is one of the most ambiguous of all the intellectual arts. Scientists, on the one hand, are required to attempt to achieve clinical objectivity and, furthermore, to assume that they have achieved it. Poets, on the other hand, or artists in any medium, have society's permission to be subjective, to consult their most private selves. But literary scholars, and particularly conceptual literary scholars,[1] must adopt both these opposing methods to uncover as many truths about artists' work and the cultural climates that helped to shape their work as fallible human beings are capable of grasping about other fallible and often elusive human beings. These scholars must thus submit to an uneasy oscillation between empathy and objectivity, allowing neither the one nor the other critical perspective to compromise their services to their subjects. In fairness to their readers, they must explicate the successes and the failures of their subjects as coolly as a technician surveys the successes or failures of an experimental protocol. At the same time, they must carefully scrutinize themselves to be sure that hidden assumptions about their own sex, their own age, or their own historical, religious, social, political, or economic mind-sets permit them to do justice, however partial it must be, to the world and the works of these writers. At best, they can also be radically moved by their subjects, but at the very least, they must seriously respect the aims and the written records of those to whom they intend to give new life.

On the whole, Hopkins has escaped the critical attention of the most mortal of scholarly sinners, the creators of "pathographies," or critical biographies that contain nothing but a hostile litany of their subjects' mental or anatomical pathologies, and thus leave a false record of defenseless writers, in which "a true malevolence seems to be the guiding motive."[2] Daniel Harris, the author of *Inspiration Unbidden: "The Terrible Sonnets" of Gerard Manley Hopkins*, is often accused of this scholarly mortal sin, and his critical biography, which challenges the accepted compositional order of the last sonnets, does indeed concentrate almost exclusively on the pathologies of which Hopkins condemned himself so often and in so much agony of spirit. But Harris's study is full of love for his subject, and its prose sometimes seems to mirror Hopkins's own pain, even while Harris achieves the objectivity toward Hopkins's distress that the poet-priest himself struggled to maintain, so as to preserve the sanity that he thought might well be in question.

Robert Boyle, S. J., subjects Hopkins to a fairly severe scrutiny concerning his sins of commission and omission, but again, Boyle's essay, which appears here, is a Jesuit professor's profoundly affectionate and respectful attempt to describe his dead colleague's difficulties as priest and poet, as well as the ultimate heroism and the triumphs, which Boyle recounts with praiseworthy evenhandedness.[3]

Nonetheless, readers do encounter difficulties with Hopkins scholarship. For instance, some Jesuits now discuss certain painful truths about Hopkins, while other Jesuits deny these same truths if they are brought forth for discussion by non-Catholics. Occasionally readers encounter scholars who concentrate entirely on the doctrine embedded in Hopkins's poetry, without any apparent awareness that Hopkins was a poet, and that most readers first encounter Hopkins as a poet, and that for most readers, even the most devout Catholics, the doctrine emerges first *as* poetry. Moreover, faithful as these poems are to the meditative aims and techniques of the Ignatian *Spiritual Exercises*, they are not sermons, lectures, or tracts; such dense yet shimmering language cannot be transposed into prose doctrine. It is important for readers to remember that Saint Ignatius Loyola himself possessed a very capacious yet subtle mind, and so did Hopkins, his disciple. Often a slight shift in prosodic techniques such as rhyme, rhythm, alliteration, or word-choice, or even the placement of a single word, indicates a subtle shift or modification of doctrine.

At times, it is quite legitimate to divorce the subject of Hopkins the poet, *as* poet, from other, wider considerations. For example, two of the essays in this collection do so, in order to offer new perspectives, one on Hopkins's parents and the other upon the topic of Hopkins's Jesuit readers and admirers, early and late. Both these essays correct mistaken assumptions about Hopkins, and therefore they both should help to modify interpretations of his poems.[4]

While some readers seem to ignore the poetry as poetry, even when they attempt to discuss it, others clearly want to divorce the poet from *The Spiritual Exercises* of Saint Ignatius Loyola, Hopkins's richest source and the most obvious shaper of his themes, his language, and all his other prosodic techniques. For example, alert readers sometimes suspect that even Robert Bridges, Hopkins's first editor, to whom admirers of the poetry owe so much, launched the 1918 edition of the poems fully as much to condemn the Jesuits for all of Hopkins's distress, as to praise the poetry of his dead friend. Hopkins's reputation as an eccentric was well-known at Oxford and it had followed him to Oxford from Highgate, his public school. As an Oxonian in Hopkins's class, Bridges should have known better. In any case, whatever his motives may have been in this publishing venture, he often misread the poetry and blamed the Jesuits for difficulties that had already afflicted Hopkins long before he joined the Society of Jesus.

Even now, after decades of Hopkins scholarship that pays tribute to the poet in the priest as well as to the priest in the poet, and thus comes closer to the readership that Hopkins craved, one may encounter such simplistic judgments as the willful assumption that Hopkins's poetry was *merely* the fruit of buried or frustrated homosexual impulses, or *merely* a sublimated record of neocommunism and a Carlylean fear that the upper classes were unfit to rule, a false assumption that William Thesing's essay in this collection neatly lays to rest.[5] Immature or biased readers will still sometimes stoutly maintain that Hopkins's poetry is *really* an eliptic admission of post-Darwinian cynicism; such readers are deaf to the difference between a poet who repeatedly calls upon his God to come to him, as troubled children cry out to their mothers, and a poet who assumes that evolution has replaced the Christian Trinity as a historical fact. Tom Zaniello's essay in this collection, "A 'Beautiful but Broken Arc,' " describes how easily, on the whole, Hopkins and other "Stonyhurst Philosophers" reconciled modern curiosity about Darwin with the teachings of Saint Ignatius Loyola.[6]

To a painful extent, Hopkins himself was responsible, not so much for any of these careless assumptions, but certainly for the controversy over whether the priest in him ruined the poet, or the poet and the eccentric in him so fatally compromised his Ignatian commitments as to leave him almost in a state of despair that constitutes mortal sin. As one Jesuit epitaph frankly stated, "It has been alleged that he ought never to have been a Jesuit," and furthermore, that "to those who knew Gerard Manley Hopkins his career will always suggest the idea of a tragedy."[7] Christopher Devlin, also a Jesuit and the editor of Hopkins's sermons and devotional writings, offered a more sanguine explanation of the distress that Hopkins so often described: "A man, in order to manage his nature, has sometimes to lay more stress in one direction than is ideally right, for fear that, if he tries merely to keep the balance, he will be overthrown. . . . But in such cases a man is a surer judge of others' problems than of his own." Not only did Hopkins inherit a considerable strain of Cartesian dualism, but, as Devlin also suggests, he had acquired an equally noticeable strain of its more modern version, "the Victorian code of ethics" and a certain "Jansenistic spirit" that "crept at times into Catholic spirituality," and that "corresponded with the severe educational and religious ideals current in England at that time." Devlin offers an ethically rich and subtle suggestion, which is almost rhetorically sylleptic: "It may be mentioned in passing that the deliberate refusal to allow desire and choice to be separated was the main inspiration of seventeenth-century religious art and poetry. As soon as the separation is sanctioned, the beauty begins to go out of religion and the certitude out of art." Devlin says quite justifiably:

"All this, it is clear, Hopkins knew very well and kept deepening the knowledge of it."[8]

Devlin's warning is useful in assisting readers to guard against forcing arbitrarily irreconcilable conflicts between the priest, the poet, and the very astute Victorian whose comments upon his age sometimes have the secular authority associated with the modern social sciences and the studies of trained environmentalists. In fact, Hopkins's empirical comments on the inevitability of global extinction, based as they were upon the evidences of history and of current human behavior, were often immensely useful to the social rebels of the 1960s and after, those heirs in many ways of the Victorian age of turmoil. Hopkins grieved as much as the secular prophets were later to do over the results of pervasive human greed and recklessness, and the misshapened relations between the men in power and various disenfranchised peoples under their control.

Nonetheless, the secular prophets of a potential apocalypse if human history were to continue in its usual fashion almost always made the same mistake, in adapting Hopkins to their own purposes, as other interpreters of the poetry who attempted to separate the Jesuit priest from the Victorian poet. Hopkins not only looked backward to the biblical account of human origins, and to the origins of these origins, but he also looked apprehensively forward to the Second Coming and to the extinction of human time. Yet he was firmly grounded in his own time, as a discrete portion of divine and human history, just as he addressed the essential need of each human's private apocalypse, which would be individually necessary as a preparation for personal death.

But when the secular prophets stripped Hopkins's apocalyptic vision from its origins in Saint John's Apocalypse, they misunderstood his sense of the apocalypse as both a private and a public event, and thus weakened his warning: individual Christians could help to forestall the end of human time on earth, if they all imitated the conduct of the first humans before the Fall, but since time's end had been prophesied in Saint John's Apocalypse, they could not prevent it forever. They could only confront it in their private relationships with the creator and with other creatures.

David Downes's essay in this collection corrects the mistakes of the secular prophets who read Hopkins at a glance and abstract what they want for political reasons, while they vigorously deny that there is anything else to be found. Downes works through the poetry to its ultimate source in scripture, and most strikingly, in Saint John's revelations. In this way Downes reveals the hope and the radiance in Hopkins's vision as well as its bleakness.[9]

Scholars of Hopkins's life and works need not accept the poet-priest's theological vision for themselves, in order to do justice to it. But if they are to remain even partially faithful to *his* vision and to *his* centers of being, rather than merely their own, which is all that most readers can achieve in the service of this prismatic Victorian, they must never set themselves in opposition to his perceptions. The essays in this collection were all selected in order to demonstrate some essential part of what Hopkins perceived himself to be, how he became what he became, and how we now perceive him a hundred years after his death.

Hopkins was not trained in both Oxonian logic and Ignatian logic for nothing. Denials of the poetry's sources in scripture thus distort not only the context, in order to stress the dualism of its radiance and its bleakness, but also Hopkins's constant search, in an almost Ciceronian way, for predictable causes and effects, as both his Oxonian tutors and his Jesuit superiors had taught him to account for the connections between them. His theological training had persuaded him that the Satanic rejection of God and the Edenic disobedience that automatically followed were the primary causes of ugly human relationships described throughout scriptural and secular history. But since free will and the ultimate responsibility of each human being is involved, Hopkins had to explain some anomalies, such as that each sinner was and was not responsible for sin.

According to classical logic, a disastrous effect of some prior cause cannot be cured unless one first cures the cause. Each generation's refusal to heed all the divine warnings of the past and the present in turn compounded the long history of human sin, and thus created fresh moral disasters, which in turn would become the primary cause of future sinning generations, whose own sins would further endanger the lives, the time on earth, and even the chance for salvation of generations to come. Since the Bible itself offers an ominous record of one human debacle after the other, and since Hopkins perceived scripture to be the precursor of postscriptural history, he felt obliged to accept the prophecies of Saint John as absolutely as he accepted the certainty of his own eventual death.

Hopkins's capacity to live with the vision of both personal and global collapse, which we find in a significant portion of his poetry, and still function as a priest and poet, especially with the brilliance and even at times the serenity that he achieved, is a courageous example of his moral endurance, which often becomes a paradoxically reassuring spectacle for troubled readers of his poetry, as they confront one postindustrial armageddon after the other. Aside from the sheen and the technical virtuosity of his poetry, and aside from its celebration of God's pastoral gifts, its record of immense fortitude in the face of many obstacles appears to be one of the profound attractions of his poetry in several different countries and continents, for his readers have spread from all the English-speaking countries to Japan, Israel, and several countries where Romance languages are spoken.[10]

It is another of those Cartesian or Hopkinsian dualisms, which Hopkins so often managed to transform into healing paradoxes, that although the priest in him would have mourned whenever modern readers separate his priestly self from his poetic self, nevertheless his gifted self would have allowed him to rejoice that his death is being commemorated in many countries, and not least for the sheer dazzling inscapes of his poetry. For he believed that recalcitrant humans could sometimes be led to their creator if they were first enticed with a cornucopia of the creator's gifts in nature and in the best of human nature, and if artists were then to recreate these gifts in their own works. His theories of inscape and instress form a lovely sanctified circle, which is the benign equivalent of the malignant forward spiral of Satanic and human sin, and which is sometimes able to keep at bay anything approaching Manichaean dualities.

The circle moves from the creator to the inscapes of natural and human objects and on to the artist's selfless reproduction of them. Artists working reverently and ordinary humans performing their assigned tasks with diligence and good will, then complete the loop or circle by dedicating their efforts to their creator. The internal selves of the inscapes of things and people cause morally sensitive artists to instress them in poetry, music, or painting. The results of this instress in turn become fresh inscapes, ready to be instressed by others, who respond to them, at least ideally, by rededicating themselves to the greater glory of God.

Nor should artists neglect to re-create various forms of human sin, including a frank admission of their own sins, for these sins are all examples of God's creatures gone astray once again. Thus artifacts of reverent human design are not only forms of prayer and thanksgiving but also didactic warnings to the self and to others in the most palatable form. During Hopkins's most sanguine moments about his double role as priest and poet, he hoped that in these ways his poems would assist him in keeping his own Jesuit mission always before him, and might even move other fallible creatures from creation to the creator.

ALISON G. SULLOWAY

Virginia Polytechnic Institute

Notes

1. Bibliographical scholars understandably leave far less room for interpreting the books and titles under their scrutiny than critics, critical biographers, and literary historians devote to the worlds and the work of writers. The responsibility of these conceptual scholars is to *conceive*, or to reconceive, discrete works, lives, or intellectual settings of particular times and writers.

2. Joyce Carol Oates, review of David Roberts's *Jean Stafford: A Biography, New York Times Book Review* (28 August 1988), 1.

3. Robert Boyle, S. J., " 'Man Jack the Man Is': *The Wreck* from the Perspective of 'The shepherd's brow,' " reprinted in this volume.

4. Norman White, "Kate, Manley, and Gerard: Hopkins and His Parents," and Joseph J. Feeney, S. J., "The Jesuit Recognition of Hopkins, 1889–1989," both reprinted in this volume.

5. William B. Thesing, "Gerard Manley Hopkins's Responses to the City: The 'Composition of the Crowd,' " reprinted in this volume.

6. Tom Zaniello, "A 'Beautiful But Broken Arc,' " reprinted in this volume. Hopkins does not belong in J. Hillis Miller's *The Disappearance of God: Five Nineteenth-Century Writers*. Hopkins's dialogues with the first two persons of the Trinity are not evidences that he thought there was no God. Instead they are conversations with beloved adversaries whose presence in *his* life was overwhelming, but who had withdrawn their favor from him. This phenomenon was perfectly familiar to medieval saints and later to Saint Ignatius Loyola, and as Father Devlin reminds his readers, it is one of those problems "which all who aim at holiness have to solve" (*Sermons*, 120). Among Miller's five writers, Emily Bronte's poetic meditations about God acknowledged some dimly outlined cosmic purposes in male form, whereas De Quincey, Browning, and Matthew Arnold are often closer to agnosticism than to a fully articulate practicing faith. The difference in context between these four writers, especially the three men, and Hopkins, is enormous.

7. *Letters*, 1: 319–20.

8. *Sermons*, 119–20.

9. David Anthony Downes, "The First Apocalypse: 'The hour of fulfilment' in G. M. Hopkins," reprinted in this volume.

10. At one international conference, "Hopkins in Dublin," Summer 1984, eleven nations and four continents were represented. One of the finest papers was Rachel Salmon's "Frozen Fire: The Paradoxical Equation of 'That Nature is a Heraclitean Fire and of the comfort of the Resurrection,' " reprinted in this volume. Because of time constraints and other inevitable conference difficulties, the paper of this excellent Israeli scholar was given scandalously short shrift. It is especially fitting that it be reproduced from the *Hopkins Quarterly* (October 1985–January 1986), and that it reappear here in this centenary commemoration.

11. The Dublin Conference of 1984 also hosted Peter Milward, S. J., Professor at Sophia University in Tokyo, and some of his protégés. Father Milward has championed a whole generation of Hopkins scholars, through his teaching and through the *Bulletin of the Hopkins Society of Japan*, to say nothing of his own fine work on Hopkins, which explicates the priest through the poet as well as the poetry through the training of the Jesuits. Mugo Takano's lovely *Gerard Manley Hopkins: The Sensuous and the Austere* (Tokyo: Chido Publishing Co., 1983) is only one of many fruits of Milward's pedagogical mission.

Hopkins, Boy and Man

Kate, Manley, and Gerard: Hopkins and His Parents

Norman White*

"A true delineation of the smallest man, and his scene of pilgrimage through life," wrote Carlyle, at the beginning of his life of John Sterling, "is capable of interesting the greatest man; that all men are to an unspeakable degree brothers, each man's life a strange emblem of every man's; and that Human Portraits, faithfully drawn, are of all pictures the welcomest on human walls." Of all biographical subjects, however, Hopkins must be one of the most difficult to judge. His poetic genius went with a manic-depressive temperament of an unusual kind, and a frequent inability to find satisfaction in his intellectual and emotional environments. His major successes were in Heaven and posthumous books.

Hopkins's life did not have a neat shape, although there have been pressures to make it appear as though it did. In his inaugural lecture at Oxford in 1971, Richard Ellmann argued that a biography must have "a pattern of explanation," and that "some idea of the space between birth and death as processive, either an exfoliation, or a sharpening definition, will have to persist."[1] Its form is associated with history, and "must retain a chronological pattern"; it is comparable to that of the novel. In fact, Eric Homberger noted the similarity between Ellmann's own biographies and the Victorian three-decker novel, "with its impressionistic sketches of the contemporary scene, profusion of characters, and commitment to the narrative idea of a life shaped by experience."[2] But in "That Nature is a Heraclitean Fire and of the comfort of the Resurrection" Hopkins implied his agreement (so far as mortal life was concerned) with Pater's conclusion to the first edition of *The Renaissance:* "That clear, perpetual outline of face and limb is but an image of ours . . . a design in a web, the actual threads of which pass out beyond it. This at least of flamelike our life has, that it is but the concurrence, renewed from moment to moment, of forces parting sooner or later on their ways."

Everything is in motion, said Heraclitus, and nothing remains. Until he reached Oxford Gerard Hopkins's progress did not have a discernible

*This essay was specifically written for this volume and is published here for the first time by permission of the author.

empirical structure; it was rather a continual seizing and outstripping of the various potentials offered by his environment. His schooldays were far from having been the happiest of his life. School never became a minor religion with him, and he was not haunted by the poignancy of leaving; he was preparing for happiness and fulfillment elsewhere. Whereas for many of his contemporaries the university would be an anticlimax, for Hopkins the mystic rapture of childhood would be at Oxford.

Hopkins's first letters home from Oxford[3] all emphasize his rise in rank; his school had failed to give him, in his own adolescent reckoning, a secure basis for self-esteem. And his home life had also left him with a psychological need to do some catching up in rank and status and fitting intellectual pursuits. "I always find home so uncivilized," he wrote, "they never seem to be acquainted with the ordinary luxuries or necessaries." But their attitude towards his finances was only one minor aspect of a larger rift. In a letter to E. H. Coleridge[4] written in the March before he went up to Oxford he showed how he had felt held back by his family, who clung, when he wanted to engage in his own nonfamilial relationships. He wanted to meet Coleridge in the Long Vacation "far from Cyril," the brother whom his family thought should be his close companion. His letters to Oak Hill in his first Oxford term all try to impress the family back home, by allying himself with the Oxford Union, or with an MP's son, or with distinguished people whom he mentions with a purposeful casualness. He tries to establish a formal distance between Oak Hill and his world, to shake off their assumption of the right to treat him as still a child, to possess him, and to tell him what to do. He tries to diminish the Oak Hill world by denigrating Grandmamma's Oxford friend, or Cyril, or his father's assumed knowledge of Oxford.

A strong resentment comes through his letters at the end of the Hilary term, showing itself in different ways. In one letter he is resentful of his mother's strictness and makes out that it is pedantic and petty: "for 10 days I think; (ten days: I am afraid you will consider the numerals vulgar"; and this letter finishes with an ironic postscript, implying that his mother regarded his independent happiness among his Oxford contemporaries as a willful unkindness to her. In an earlier letter he had shown a sharpness and resentment at Mamma's telling him off for breaking a lamp, and a determination to be self-sufficient. His third and last surviving letter from that term started off with an open sharpness and resentment which had been somewhat submerged in the first two. He had been required by his parents to write to Aunt Kate, who had been widowed recently, and he had been blamed for not having written. To pay off this "gratuitous blame" and assert his independent rights he announced his decision to delay his return to Hampstead. His new world had become all-important, and Oak Hill more limited. At Hampstead, he wrote, "you can only see *The Times* and *Saturday* and nothing else, and the Church is dreary and friends talk of Oxford as if it were Samarkand or Bothnia Felix."

The relationship of Gerard Hopkins to his parents was described by Father Lahey in terms of neatly shaped direct influence. He was "a happy reincarnation of the many characteristics which gave to each of his parents a rare charm." Manley Hopkins's "love for the original and abstruse found an easy way into the mind of his son, as did also his poetic instinct." Kate Hopkins ("an unusually well-educated woman for that generation") "gave to her son her gentle nature and love for metaphysical speculation." She was "a keen student of philosophy, history and politics."[5] It would be unfair to be harsh with Lahey's brief and hasty pioneering study, but a different picture now needs to be drawn — one in which Kate and Manley Hopkins are seen as typical of their age, and their son as an extraordinary individual who was very different from them in most ways.

Kate Smith[6] had met Manley Hopkins while they were neighbors at Tower Hill, in the south-east corner of the City of London. This was Kate's area of London, though not Manley's. She was brought up almost on the north bank of the Thames, at one of its busiest and most filthy stretches, lively with boats, barges, and sailing-vessels. She lived in a large and mysterious Queen Anne house in Trinity Square, which lay between the river and the commercial part of the City. Kate and her six younger sisters and brothers were familiar with noisy lanes of a narrow, medieval pattern, cramped churches and alleyways, quays and wharves, warehouse-blocks, heavy wagons, cranes, and the smells of salt, rope, and cargoes.

Kate and her sisters used to go every day in fine weather to the Tower of London, on the opposite side of the Square to their home. They wandered within its walls, in the shade of the Beauchamp Tower, or along the pavement in front of the Armoury, and watched the soldiers at drill in a courtyard. It was an overwhelming and sombre experience for Kate:

> Raleigh's lodgings and the Bloody Tower were at the other side of the walk, which we approached under the archway of the Bloody Tower — I never once passed under it without a shudder or an awe-struck thought of the murdered princes. The very self-important Beefeaters filled me with a different but quite strong alarm. Sometimes we went on to the Tower Wharf and I used to have a vague fear that if I stayed anywhere I should be taken through the Traitors' Gate.

Her day was punctuated by drum-rolls, the 9:00 P.M. one being the signal for going to bed. Some of the most poignant and bloody moments of English history had been enacted at the Tower. Thirty yards from the Smiths' front door was the site of the scaffold on which More, Wyatt, Surrey, Laud, and the Duke of Monmouth had died. The Governor of the Tower had lived in their house during the 1745 rebellion, and the rebel lords had been executed just in front of it.

Trinity Square was still close to the center of some public events in Kate's childhood. On Tower Hill she witnessed the proclamation of William IV by a quaintly costumed herald throwing down a glove.

Cannons boomed and blazed on royal birthdays, or to celebrate an accession to the throne, or military victories. The whole family once lined up to see the Duke of Wellington emerging from a coach to visit Trinity House, the headquarters of the British lighthouse authority, on the same side of the Square as their house. She witnessed the burning of the Houses of Parliament in 1834. Secondhand versions of events meant little to her, and in any case she had few books in her childhood.

Dolls though were pieces of life to Kate and her sisters Maria, Tillie, and Laura (known as Poppy). They invented histories for them, which they wrote down in irregular parts, imitating the publication methods of Dickens. They had their own plays and other occupations which took place in the schoolroom, at the very top of the house. Although they had a governess, she was unable to discipline the strong-willed girls, who gave her a hard time. The girls also ruled over the nursery, where they went down at teatime to eat with the younger children. Tillie kept discipline at the table while Maria read Dickens aloud.

As an occasional treat their father, Dr. Simm Smith, would take two of the girls in a hackney-cab to the theater; "Black-Eyed Susan" was the play over which they nearly broke their hearts. Some winter evenings he set Maria and Kate on his knee, and would "throw a large silk handkerchief over our heads, which he called our tent, and dramatise for us 'Morgiana and the forty thieves' alternately with 'Bluebeard.' " They usually went on holidays without their father, however, either to a country cottage, or to a farm at sheep-shearing, or by stagecoach to the seaside at Southend or Eastbourne. In 1832, when the cholera epidemic seemed to be threatening all England, Dr. Smith built a gable-ended holiday cottage at Chigwell, on the edge of Hainault Forest, where the freedom and natural surroundings were luxuries after the lack of even a garden in Trinity Square. In July every year Fairlop Fair was held beneath a huge oak in the forest. There were roundabouts, stalls, twenty-minute melodramas, and gingerbread. After she was married Kate took her own children to the fair, and Gerard remembered it for the rest of his life. "Ah, life, what's like it?" he asked in the late 1880s, and gave the answer: "Booth at Fairlop Fair; / Men / boys brought in to have each our shy there." When he was at his most despondent in Dublin he wished he could revisit the Essex forest.

There were two Dr. Smiths in Trinity Square. The other one, Southwood Smith, was concerned with the conditions of factory workers and child-miners, and he was associated with Dickens in pressing for public health reform. Simm Smith, however, was at the center of a full and lively social life, gave large parties with entertainment by professional singers, and he was good at visiting patients in their homes and accumulating wealth. In an 1867 court case it was revealed that a wealthy widow, Mrs. Thwaytes, whom he had attended since she developed a "nervous fever" in 1832, had been paying him an annuity of £2,000 for the last thirty years, besides giving him gifts of almost £50,000. He had helped her manage her property, and she had been generous in many ways to other members of the Smith family; Kate, for instance, had spent all October 1839 as her guest at Herne Bay, and Blunt House, the mansion at Epsom to which the Smiths eventually moved from Trinity Square, and which became a second home to Gerard Hopkins, was built with her money. Her will, in which she left Simm Smith an additional £180,000, was declared invalid by the court, owing to her diseased state of mind. She had prepared the drawing-room of her London house for the Last Judgement, and believed that she herself was the Holy Ghost and Dr. Smith God the Father. The episode indicates some circumscriptions of Kate's upbringing, with its lively and carefree round.

Another limitation which runs counter to Father Lahey's picture of Kate Smith was in her religious upbringing, which was probably as undeveloped as would be compatible in the 1820s and 30s with the importance of conventional social behavior to their father's medical practice. When in middle age Kate and her brother and sisters wrote accounts of their childhood, none of them bothered to mention going to church, except Edward, who merely remembered an interesting monument opposite their pew in All Hallows', Barking.

Kate's two brothers were very much younger, and as her father was habitually absent from his children, it meant that she and her sisters were unusually free from dominant males. They possessed highly cultivated abilities to twist both men and women into indulging them, and on the occasions when their willfulness came up against an uncompliant adult, such as Grandmamma Hodges, they reacted with silent hatred and long sulks. They were accustomed to their own kinds of amusements and people and places. In many ways their actions were governed more by the directions their imaginations and wills dictated than by externally imposed precepts.

Like other girls of their time and station, Kate and her sisters sang, played the piano, drew, and painted. But they had comparatively little formal education. It was before the days of cheap printing and the new breed of publishing entrepreneurs. The Smith household did not have the wide range of periodicals and books that would soon become part of every middle-class household's daily imaginative diet, although the girls were hooked on the green monthly parts of Dickens, waylaying the postman before he had reached their door.

Kate was said to have taught herself to read when she was three. She was quick-minded and, like her sisters, was observant and remembered detail. Her writing style was strong and energetic, punctuated by frequent dashes, and it raced along by association rather than by deliberate thought. Unlike her sister Maria's it was unliterary and unself-conscious. She went to a small, educationally modest, private school at Brixton from the age of eight until she was fifteen or sixteen. Neither she nor her sisters liked school. She won a few second and third prizes in very small classes. But by the age of eighteen she could read French and Italian, and must have practiced cross-translating, as when she was seventeen (with a mass of ringlets either side of her head) her father gave her a French-Italian dictionary. After she left school she privately studied Italian during summers at Chigwell, working on Tasso, Metastasio, and the *Divina Commedia*, and she owned four volumes of Alfieri's tragedies. She and Maria had a few German lessons one winter, but never became very learned or read much in it, although in her late teens or very early twenties she stayed for a time with a family in Hamburg.

Apart from that her reading was casual. Her uncle Sam Smith collected together four miscellaneous volumes of different editions of Mrs. Hemans and had them uniformly bound as a present for her once, which might indicate a passing taste of hers, and she also had the complete works of Washington Irving and Mrs. Jameson's *Memoirs of Celebrated Female Sovereigns.*

Shortly after her marriage Kate owned Chateaubriand's *Le Génie du Christianisme*, which may have been part of a drive on Manley's part to educate his new bride, and she later encouraged her children to read French. But once she was married she either had little time for reading, or lacked the inclination. When the family library was eventually broken up, whereas Manley's books show that he did a large amount of reading, some of it grouped within particular subjects such as religion and English poetry, the few books belonging especially to Kate are nearly all ones she had kept from childhood, or which had been given her as birthday presents from the family, particularly from Manley early in their marriage. They form no other pattern, although there are two Tennyson volumes given to her at different times.

After her death, Kate's children spoke of her love for and memory of history, rather than of books. And if we are searching for similarities between Kate and Gerard the strongest for which there is still evidence seems to be this preference for objects rather than ideas, for the confrontation between the real and the self, rather than a secondhand version of things: "a flogging, which is terrible and instructive *and it happened* — ah, that is the charm and the main point."

Although Gerard was said by his brother to have been particularly close to his mother, apart from that one feature his life seems to have been — as far as she was concerned — a disproof of hereditary principles; rather, it demonstrates the determining forces of education and individual genius.

The influence of his father was more noticeable. Kate Smith's was a rich and stable background, whereas Manley Hopkins's was nomadic and insecure. Just around the corner from 17 Trinity Square was Savage Gardens, and in the early 1830s Martin Edward Hopkins, an apparently respectable indigo merchant, moved into number 4. His slightly older wife, Ann, had a noticeable Devonshire country accent, and they had five children. Manley, the oldest boy, had already left school and was working in the City; he was three years older than Kate.

The Hopkinses' move to Savage Gardens may have been partly due to the horrifying spread of the cholera epidemic from 1830 to 1832, and the consideration that their previous home had been in Stratford, a low-lying, marshy, and reputedly unhealthy village in Essex. But there were also economic reasons; the fact that Manley had left school probably when he was only fourteen — four years before his father's death — suggests that the family could not afford to send him to the university, for which, like his more fortunate younger brother Marsland, he would have been well-suited.

On leaving school Manley knew a small amount of Latin, Greek, and French, although afterwards he read classical works only in translation. But he had a talent for mathematics, and went into an insurance broker's office for a short time. He then moved to a more specialized branch of insurance. William Richards' was possibly the first firm openly to call themselves Average Adjusters, "average" being an old technical term of marine law. In the event of a ship's wreck or damage or putting into port in distress, an average adjuster distributed the expenses and losses among all the interested parties.

During his ten years at Richards' Manley developed enough experience to become a leading member of the firm, and the self-confidence to start his own business. His advertising circular stressed his "punctuality and correctness" (prosaic qualities he did not pass on to his poet son); and it could be assumed that he now had a skilled mathematical mind, a wide knowledge of shipping and cargoes and mercantile law, besides being a competent accountant. To be successful in a role where he had to discriminate between rival interests and yet maintain the confidence of all parties suggests that he must also have possessed considerable diplomatic abilities. His firm prospered and developed until it had branches in all the principal English ports. "What fun," Manley's eldest son remarked to Robert Bridges one day, "if you were a classic!" By that time Manley already was a classic, having published in 1857 *A Handbook of Average*, which became the standard reference book, and ran to several editions. He became a leader and definer of his profession, and helped bring into existence the Association of Average Adjusters, which instigated and administered searching professional examinations.

Manley's business judgment seems to have been a great deal better than his father's. Martin Hopkins had died in 1836, aged fifty. His commercial speculations had been unsuccessful, and he left a paltry estate of £200 for his widow to live on and bring up the five children. When he was only eighteen Manley had to assume the role of eldest male and head of the family. A poem of his expresses baldly the sudden shock of his father's death:

> My father built a house and died.
> He wedded to a lovely bride.
> In one short year, a widow, she —
> And he decayed mortality.[7]

The telescoping of his parents' married life to "one short year" brings home more powerfully than the truth would have done Manley's feelings of the tragic nature and shock of the death and bereavement; and his denial by the same phrase of his three brothers and a sister also makes his suddenly forced assumption of an adult responsibility more lonely and frightening. The poem then makes the judgment that the Hopkins family suffered from what later came to be known as manic-depression: "Somewhat too rash in love and hate; / Too soon depressed, too soon elate." Although Manley claimed in this poem to "bear the one ancestral face," there is no other evidence that he had this temperament; but his son Gerard was noticeably liable to be "too soon depressed, too soon elate."

It is likely that Manley learned from the example of his father in two ways: first, he knew the results of failure at close hand, so that he himself was realistic and hardworking in order to avoid them; and second, as opposed to his father's widespread speculations, he stuck to one narrow area of business and applied all his efforts there, putting aside any disappointment he had felt at not being able to go to Cambridge University to develop his intellect in wider and more speculative areas. Gerard Hopkins never mentions his father's job in all his surviving letters, and makes no sign of awareness that his own privileged and comfortable home life and education were dependent on his father's income, and on the social class and material position that Manley had won the hard way.

Two of Manley's three brothers also had to leave school early, with the intention of training up from humble beginnings into some secure professional City job. But the youngest, Marsland, was sent as a pensioner to Peterhouse, Cambridge, near the time when Manley and Kate were married. It might be wondered how Manley could afford to send his brother to college and also set up a new home for the rest of his own family as well as the new one he was starting, all before he was earning money as his own boss. One suspects that the Smith alliance was proving useful.

Considering his family's recent history, it was understandable that Manley desired not only to build a place in middle-class society, but also to draw attention to it with proud, challenging flags. Martin Edward had discovered a Hopkins family crest, coat-of-arms, and motto, "Esse quam videri," "to be rather than to seem," which he had had printed on a specially designed bookplate. Manley resurrected this crest and motto, and transferred them to his own letter-headings and bookplates; he also had an embossing machine made, and practiced drawing the arms in pen and ink. A common medievalist practice of the day (John Simm Smith also had his own bookplate, with crest and motto, "Propositi tenax"), its childish showing-off aspect was demonstrated when Gerard as a schoolboy took up the idea, and wrote the motto in the front of many of his books; later he would automatically write A.M.D.G. ("An Maiorem Dei Gloriam"), following a more meaningful tradition.

As if to apologize for the masculine concentration and narrowness of his everyday business world, Manley continuously cultivated his talents in several other areas, where his family in particular and sometimes a more general public could appreciate his abilities. Unfortunately, in this feminine household realm, he still admired those qualities which had made him successful in business; he became in most of his extraprofessional writing the conventionally chivalrous figure, leaving it to his "effeminate" eldest son to write with original ideals and force. Freedom of expression, extravagance, and individuality had no part in Manley's respectable and derivative poems; his poetry and his other nonprofessional publications had a part to play in forming a refined bourgeois household.

But there are many of Manley's abilities and leanings which it is possible to see in Gerard, the most obvious one being a voracity of mind. The width of Manley's interests is shown by the extraordinary variety of his publications—besides the books on average adjustment, marine insurance, and maritime procedure, he produced two books of poetry, which themselves include attempts at a large number of different types and moods of poem, a drawing-room play called *The New School of Design*, a historical account of Hawaii, a book on the cardinal numbers, and with his brother Marsland a book of religious poems, very different from his other verse. He wrote book reviews for the *Times*, including a review of *In Memoriam*, articles for the *Cornhill* and *Once a Week*, dramatic monologues, hymns, and letters and poems to newspapers. He had a regular column in the official Hawaiian newspaper commenting on political and social events in London, and two other works—an essay on Longfellow and a novel—were both rejected by publishers. Some of his poems were printed in anthologies such as *Lyra Eucharistica* and *Lyra Mystica*, alongside poems by Christina Rossetti. He was also an assiduous sketcher and a composer of songs. Other interests of Manley's are reflected in the variety of books in his library, which included works on the orders of chivalry, rose-growing, astronomy, and piquet.

The range of Gerard's interests while he was at Oxford, and also over his Jesuit life after 1874, is similarly remarkable for the unpredictability of the subject of his next enthusiasm—music, Egyptology, Greek choral odes, the Welsh language, religion, painting, botany, meteorology, etymology. In Gerard's case, though, it was combined with a fatal inability to complete projects, a flaw that his father did not share.

At the end of Gerard's life, father and son combined in a book, and to such a degree that—despite the unlikelihood—it is difficult to say with absolute certainty where Manley's contributions ended and Gerard's began. In 1887 was published *The Cardinal Numbers* by Manley Hopkins. On page v the author expresses his thanks "for valuable aid and useful criticism afforded me by my friend the Rev. Sherrard B. Burnaby . . . and in like manner to my near relative the Rev. G. M. Hopkins, of University College, Dublin." I have not been able to trace "the Rev. Sherrard B. Burnaby," and I suspect that this was the name chosen to mask other contributions that Gerard made but did not wish to be credited with.

"With much modesty," concludes the preface, "these pages are offered to the public." With defined subject-matter to write on, Manley's prose is direct and lucid for most of the body of the book, after an introduction written in a manneristic style that pallidly imitates the style of a courteous aristocrat with more of a critical education to draw on than Manley himself had had. Sometimes his mind runs on into a minor essay on a word, as so often occurs in Gerard's early journals. The word "Cardinal," for instance, "is also used in respect of other things. In the crypt of a cathedral, the principal pier is sometimes spoken of as the cardinal column. In the Roman Church the most exalted of the Clergy are by preëminence Cardinals — though other derivatives have been claimed for this title. In the same sense of superiority there are cardinal virtues, cardinal colours, the cardinal points in the mariner's compass, & C." At other places in his arguments, too, Manley cannot resist the temptation to elaborate on inferences, tendencies, and connections; facts become isolated from the argument in which they had arisen, and become things to be marvelled at in their own right (as are encyclopedic facts noted in Gerard's diaries). Within two pages of his book Manley uses examples of parallel numerals from the Indian, Arabic, Phoenician, Hebrew, Greek, Egyptian, and Roman, all with a charmingly careless and spurious fluency, just as his son would love to startle with a parallel in a completely unexpected language.

Sometimes also the life of an anecdote develops more power than the argument it illustrates, and is continued sideways by elaboration or in a footnote. The habits of Rover (a retriever at Oak Hill) take their place among a remarkably miscellaneous mass of sources for Manley's references and analogies, much like Gerard's: Sir Henry Bessemer, Sir William Hamilton, Frank Galton, and other mathematicians; Aristotle, Plato, Pythagoras, and Varro; Greek and Roman mythology, Hinduism, Buddhism, Roman Catholicism; Brahmans ("I have been told by one who tried them"), German, Welsh (supplied by Gerard), Irish legends, Algonquin legends, Kashmiri proverbs; architecture, botany, astronomy; the Old and New Testaments; Pope's epigrams; cricket umpires; the *Athenaeum* and the *Times* (on a cat living in a Swiss hotel, and on a hybrid cat-rabbit produced in Australia).

The contributions to the book that are acknowledged as being Gerard's are connected with Welsh methods of reckoning and with "spectral numbers," or "the mental visibility of numbers"; neither father nor son appears to see anything extraordinary about the following passage of Gerard's, although the *Saturday Review* made fun particularly of this section:

> From No. 1, which as scarcely seen, to 12, the numbers rise either uprightly, or leaning a little to the right, in a gloomy light. From 12 to 20, they run to the right, rising a little, and are in a cheerful day-light. . . . On the left of number *one* are a few minus numbers, and below it, swarms of fractions. The place where they appear is gloomy grass. Backgrounds or rooms and remembered open-air scenes appear in different parts of this picture or world.

Gerard's name appears only once in the preface. Elsewhere he is referred to, with perhaps some pride, as "my relative," and the relationship between the minds of Manley and Gerard is plain in *The Cardinal Numbers*. Several other parts of the book could be examples of something Gerard had noted, rather than his father. The possible derivation of "Mind your Ps and Qs" from a landlord's act of chalking up his debts in pints and quarts, for example, or a rural numerical jungle, used for scoring sheep or counting stitches: "iny, tiny, tethery, fethery, phips, ither, lather, cother, quather, dix, iny-dix, tiny-dix. . . ." And parts of the second chapter, on "one," besides having a certain eloquence, also bear a relationship to Gerard's ideas of *one* and *selfhood*, as well as containing rhythms which are strangely similar to some of the son's.

It is plain, too, from the consciousness Manley's book shows of the part numerical symbols play in religion, and particularly in Christianity, that the mind that would leap with recognition at the significance of there being exactly five nuns in the *Deutschland*'s wreck had other common roots with his father.

Religion in fact was present to some degree in all the books Manley wrote which were not concerned with his profession. In the Hopkins family library at Manley's death were books that reveal his continual though not extensive reading in religion and religious controversies of his day. Among his earliest books were the works of Paley and Jeremy Taylor's *Holy Living*. There were the *Pilgrim's Progress* and the odd volumes of Church history, biblical comment, and late-Victorian questions of belief. More practically there were also a book of hymns, the Book of Common Prayer, and at least two Bibles, and he had given his wife as a thirty-fourth birthday present a book of meditations and prayers on the Holy Eucharist.

In 1849, with Marsland, who had just been ordained but who had not as yet been assigned to a particular parish, Manley published *Pietas Metrica; or, Nature Suggestive of God and Godliness. By the Brothers Theophilus and Theophylact*. The dedication read: "To the Church This little Volume is dutifully offered, by two of her sons." It was the aim of the book "to blend together two of Man's best things, Religion and Poetry," and to that end "the books of Nature and Revelation have been laid side by side and read together." It consisted of fifty-eight poems, each with a biblical text between its title and the body. The poems have little force when read today. But in many ways, from the carefully designed title page, with red gothic type Puginesquely used for title and authors, the spacious and neat printing, to the way every poem, however trite, emerges from a carefully selected solid biblical text, the solemnity and sincerity of the book is nevertheless impressive. His religion was a real everyday presence to Manley: "O Omnipresent Eye, how dread, how sweet, / Is They companionship! About our bed, / Our path, our converse, ever standing near." It was also, as the poem "This Histories of Saints on Earth" makes clear, not merely a background to life, but something in which one should take an active part: "The weapons of *their* warfare, lo! are thine, / Gird up thy loins, *and be thyself a saint.*"

Although once he was at Oxford Gerard rejected it, he had been brought up in a strong religious environment, largely the creation of Manley.

Notes

1. Richard Ellman, *Golden Codgers: Biographical Speculations*, (Oxford: Oxford University Press, 1973), 15.

2. Eric Homberger, "Details, Details," (London) *Times Higher Education Supplement*, (9 October 1987), 11.

3. *Letters* 3:68–81.

4. *Letters* 3:15–16.

5. G. F. Lahey, S.J., *Gerard Manley Hopkins*, Oxford: (Oxford University Press 1930), 1.

6. Material on Kate Smith's childhood in this essay is partly from "The Book of Memories," unpublished recollections of their childhood by Kate Hopkins and her brothers and sisters, in my possession. Otherwise, for Kate's and Manley's background this essay draws on researches undertaken for the *Life* of Hopkins commissioned by the Oxford University Press.

7. *Spicilegium Poeticum* (London: Privately printed, 1892), 147–48.

Hopkins as Poet

Frozen Fire: The Paradoxical Equation of "That Nature is a Heraclitean Fire and of the comfort of the Resurrection"

Rachel Salmon[*]

"That Nature is a Heraclitean Fire and of the comfort of the Rescurrection"[1] has frequently been seen as both closing the "terrible sonnets" and as reconciling them with the apparently very different "nature sonnets" written nearly a decade earlier in Wales. As a rule, critics have attempted to offer a sequential or diachronic interpretation. They have sought to demonstrate how Hopkins progressed (for the better or for worse) from one sort of sensibility and mode of expression to another by equating the two sonnet cycles with oppositions frequently drawn between Hopkins's baroque and plain style, between priest and poet, and between the sacramental and self-reflexive functions of poetic language. It has become common to use the significant differences between Hopkins's earlier and later poems — and their possible synthesis in HF — as the means for constructing Hopkins's aesthetic and spiritual biography. The purpose of this paper, on the other hand, is to examine the sort of relationship that HF brings to light between the two groups of poems when we think of them from a synchronic point of view, and the sort of poetic function that HF performs within such a context.

I wish to make clear, at the outset, that my adoption of such a point of view — which treats the poems as if they were written simultaneously because it refrains from attributing *essential* significance to their chronology — is motivated not by reasons of critical fashion, but by a personal concern that sequential interpretation cannot satisfy.[2] Like many of Hopkins's readers and interpreters, I read his poetry as one who does not share his specific theological beliefs, and who, therefore, does not seek an entrance into his work through his biography. Yet the response that his poetry elicits convinces me that there is a significant structure communicated — and not merely intellectually — across the barriers of these specific tenets and behaviors.

I believe that the best way to describe such a structure in Hopkins's work is to remove the poems — at least momentarily — from the context of that sequential development that shaped the man's particular way in the

*From *The Hopkins Quarterly* XII, 324 (October 1985–January 1986): 65–79.

world, in order to trace their effect when read as if they were simultaneous creations. Objections may be raised to this procedure on the grounds that it diverts attention from the poet or poem to the reader. I cannot take up the theoretical issue in this context,[3] but can only recall that for Hopkins there could be no "inscape" until there was a "beholder" to perceive it, and that there is a genuine mutual relationship between "inscape" as a noun (which is to be found in the poem as object) and "inscape" as a verb (which is the responsible act of the reader.)[4]

HF is the single poem that combines in one unit the features that characterize poems of diverse periods. It can, therefore, be studied as a model of the synchronic relations between the individual poems in the Hopkins canon. Furthermore, the "and" in the title "That Nature is a Heraclitean Fire and of the comfort of the Resurrection" can be seen as supporting synchronic study, for it abrogates the temporal sequence in which later time replaces earlier, and suggests a composite figure, rather than one that invites choice between alternatives. This inconspicuous conjunction is the first sign that the reader is being called upon to recognize and accept a paradoxical combination of contraries. Although it may not be noticed initially, this "and" in the title of the poem is reinforced by subsequent signs, which work upon the reader in a similar way. Neither the combination of opposites—"Nature" and "Resurrection"—in the title, nor the other "impossible" combinations found in the body of the poem can be resolved by extending the opposing poles into a temporal narrative in which each term or event supplants the one that preceded it.[5] HF, then, forces the reader to confront, in a single poem, the paradox that he meets when he tries to trace the way that the different sorts of poems, written by Hopkins at different times, relate to each other.

1

We shall begin with the "nature" sonnets, in which Hopkins appeared effortlessly to achieve the end for which man was created: the praise of God. If, for Hopkins, only "usefulness" could justify the diversion of time and energy from ordinary priestly tasks to the writing of poetry, the nature sonnets must surely have fulfilled his stringent criteria.[6] In addition, as scholars have frequently suggested, these poems follow the format of an Ignatian meditation quite closely.[7] They are, therefore, instrumental in accomplishing the purpose for which such meditation is undertaken: the joyful bending of the will of the individual to that of the subject of his meditation, Christ. Hopkins's poetic structure—like the structure of an Ignatian meditation—is informed by the three powers of the soul: memory, understanding, and will. In the "nature" sonnets, each of these powers carries out its respective task: the memory accomplishes the composition of place, the understanding undertakes an analysis of the vividly presented scene, and the will finds its voice in a direct colloquy with God—a soul-felt request of a paean of praise. As Hopkins explains in his unfinished commentary on Loyola's *Spiritual Exercises*, apprehension, comprehension, and the expression of reverence are the functions of the memory, understanding and will (S, 173–76). Naturally, Hopkins would have hoped that his poetry in this mode would be more than mimetic of his own personal experience — that it might act upon others as well.

Long before Hopkins read Duns Scotus, his sense of the "thisness" or individuality that links everything in the created universe with God is present in his journals, his art work, his theological writing, and his poetry. The terms he coined — "inscape," "instress," "selving," "sake," "doing-be" — all express his feelings for the ultimate presence waiting to be discovered at the core of every created thing. The excitement with which he greeted the medieval theologian, when he finally read Scotus, bears witness to the gratitude and exhilaration he felt at discovering a forefather who could help him to unite the priest and the poet aspects of his being.[8] If each thing is Christ at its core, the poet who reveals how the creature, through "selving," joins its Creator, draws the memory, understanding and will of his reader home with him to "abrupt self" (P, 45), to Christ. Hopkins is most explicit about this process in "As kingfishers catch fire" (P, 57):

> Each mortal thing does one thing and the same:
> Deals out that being indoors each one dwells:
> Selves — goes itself: *myself* it speaks and spells.
> *Crying What I do is me: for that I came.*

"Each mortal thing" is not a metaphor for Christ, but precisely something that has achieved identity with Christ by becoming fully itself. On the one hand, Hopkins is not speaking of analogy — of a finite being trying its best to imitate Infinite Being. Nor is this "selving" a mystical union in which the individual self loses itself in God. On the contrary, the achievement of utter and absolute selfhood enables the self to "know" (in the intimate, biblical sense) the Utter and Absolute within itself. In the same poem, the human self:

> Acts in God's eye what in God's eye he is —
> Christ. For Christ plays in ten thousand places.
> Lovely in limbs, and lovely in eyes not his
> To the Father through the features of men's faces.

Therefore, the "selving" of birds, leaves, clouds, and "all the air things wear that build this world of Wales" (P, 34), caught in the "nature" sonnets, may accomplish the painstaking task assigned to the composition of place in the discipline of Ignatian meditation. The exuberant compositions of the "nature" sonnets could have quieted Hopkins's qualms about writing poetry, by holding out to him the hope of furthering the work of salvation in the world.

2

However, the sonnets that Hopkins wrote in Dublin in 1885 contrast sharply with the "nature" poems, and raise the baffling question of how he allowed himself to write them, not to speak of how he allowed himself to send them to friends. If — as we may surmise from the fact that he all but stopped writing nature sonnets, and began severely to ration his contact with the beauty of the world — Hopkins found something damning, or at least impossible, in his earlier celebration of the created world, how did he find sanction for the extreme concentration upon the self evident in the Dublin poems? Despite the striking disparity in content and linguistic form, the later poems exhibit the same meditative format typical of the sonnets composed in Wales. Although the Dublin sonnets are personal and painful, rather than objective and joyful, they are also based upon the three powers of the soul that characterize the meditative genre and produce "selving" in the nature sonnets. Why, we may ask, did the selving of other creatures, in the poetry he wrote in Wales, finally strike Hopkins as more pernicious than the self-serving that dominates the Dublin sonnets? One would imagine that such personal material most decidedly runs the risk of becoming a form of the damning self-celebration that Hopkins describes in his commentary on *The Spiritual Exercises*: "This song of Lucifer's was . . . an instressing of his own inscape, and like a performance on the organ and instrument of his own being: it was a sounding, as they say, of his own trumpet and a hymn in his own praise. Moreover it became an incantation: others were drawn in" (S, 200–201). The later sonnets do indeed suggest that an "instressing of his own inscape" has replaced the instressing of the inscapes of creation to be found in the "nature" sonnets.

Whereas the "nature" sonnets typically record the way that the individual's apprehension of the particular places or creatures becomes, suddenly, the comprehension and celebration of inscaped divinity, the "terrible" sonnets are confined within the self: a despicable and despised self, but a self nonetheless. The first-person pronoun — which appears in only half of the "nature" sonnets — appears in every one of the "sonnets of desolation." In the earlier poems that "I" is an *eye* perceiving and composing a scene: in the late poems the "I" is itself the scene to be composed. While the nature sonnets strive for mimesis of already achieved inscapes through memory, the "terrible" sonnets directly present a state of soul in which selving has not yet taken place. The outcome, too, is different. Instead of issuing in a peal of joyful praise, the "terrible" sonnets cause us to "hear our hearts grate on themselves" (P, 68); to utter the cries that "on an age-old anvil wince and sing" (P, 65); and to feel the "lonely began" (P, 66) of our "sweating selves" (P, 67). The self is highly prominent in these poems, although it is rejected because it fails to reach God through itself. If we view these poems as mimetic of personal crisis, we must wonder why Hopkins allowed such "non-useful" work to supersede his "nature" sonnets, and even more wonder why he sent them to Bridges whom, after all, he hoped one day to convert.[9] Surely, one would have supposed Hopkins to have feared that "others [would be] drawn in," and led along a barren and dangerous path.

Most critics have dealt with this problem biographically, as the very terms "terrible sonnets" or "sonnets of desolation," used to designate the core group of poems written in Dublin, indicate. On the whole, readers unsympathetic to Hopkins's decision to become a Jesuit have viewed the agony of these poems as a sign of spiritual regression or deterioration, which they link causally to his depressing accounts of life in Dublin. They postulate that Hopkins's well-established scruples were overcome, at this point, by a degree of suffering sufficient to cause the loss of his customary self-control.[10] Some of them, even, go so far as to suggest that his poetic or priestly powers — or both — were in decline.[11]

On the other hand, critics who sympathize, or identify, with Jesuit life tend to interpret these sonnets within the context of the Ignatian "way of desolation" — a state of soul often considered to be more elevated than the "way of consolation" so prevalent in Hopkins's "nature sonnets." This trial of desolation is reserved by God for those who can submit to the test of purification at the threshold of mystical union. "Desolation" is thus viewed as superior to "consolation" and, in fact, takes its place.

Both sorts of interpretation — whether leading to positive or negative judgments about Hopkins's personal and spiritual progress — posit a mode of chronological development in which one stage succeeds another, and the later stage is thought of as more significant than (perhaps even the annulment of) the earlier one. Within the parameters of such an approach, HF tends to be regarded as in some sense definitive, because it is the final poem of the later sonnet cycle, and thus seems to come "to lash with the best or worst word last" (P, 29). One's view of the relationship between the "nature" and "terrible" sonnets will thus determine, in advance, the context within which HF is read. If we are dissatisfied with the conventional model of chronological supersession presupposed by biographical explication, the burden rests upon us to suggest an alternative way of explicating the relations between the two sonnet groups, and the role that HF plays in respect to them.

3

I believe that we gain a new understanding of the reconciliation effected in HF if we consider the "nature" and the "terrible" sonnets within the framework of a non-chronological model. Thinking of them synchronically, rather than diachronically, we need not imagine that one form replaces the other, but that they are two simultaneous aspects of a single whole. Actually, the features that distinguish the "nature" sonnets from the "terrible" sonnets are also discernible — and in no particular temporal arrangement — in the descriptions of the two different kinds of meditations found in Loyola's *Spiritual Exercises*.[12]

One form of meditation, while taking place within the self, aims at participation in a scene from the life of Christ, and thus locates the self in relation to a fully selved Other. The second form engages the self within the self in the self-analysis of one's sinfulness and impotence. By emptying the soul of pride and self-reliance, it prepares the sinner to receive the grace of God. The purpose of the former type — to arouse the love, service, and praise of God that are natural to man's true instincts — corresponds to the "usefulness" of the nature sonnets. Both draw upon and express the affective will, which is the will natural to each creature by virtue of its having been created thus. The "affective will" is neither free nor unique to man; it is that in each creature which enables it to embrace, by necessity, that good which naturally pertains to it. The purpose of the latter form of meditation is to enable an individual to choose his state of life. Choice is possible only through the activation of the "elective will," which is peculiar to man among the creatures. All creatures choose as they must, according to the dictaes of their affective wills. Only man — whose will has been created free, to some degree, in the image of his Creator — has the *will-power* to oppose the will of God. He can pit his own elective will against the divinely given affective will. However, the elective will can also be employed in a positive manner. By choosing freely what God determines, man becomes a partner in his own salvation. The meditations and the poetry that draw upon the elective will thus have a most exalted function of their own.[13]

Although Hopkins's "terrible" sonnets follow his "nature" sonnets in his own history, in *The Spiritual Exercises* the contemplation of one's sinful wretchedness belongs to the exercises of the first week, preceding the meditations on the Nativity, the Passion, and the Resurrection of the second, third, and fourth weeks. However, in the instructions to be given to one who is meditating, there is no necessary sequence. The two types of meditations alternate and recur, because each applies to a constant aspect of the spiritual life of man. Therefore, the two types of sonnets that Hopkins wrote — the "nature" sonnets that spring from the affective will and the "terrible" sonnets that originate in the elective will — can be seen as complementary aspects of a single whole, and not as self-exclusive, successive phases. The human being is paradoxically free and determined; only simultaneity can express the paradox in which neither pole can ever obliterate its opposite.

4

HF has been subject to exactly the differences in interpretation that characterize the readings of the "nature" and the "terrible" sonnets. This is not surprising, for this poem, more than any other, is a composite one in which the elements of both sonnet cycles find expression.

HF opens with an inscape of clouds reminiscent of the earlier poems. The reader is carried along in pure affirmation and praise until the fifth line. There, already (although often overlooked), the transition between the mood of the "nature" sonnets and the "terrible" sonnets begins. A complication sets in with "the bright boisterous wind" that is inscaped not in itself, but in its relation to the earth — in action, rather than in essence. It acts, we are told, "delightfully" — apparently as nature does in Wales — but what it is actually doing, in this Dublin poem, is roping, wrestling, beating bare, parching, squandering, stanching and starching the poor, passive earth. And, if that is not enough, it also obliterates, on the earth, not only "yestertempest's creases," but any mark or inscape of himself that man has imprinted there. "Man," who is "nature's . . . bonniest, dearest . . . clearest selved spark," is powerless to resist. We are, here, one step further into despair than in the "terrible" sonnets, which writhe with resistance.

In "Spelt from Sibyl's Leaves," the poem which suggests itself, both formally and thematically, as the companion-piece of HF — and which opens the series of the "terrible" sonnets just as HF closes it — "our evening" may be "over us . . . quite / Disremembering, dismembering all now," but opposition between "black, white: right, wrong" is still possible. On the one hand, life has lost its "dapple" and "pied beauty," "her once skeined stained veined variety." The lack of commas in this list indicates the blurring of distinctions in an "all through her" that makes it impossible to hold oppositions into a paradoxically united inscape. On the other hand, it is still possible to struggle on: "a rack / Where, selfwrung, selfstrung, sheathe- and shelterless, thoughts against thoughts in groans grind." In this series, the commas mark oppositions, and the stress marks concretize the dislocations by disrupting rhythmic and syntactical expectations. This is the struggle that is waged, in the "terrible" sonnets, by the elective will. In HF that struggle, too, is obliterated: "firedint [and] . . . mark on mind, is gone! / Both are in an unfathomable, all is in an enormous dark / Drowned." "Our tale" is still inscaped in "Sibyl's Leaves" and in the "terrible" sonnets — even if it is only marked in black on black — but in HF all trace of man "death blots black out: nor mark / Is any of him at all so stark / But vastness blurs and time beats level." Although the "composition of place" in the latter poem initially presents us with a vivid image of air and water in the clouds, the understanding's analysis of the situation disintegrates them into a "squandering" wind, and an "unfathomable," "dark" "vastness" of water that drowns and "blots black out" all of creation. There is nothing left for the "affective will" but to moan, "O pity and indignation!"

Far from leading men to praise God, this inscape of nature seems to produce a colloquy of quiescent despair. The abrasiveness of the elective will's struggling to inscape the self against all odds in the "terrible" sonnets seems to have been rubbed smooth or burnt to "ash." "Million-fueled, nature's bonfire burns on," but, whereas for Heraclitus nature and man are both renewed in the cycle of fire, for Hopkins, the self that seeks to inscape itself through the elective will appears to be lost entirely in such a world. In the "terrible" sonnets, that self that grinds against itself may produce a "spark." Here the affective and the elective wills no longer struggle — man is pushed to extinction. So far in the poem, we have not heard the voice of a single "I."

So far in the poem, also, there is little issue for critical controversy. But with the outbreak of the imperative voice in "Enough!" and "Away," the controversy begins. For readers who find that the Dublin years mark progress in Hopkins's spiritual state and aesthetic creativity, the poem achieves, here, a decisive triumph because it encounters despair fully and directly, and overcomes it through transfiguration. Interpreters who work within the presuppositions of Hopkins's religious convictions claim that the poet, having trusted God "Enough" to be led by Him through the "Heraclitean Fire," emerges as the "clearest-selved spark" not of nature, but of God.[14] Only thus can the fully inscaped "I" appear, that "I" which is fully itself and fully Christ at the same time, and to which Hopkins referred in his commentary on *The Spiritual Exercises:* "It is as if a man said: That is Christ playing at me and me playing at Christ, only that is no play but truth: That is Christ *being me* and me being Christ (S, 154).

Having willingly surrendered his "mortal trash" to the "world's wildfire" that changes all from state to state, man suddenly discovers the fate of residual "ash." Ash — the least form-holding, most worthless, most unsubstantial state of carbon — is transformed, "in a flash, at a trumpet crash" into its most compressed, most permanent, most precious state — "immortal diamond." This, in brief, is the sanguine reading of the end of the poem — a reading that would close the "terrible" sonnets, as a group, upon a note of comfort.

There are, however, readers who reject such a reading of HF. The transition, they claim, is too sudden: it does not grow out of the poem. Although they cannot but admit the explicit imagery and statement that dominates the final third of the poem, they claim that it does not work, because the previous two-thirds of the poem do not prepare for it. Human time and human space — the human body itself — seems to them to have been too convincingly destroyed in the bulk of the poem simply to be restored by the word "Enough!" They read that word as a sign of Hopkins's weakness and escapism — a willful, ungrounded denial of the disorientation and dislocation that he so convincingly portrayed. Hopkins, they assert, unable to bear any more pain and strain, manufactured a spurious comfort out of his own need and wishful thinking, rather than out of any genuine experience in the real world. For them, Hopkins is pushed by his desperation to choose an easy way out. At best, they maintain, Hopkins could have hoped for such an event in the future; to place it in the present tense is to be, of necessity, insincere.[15]

It is worth emphasizing that this sort of reading is every bit as diachronically biographical as the affirmative one: its aim is to damn Hopkins, instead of redeem him. I use these terms advisedly in order to bring out the utter seriousness of the charge. If Hopkins's "heart's clarion!" is in any way forced or artificial, he has tread upon very dangerous ground. To speak in such a way without the strongest personal evidence would be tantamount to blasphemy in any religion, and most surely so for Hopkins as an educated priest. It would make Hopkins guilty of a preposterous pretension to force God's hand, which amounts to a denial of God's power to initiate salvation in His own way. Furthermore, the critics who find the climax of the poem unanticipated reveal both a simplistic view of grace as a natural process that must obey the laws of sequence and decorum, and a highly restricted conception of the function of the will in the colloquy. The term "willful" is often employed in a pejorative sense without an exposition of the specific concept of the "will" assumed in its usage.

To claim that the poem does not prepare for the outburst of the colloquy is to assume that only the affective will — which must choose in accordance with its present nature — has a voice. Were this the whole truth, man could play no part in his transformation from ashy carbon to diamond. No act of his will could enable him to extract himself — through meditative or poetic means — from the flux of constant disintegration and refiguration in order to enable him to experience the permanent integration of his identity with Christ. Had man only an affective will, this sort of transformation could be achieved — if at all — only through an infinite series of minute changes in which the creature affirms, at each stage, the better aspect of his present self, and rejects the worser. The alternative to this long slow process of evolutionary adaptation would be a sudden mutation, for which the creature himself is in no way responsible. Grace — which issues solely from God in this way — would annul the freedom of the creature it saves. The affective will might surely exalt in and give praise for such salvation, but it would have played no part in producing it. In HF, however, as the critics have complained, the voice of the poet does appear to be instrumental (for the taste of some, too instrumental) in effecting radical change.

5

I suggest that it is the elective will — the *arbitrium* — that speaks out in the last section of this poem. When the inscaped world dissolves, only the *arbitrium* is left. Whereas the affective will is the expression of present inscape, the very condition of the *arbitrium*'s freedom is that it has no fixed form or inscape to dictate its choice. It is always open, potential, always in that very act of "doing-be," through which it strives to create a future self that will correspond to, or oppose, the will of God. Hopkins is most explicit about the role of the *arbitrium* in his comments upon *The Spiritual Exercises*:

> For there must be something which shall be truly the creature's in the work of corresponding with grace: this is the *arbitrium*, the verdict on God's side, the saying Yes, the "doing-agree" (to speak barbarously), and looked at in itself, such a nothing is the creature before its creator, it is found to be no more than the mere wish, discernible by God's eyes, that it might do as he wishes, might correspond, might say Yes to him; correspondence itself is on man's side not so much corresponding as the wish to correspond, and this least sigh of desire, this one aspiration, is the life and spirit of man. . . . And by this infinitesimal act the creature does what in it lies to bridge the gulf fixed between its present actual and worser pitch of will and its future better one (S, 154–55).

The soul, in freeing itself from "its present actual and worser pitch of will," frees itself also from its affective will that irresistibly complies with the past that has formed that "pitch." The elective will thus occupies a timeless "moment" between present and future; it is not a phase that needs to be prepared for through a past, nor can it be passed in order to establish a past to be recalled by memory. On the contrary, it is always in pilgrimage, "in via" (S, 156). That, exactly, is the condition of its freedom. Only in this way can Hopkins express the participation of the creature in the salvation that comes, ultimately, from the Creator. What we hear at the end of HF is the "Yes" of the *arbitrium*, which breaks through time and sequence to find its own "absolute which stands to the absolute of God as the infinitesimal to the infinite" (S, 153). The soul thus realizes its identity in God while preserving its individual identity. In this way Hopkins is able to maintain the precarious balance between God's omnipotence and man's freedom. If there were only the affective will, absolute divine power would be preserved, but man — choosing always what he was made to choose — would not be responsible. On the other hand, if the elective will is overemphasized, God's power appears to be contingent. It seems clear, both from Hopkins's prose and from his poetry, that he never regarded the "affective" and "elective" wills as opposed or competing forces, one of which might replace the other. On the contrary, he seems to have thought of them as coexistent and complementary. I have thus argued for a synchronic rather than diachronic reading of the sonnets that came out of Wales and Dublin.

In this light, HF appears to be to me *the* poem that reconciles the affective and elective wills, while denying neither. Aside from the thematic material already examined, we see this reflected in the way the language behaves — in the verb tenses, and the ways words relate to each other. Up to the first "But," all of the verbs are in the present tense and active. Although "nature's bonfire burns on," causing everything to move and change, the inscapes of nature are not destroyed. The individuality, the "thisness" of clouds and elms resides in the species. In contrast to Heraclitus, however, for Hopkins man is not at one with nature. Whereas the things of nature are active participants in the process of flux — the clouds flaunt forth and chevy, the elm arches, etc. — man is the passive victim of flux — his "spark" is quenched by nature, the "firedint" and "mark" of the individuality that he strives to imprint "is gone," "is . . . drowned." Blurred and beaten by time and vastness (space), his glory — "a star" — exists within the natural world already in the past tense — "shone." He cannot, now, find the presence of his inscape in the world of nature. He no longer corresponds to anything on the level of his affective will alone. It is only when he chooses to follow not the effervescent shining of his own "star" but "a beacon, and eternal beam" that has "shone" in the past as it shines in the present is he able to reverse "all at once" both temporal process and material flux. The strong imperatives — "Flesh face . . . mortal trash / Fall . . . leave but ash" — herald the activation of man's elective will over the resistance offered by the affective will that is at home in ordinary temporal sequence.

At this point the diction of HF also changes. In the first two-thirds of the poem there are many metaphorical comparisons — the clouds are *like* "tossed pillows," "heaven-roysterers," "gay-gangs," man is *like* a "star" — and in a metaphor there are elements always of difference as well as similarity. In the last part of the poem, however, as in the "nature" sonnets, analogies disappear, and we find equations of identity. The self and Christ are one — "immortal diamond. / Is immortal diamond" — just as the windhover was not analogous to Christ, but somehow inscaped Christ himself. Man may strive to imitate God, but his creaturely affective will cannot stave off the flux, or bridge the gap between like (but different) and the same. Only the grace of God can perform this miracle and this paradoxical mystery. There is a divine, not a human, preparation that overrides human time and causality making "I am . . . what Christ is, since [the time] he was what I am" and "I am . . . what Christ is since [because] he was what I am" simultaneous, but in no way unprepared for. Yet, although the preparation is not his own, man can embrace it only in freedom. Through his elective will man says "Yes" to what he may accept, although he cannot fully grasp its ways. In doing so, he assists grace in raising him out of time — thus making the problem of "too sudden" into no problem at all.

As some critics have noted, the members of the series "Jack, joke, poor potsherd, patch, matchwood, immortal diamond" modulate into one another phonetically, although they are separated by punctuation.[16] It is precisely this double-featured aspect of human mortality that is maintained in the "immortal diamond" equation. The preservation of the "Jack, joke" self through its loss in "ash," is exactly the same as the preservation of "matchwood" in "immortal diamond." I imagine that

Hopkins chose the diamond because here — in frozen fire — flux is paradox-ically arrested in a meeting between heaven and earth in which neither loses its peculiar inscape. Whereas the Resurrection is indeed future for man at his "present actual and worser pitch of will" (the affective will), it can, for Hopkins, become present for the man who is able to say "Yes" through the "future better one" that God reveals to him via the *arbitrium*.

This capitalized "Yes" of the elective will stands out in sharp contrast to the lower-case "comfort" in the title of the poem. Milward explains the spelling of "comfort" as a sign of Hopkins's "humility" — "recognizing (with St. Paul) that what he feels on earth 'as it were in a glass darkly' is not to be compared to that true Comfort (appropriately spelt with a capital letter) which remains to be revealed in heaven."[17] I suggest, none too fancifully, I hope, that this small "c" pulls against the tendency towards transcendence in the resolution of the poem, just as does Hopkins's consistent spelling with small letters of the pronouns that refer to God. Although man is equated with God (transcendence), God is equally joined with man (immanence). The linguistic signifiers are thus coaxed into figuring the same configuration of paradox that themes the specifically Roman Catholic signified. Thus, by reading synchronically, a non-Catho-lic reader can participate in (and not merely acknowledge intellectually) a basic theological structure — paradox — even if he does not accept the contents of its particular manifestation.

Notes

1. All references to and quotations from Hopkins's poetry will be from *Poems* (hereafter cited with the text as (P, number of poem)) "That Nature is a Heraclitean Fire and of the comfort of the Resurrection" will be abbreviated throughout as HF.

2. My treatment of HF in this paper is a further instance of the concerns that motivated a previous article. "Prayers of Praise and Prayers of Petition: The Sonnets of Gerard Manley Hopkins," *Victorian Poetry*, 22:4 (Winter 1984), 283–306. There I have worked out, at some length, my rationale for a synchronic reading. I shall also draw upon some of my previous findings about the "nature" and "terrible" sonnets in the present attempt to define and explore HF's relation to them.

3. I have more fully discussed the way that interpretations inevitably reveal the configuration of personal concerns — with specific reference to Hopkins — in "Basic Herme-neutic Structures and Readings of Gerard Manley Hopkins's *The Wreck of the Deutschland*," *Hebrew University Studies in Literature*, 12:3 (Summer 1984), 31–44.

For basic expositions of reader-response critical theory see especially: Stanley Fish, *Is There a Text in This Class? The Authority of Textual Communities* (Cambridge, Mass.: Harvard University Press, 1980); Wolfgang Iser, "Indeterminacy and the Reader's Response," in J. Hillis Miller (ed.), *Aspects of Narrative: Selective Papers from the English Institute* (New York and London: Columbia University Press, 1971), pp. 1–45; "The Reading Process: A Phenomenological Approach," in Iser's *The Implied Reader: Patterns of Communication in Prose Fiction from Bunyan to Beckett* (Baltimore and London: Johns Hopkins University Press, 1974); *The Act of Reading: A Theory of Aesthetic Response* (Baltimore and London: Johns Hopkins University Press, 1958); and "The Current Situation of Literary Theory: Key

Concepts and the Imaginary," *New Literary History*, 11:1 (1979), 1–20; Hans Robert Jauss, *Aesthetic Experience and Literary Hermeneutics*, trans. Michael Shaw (Minneapolis: University of Minnesota Press, 1982); and *Toward an Aesthetic of Reception*, trans. Timothy Bahti (Minneapolis: University of Minnesota Press, 1982).

For comprehensive collections of essays see: *The Reader in the Text: Essays on Audience and Interpretation*, Susan Suleiman and Inge Crosman, eds. (Princeton: Princeton University Press, 1980); and *Reader-Response Criticism: From Formalism to Post-Structuralism* (Baltimore and London: Johns Hopkins University Press, 1980).

For an excellent study of the issues involved see: Robert C. Holub, *Reception Theory: A Critical Introduction* (London and New York: Methuen, 1984).

4. The frequent syntactical ambiguity in Hopkins's usage of this term certainly suggests this mutuality — as does its complex relationship with the analogous term "instress" evident in Hopkins's prose writings. See especially: *Journals*, pp, 127–30, 199, 241–8, 271, 289; *Sermons*, pp. 125, 146, 168, 210 (quotations from this work will hereafter be indicated in the text as (S, page number); *Letters I*, p. 66; and *Letters II*, pp. 37, 63, 68, 135.

Critics have commented extensively on this problem. See, for instance: James Finn Cotter, *Inscape: The Christology and Poetry of Gerard Manley Hopkins* (Pittsburgh: University of Pittsburgh Press, 1972, pp. 3, 18–20, 99–100, 125–6, 143–5; David A. Downes, *Victorian Portraits: Hopkins and Pater* (New York: Bookman Associates, 1965, pp. 84–127); W. H. Gardner, *Gerard Manley Hopkins: A Study of Poetic Idiosyncrasy in Relation to Poetic Tradition* (London: Martin Secker and Warburg, Vol. I, 1944, pp. 11–15, 22–7; Vol. II, 1949, pp. 122–3, 128–30, 133–9); Alan Heuser, *The Shaping Vision of Gerard Manley Hopkins* (London, New York, Toronto: Oxford University Press, 1958, pp. 23–39, 80); Donald McChesney, *A Hopkins Commentary* (London: University of London Press, 1968; pp. 22–9); J. Hillis Miller, *The Disappearance of God: Five Nineteenth Century Writers* (Cambridge, Mass: Harvard University Press, 1963, pp. 281–3); James Milroy, *The Language of Gerard Manley Hopkins* (London: Andre Deutsch, 1977, pp. 100–13); W. A. M. Peters, S.J., *Gerard Manley Hopkins: A Critical Essay towards the Understanding of His Poetry* (London, New York, Toronto: Oxford University Press, 1948, pp. 1–29); John Robinson, *In Extremity: A Study of Gerard Manley Hopkins* (Cambridge, New York: Cambridge University Press, 1978, pp. 22–4); and Austin Warren, "Instress of Inscape," in *Hopkins: A Collection of Critical Essays*, Geoffrey H. Hartman, ed. (Englewood Cliffs, New Jersey: Prentice-Hall, 1966, pp. 168–77).

5. For a fascinating theory of how the human mind has actually attempted to "solve" paradox through narrative, see Kenneth Burke, *The Rhetoric of Religion: Studies in Logology* (Berkeley and Los Angeles: University of California Press, 1970), especially pp. 223–54). For Burke's discussion of the same issue in another context, see also his *The Philosophy of Literary Form: Studies in Symbolic Action* (New York: Vintage Books, 1957, pp. 42–51).

6. See: *Letters II*, pp. 14–15; *Letters I*, pp. 66, 135; and *Letters III*, p. 231.

7. For the pioneering study of the relevance of Ignatian meditation to an understanding of Hopkins's poetry, see Louis L. Martz, *The Poetry of Meditation: A Study in English Religious Literature of the Seventeenth Century* (New Haven and London: Yale University Press, 1954, pp. 14–39, 321–6); and the introduction to his anthology *The Meditative Poem* (New York: Anchor Books, 1963, pp. xxxi–xxxii). For more recent discussions, see: David A. Downes, *Gerard Manley Hopkins: A Study of His Ignatian Spirit* (New York, 1959), pp. 20, 54, 74–5, 141, 166); Daniel A. Harris, *Inspirations Unbidden: The "Terrible Sonnets" of Gerard Manley Hopkins* (Berkeley, Los Angeles, London: University of California Press, 1982, pp. 72–125); John Pick, *Gerard Manley Hopkins: Priest and Poet* (London, New York, Toronto: Oxford University Press, 1966, pp. 25–37, 127); Robinson, pp. 22–4; and Alan M. Rose, "Hopkins' 'Carrion Comfort': The Artful Disorder of Prayer," *Victorian Poetry*, 15 (1977), 207–17.

8. For analysis of Hopkins's relation to Scotus see especially: Robert J. Andreach, *Studies in Structure: The Stages of the Spiritual Life in Four Modern Authors* (New York:

Fordham University Press, 1964, pp. 3–38); and Christopher Devlin, S.J., "The Image and the Word," *The Month*, n.s. III (1950), 114–27, 191, 202; *The Psychology of Duns Scotus*, Aquinas Paper 15 (Oxford, 1950); and his Introduction and Appendix to *Sermons*, pp. 118–20, 338–51. See also: Cotter, pp. 121–33; McChesney, pp. 20–2; Pick, pp. 32–7, 51–4, 83–4, 156–9; and Robinson, pp. 36–41.

A succinct statement of the spiritual-aesthetic implications of Hopkins's Scotism is to be found in J. Hillis Miller's *The Disappearance of God:* "In this view natural things, instead of having a derived being, participate directly in the being of the creator. They are in the same way that he is. Each created thing, in its own special way, is the total image of its creator. . . . Such a view of nature leads to a poetry in which things are not specific symbols, but all mean one thing and the same" (pp. 314–5).

9. See *Letters I*, pp. 60–4, 117–18, 186–7.

10. The critics rely heavily upon Hopkins's descriptions in letters of his physical and mental state at this time. See especially: *Letters I*, pp. 189–270; and *Letters II*, pp. 63, 184, 446. For critics who follow this line of explication see: Bernard Bergonzi, *Gerard Manley Hopkins* (New York: Macmillan, 1977, p. 54); Gardner, vol. I, pp. 32–7, and vol. II, pp. 339–47; Miller, pp. 324–59; Robinson, pp. 142–50; J. F. J. Russell, *A Critical Commentary on Gerard Manley Hopkins's Poems* (London: Macmillan, 1971, pp. 13, 36); Elisabeth W. Schneider, *The Dragon in the Gate: Studies in the Poetry of Gerard Manley Hopkins* (Berkeley and Los Angeles: University of California Press, 1968, pp. 186–90); and Yvor Winters, *The Function of Criticism* (London: Alan Swallow, Routledge and Kegan Paul, 1957, pp. 107–8).

11. The most striking elaborations of this position are Harris, pp. 35–41, 129–44; and Michael Sprinker, *"A Counterpoint of Dissonance": The Aesthetics and Poetry of Gerard Manley Hopkins* (Baltimore and London: Johns Hopkins University Press, 1980, especially pp. 64–5, 127–33, 142–3).

12. St. Ignatius of Loyola, *The Spiritual Exercises*, trans. Anthony Mottola (Garden City, New York: Image Books, 1964, especially pp. 48–80). I briefly summarize here the argument worked out in my *Victorian Poetry* article, in order to establish the critical framework for my reading of HF.

13. For Hopkins's most explicit discussion of the "affective" and "elective" wills, see his "On Personality, Grace and Free Will," in *Sermons*, pp. 146–8. Devlin's commentary on this issue (pp. 118–20, 338–51) is quite helpful.

14. For critics who view the suffering of these poems as a sign of spiritual triumph, see: G. F. Lahey, S.J., *Gerard Manley Hopkins* (London: Oxford University Press, 1930, pp. 140–3); Pick, pp. 129–30, 143–50); Stephan Walliser, *"That Nature is a Heraclitean Fire and of the comfort of the Resurrection": A Case-Study in G. M. Hopkins' Poetry* (Basel: Francke Verlag Bern, 1977, especially pp. 15–41, 98–124, 167–72); and Patricia A. Wolfe, "Hopkins's Spiritual Conflict in the 'Terrible' Sonnets," in *Gerard Manley Hopkins's Poems: A Casebook*, Margaret Bottrall, ed. (London: Macmillan, 1975), pp. 218–34).

15. See especially: Howard W. Fulweiler, *Letters from the Darkling Plain: Language and the Grounds of Knowledge in the Poetry of Arnold and Hopkins* (Columbia, Missouri: University of Missouri Press, 1972, p. 161); Harris, pp. 38–9, 46; Paul Mariani, *A Commentary on the Complete Poems of Gerard Manley Hopkins* (Ithaca, New York: Cornell University Press, 1970, p. 289); and Harris, pp. 124–6.

16. See Jacog Korg, "Hopkins's Linguistic Deviations," *PMLA*, 92:5 (October 1977), 977–86, here p. 979; and Sprinker, pp. 32–3, 62–3.

17. Peter Milward, "Hopkins' 'comfort,' " *Hopkins Research*, no. 13 (July 1984), pp. 1–7.

"The shepherd's brow":
Hopkins "disparadised"

Richard F. Giles*

Hopkins' penultimate completed poem—"The shepherd's brow"—was composed a few months before his death in Dublin on June 8, 1889. His health had been deteriorating quickly during the time he composed the poem; his duties as examiner at University College were proving to be both a physical and, ironically, spiritual burden he could hardly bear;[1] and his creative projects were lacking inspiration and fulfillment, as he often and candidly complained to Robert Bridges in letters and in his final sonnet. It is apparent that Hopkins was made daily aware of his physical weakening, and it is also very likely that the texture of "The shepherd's brow"—rich, interwoven, and simultaneously striving to conceal and to reveal—reflects that awareness in Hopkins. Whether the poem is "cynical," as Bridges as first editor insisted, or whether it is merely realistic in its rendering of the image of man, it presents a summary of Hopkins' lifetime preoccupations and it reveals, as much by what it does not literally say as by its actual verbalization, the state of a poetic mind nearing its physical and creative death. "The shepherd's brow" combines personal and universal elements in a way unique to the poem; it is—at once—one of Hopkins' most personal communications and one of his most detached poetic exercises. The melding of these two very different modes contributes to the inordinate tension in the poem.

It is a poem built upon ambiguity, dichotomous contrast, and inversion, with each of these factors contributing to the tension created in the first line and left unresolved in the final line. That feeling of tension is even more powerful when the highly personal nature of this poem is considered; it is a sonnet-letter written to Hopkins' audience, his literary friend Bridges.[2] The poem went through four drafts before Hopkins was satisfied that its fifth version communicated to Bridges the sentiment and passion Hopkins felt at the approach of his own death. What now seems uncertain is exactly what Hopkins was attempting to convert his reader to in this troublesome piece, or what darkened vision he was admitting to himself and Bridges.

1

The poem begins on a note of ambiguity: "The shepherd's brow, fronting forked lightning, owns / The horror and the havoc and the glory / Of it." The image that emerges from these lines is that of a shepherd in a field tending his flock while a storm rages about[3] (the definite article either creates the class of shepherds or restricts the meaning to one in particular);

*From *Victorian Poetry* 23, no. 2 (Summer 1985): 169–87.

the words are too brief, however, to create as detailed a picture as Hopkins often did in, say, his nature sonnets of 1877. The deliberately cryptic quality of these lines suggests that Hopkins is evoking an archetype as well as a specific (as he will do later with "Man Jack"). "Forked" functions to depict lightning that has split.[4] Symbolically, the fork introduces the first of the dichotomies that abound in this poem and from which it draws much of its strength. The lightning has been divided, has dissipated its unified strength into two spears. The shepherd, facing this lightning, "owns" its "horror and the havoc and the glory," in the sense of both possessing and recognizing[5] the potentially destructive element as well as its visually striking display (another contrasting dichotomy).

Further ambiguity surrounds the identity of the shepherd. He may well be merely a human figure. However, as the remainder of the first quatrain shows, Hopkins is setting up a contrast between the human (which does not appear until the second quatrain) and the superhuman or the angelic (which appear in the first quatrain).[6] Many critics have asserted that the shepherd may be Christ,[7] Moses,[8] St. Peter,[9] simply a shepherd,[10] or even Hopkins himself.[11] One critic has even suggested that "the shepherd is cited as a symbol for men who recognize God's grandeur when it flames out and who do 'reck his rod.' "[12] However, the divisions of the poem are much too sharp and definite to allow for such a mingling of human-but-different with divine as one group that is then contrasted with the simply human. Such a mingling would destroy the deliberate structuring Hopkins carefully applied to this oft-revised poem.

Hopkins gives us a clue as to which shepherd he had in mind in the second line, "The horror and the havoc and the glory," which is rhythmically, verbally, and imagistically an inversion (perhaps even a perversion) of the line from The Lord's Prayer: "For thine is the kingdom, and the power, and the glory, for ever" (Matthew 6.13; King James version). "Kingdom" becomes "horror"; "power" becomes "havoc"; and (significantly for the poem) "glory" (a characteristic dependent upon mutual perception) remains the same in both. The shepherd for whom this perversion has occurred must be Christ,[13] confronting the "forked lightning" — the meaning of His Sacrifice on Calvary — just as He had earlier confronted the Fall of Lucifer: "I was watching Satan fall as lightning from heaven" (Luke 10.18; Douay version). For Him, conceivably, the words of His earlier prayer have become a reminder of what He perceives to be a betrayal, just as Hopkins, throughout his years in Dublin and especially in his final months, was feeling more and more the emptiness of the earlier words he had uttered in praise of "The roll, the rise, the carol, the creation" ("To R. B."). Appropriately, the facts that Christ's brow would be the part of His body closest to the sky and, therefore, the part most likely to turn to front the lightning, and that, as One of the Trinity, He would own all those traits of the lightning Hopkins lists as well as —

because of His human form — recognize them for their intrinsic power, lend further weight to the identification of Christ as the shepherd.[14]

This identification is enforced by the next sentence in the opening quatrain: "Angels fall, they are towers, from Heaven — a story / Of just, majestical, and giant groans." Christ's incarnation — as a descent into flesh — was a type of fall; in fact, the poem begins on an image of Christ at His most fallen and then adds that angels fall as well, and not just from a great height, but from the greatest height: heaven. Their rebellion and their fall constitute — a story. "Story" in its placement at the end of the poetic line and following immediately upon a dash is deliberately ambiguous and extraordinarily effective. While the final line of the quatrain informs the reader rather quietly that the groans of the fallen angels are "just" (deserved), "majestical" (grand, stupendous), and "giant" (large, deafening, worthy of attention), the word "story" serves to undercut those very characteristics. A story can be epic, dynamic, charged, but it can also be merely a story: a fable, a tale, an entertainment, a mere speaking of words to while away time. Just as Christ's crucifixion is reduced to a divine forehead fronting forked lightning (Divine Wisdom and Power?), so too is the Angelic Rebellion rendered into its smallest components: words in a story.

The poem, then, begins in a kind of deception. It presents a shepherd confronting a natural phenomenon and follows that image with one of the Fall of Lucifer, only to begin the second quatrain with indications that the first must be regarded as a homogenous whole and that the shepherd cannot be merely human; there must be some common bond between the angels who fall and the shepherd. That bond is, obviously, the divine origin of both, but it is also, within the poem, the subject of much of its concern: lamentation and complaint. Christ on the cross lamented and complained, and with good reason, according to the rationale of this poem. So too did the angels who lost their bliss in heaven and who fell to eternal torment have just reason to groan. These grand lamentations make up the first quatrain, but their grandness is kept in check (even undercut) by the poet's referring to them as a mere story, as almost a bit of myth-making. In all of this, the first quatrain is one-half of a comparison-to-be-made. The contents of this quatrain must, then, be exclusively divine according to the structure of the poem.

The second quatrain immediately presents the comparison between the angelic creatures of the first and the subject of this one:

> But man — we, scaffold of score brittle bones;
> Who breathe, from groundlong babyhood to hoary
> Age gasp; whose breath is our *memento mori* —
> What bass if *our* viol for tragic tones?

The dramatic workings of the poem are no more clearly displayed than in this quatrain. The poet begins at some distance from his subject ("But man") and then decides that he cannot "afford" such distance; he is no longer the privileged singer of songs or teller of stories; he has become both subject and object of the poem he is himself composing.[15] The dash represents this moment of illumination, provides the pause the poet took to discover it, and gives us the "false start" needed to show that this composition is dramatic in that it presents the mental and emotional workings of the poet as they occur. "We" — the category rests in the poet's mind and he is unable to follow it with any statement of activity. Rather, he offers an appositive: "scaffold of score brittle bones." That image looks back to and contrasts with the preceding "towers," those angelic creatures so magnificent in their heavenly surroundings. Towers must be constructed; God makes all towers; He made the angels grand; He made us a feeble "scaffold"[16] of fragile bones. There is bitterness in and under this line, and that bitterness continues, with the poet still unable to articulate a statement of activity on the part of man: "Who breathe, from groundlong babyhood to hoary / Age gasp." Angels groan, and we hear it in the story; man breathes, rhythmically and weakly from the time he crawls along the ground as a child until he stands and gasps for breath as a hoary creature. Still unable to formulate his sentence, the poet adds yet another description: "whose breath is our *memento mori.*" Finally, the poet musters his powers to form — not a statement but — a question: "What bass is *our* viol for tragic tones?" Several critics have pointed out the ambiguity in these lines (see, e.g., Mariani, [*A Commentary*,] p.307), and that ambiguity further enhances the strong dichotomous content of the poem. Man is contrasted with angels; breath in youth becomes gasping in age; breath (that which allows us to live) actually serves as a reminder of our mortality; even though our complaints seem justified, are they "bass" (base) enough to allow us to reach tragic heights in our or God's estimation? The poet only asks the question as a form of complaint that simultaneously declares and inquires and thus serves to bridge the distance between the questioner and the questioned and to increase that distance. Hopkins continues his spiritual battles actively on paper, to pursue colloquy with God.

That battle leads to a distancing that takes place between the end of the second quatrain and the beginning of the first tercet — a place where some volta should occur but does not (Mariani, p. 310). Rather, the distancing is Hopkins' speaking directly to Bridges, directly to his larger audience, but mostly to Bridges: "He! Hand to mouth he lives, and voids with shame; / And, blazoned in however bold the name, / Man Jack the man is, just; his mate a hussy." The "our" in line eight has — dramatically and emphatically — become "He," almost shouted and soon to be repeated within the same line. Hopkins now steps back from his subject (man, himself) and manipulates the object of the poem (now himself, his audience but especially Bridges) by introducing a hidden, very personal meaning.[17] He — Hopkins the Jesuit and poet — cannot be included in this category of Man not because he does not also live "Hand to mouth" and "voids with shame" (he does),[18] not because he does not have a name "blazoned" boldly (perhaps a reference — however obscure — to Bridges' growing reputation as a poet), but because he does not (indeed cannot) have a mate who is a "hussy." He can, of course have no mate and remain true to his vows to his order, and so he becomes like man and unlike man, like men and unlike men.

The picture of man that emerges in this communication is somewhat shocking, at least unsettling. He lives "Hand to mouth," meaning precariously and day by day; but the image of a man almost grazing, scooping his food with his hand and stuffing it into his mouth is just below the surface of this line. What he takes in this manner he must excrete in an equally shameful way, and so he seeks privacy when he must void. And whatever claim to glory he may have, man is "just" (an echo of the other "just" in line four and a playing-off of the one against the other) — merely — man. This tautology is made even more effective by Hopkins' capitalizing Man Jack, only to follow it immediately by the resigned statement that no matter the title, man is but man.[19] Hopkins goes even further and undercuts one of his most fondly held notions. "Man Jack" (the type, the individual as well as, apparently, the majority) mates himself to a mere hussy. The word is so placed that its pejorative value cannot be ignored. In this single line Hopkins reduces to ridicule a notion he had held for many years. The sacred bond of marriage to which he had often and fondly referred (see *Letters*, I, 194, 198, 298) becomes in the poem a mere physical coupling of the sexes of the species — for the purpose of procreation or of pleasure only. Bridges would surely have been more than a little uncomfortable over this rather sudden and abrupt undermining, and Hopkins was surely aware of the discomfort these lines would cause in his most faithful (at that time practically only) reader.

Hopkins turns to himself in the final tercet: "And I that die these deaths, that feed this flame, / That . . . in smooth spoons spy life's masque mirrored: tame / My tempests there, my fire and fever fussy." Again in the realm of the merely human, he must begin with a conjunction, as he did in lines five and ten.[20] The poet resumes his thoughts on his own life. The first line of the tercet presents an image of death, but death becomes plural. "These deaths" the poet dies are, no doubt, of the same kind that ended an earlier sonnet: "Life death does end and each day dies with sleep" (*Poems*, p. 100). But "these deaths" function on many levels, as did the shepherd with his unclear identity who began the poem. Each day of the poet's life may die with darkness; each day's activities may die in sleep; each breath may become a reminder of death as well as a shortener of the life remaining; each doubt about his life and its value may be a type of death to a religious; each "resolved" spiritual crisis may be a form of death; in the renewed spirit of identity between the poet and man, each death of a man may be suffered by the poet, may be felt as a kind of stigmata; each poem may represent, upon completion, a *memento mori* of creative demise; or, referring to the immediately preceding hussy mated to her man, the poet may suffer a kind of sexual stigmata each time fallen man fornicates, or even procreates within the bonds of marriage (either act being a sordid reminder of his fall in the Garden). Regardless of what these deaths are, they contribute to the image of decay that is picked up by the remainder of the line: "that feed this flame." Death and decay can feed a flame in that gases (groans, breaths, gasps) are created by decomposition of organic material. The image is ugly even if the exact reference of this flame is not known. The ambiguity continues as "this flame" could be any number of things: the "fire" of inspiration; the flames of hell; the agony of doubt; the heat of desire; or the internal "combustion" of the human body, fed hand to mouth and excreting noisily (the rhyming of "shame" — to describe "void" — with "flame" reinforces this idea).

The end of the first line of this tercet is the second of what starts out to be a series of clauses describing the poet (similar in structure to the clauses describing man in the second quatrain). The dramatic break — and the real volta of the sonnet — occurs in the next line. The poet is able to utter the first conjunction in the next clause in the series, and then stops, pauses, reflects on not only the poem in which he is struggling to create and to understand a vision of his life in the context of the lives of all other human beings but on that vision itself. An ellipsis indicates the pause, and the resumption, while altering the proposed parallel structure, retains enough of the grammatical structure to end the poem quietly and with a great deal of cynical resignation. The poet sees reflected in "smooth spoons" "life's masque." This is one of Hopkins' more troublesome images, and because it is in his penultimate poem, it is one worth exploring.[21]

"Spoons" is to be taken literally. The poet sees himself (no doubt) reflected in a spoon, either an empty spoon being taken from the mouth and returned to the plate or bowl, or perhaps an inverted spoon resting on a table beside a dish.[22] The appropriateness of this strange instrument as part of the final image in the poem may be accounted for in several ways. First, spoon balances the fork of "forked lightning" in the first line of the poem. It also picks up with the "Hand to mouth" cliché of line nine. And it also picks up with the feeding of flames in the preceding line. Finally, it looks ahead to the "fever" in the final line evoking an image of a sick person feeding himself (or being fed) some sort of medicine to help effect a cure. (An earlier version of this line, "In spoons have seen my masque played," was even more personal but less specific; in the final version the poet sees all "life's [not just his own] masque" played out on this minute stage.)

A further personal connection — and one Hopkins may have had in mind — is his use of "spooniness" in a letter to Bridges to describe his (Hopkins') feelings about married people (see *Letters*, I, 198). "Spooniness" means "silliness" or "foolishness" and, in its context in the letter, diminishes Hopkins as a sentimental, somewhat naive fool. "Spoon" in this poem functions similarly to diminish the value of the life by diminishing the image of the stage upon which the life is acted out. But the spoon does even more. It reflects "life's masque"; in other words it is an image of a play. To untangle this web of perception would require superhuman power, and the poet does not have such power, nor does he pretend to. He merely states that in such smooth surfaces on such everyday items as spoons he sees what the whole drama of life is: a simple reflection, a refraction. This thought essentially ends the poem; it is followed by a colon that is in turn followed by another appositive ("tame" is neither an imperative nor indicative verb; it is an adjective, as an earlier version of the line shows: "and how tame / My tempest and my spitfire freaks how fussy"), further describing what the poet sees in these spoons.

What the poet "sees" (in the sense of "perceives") is this: there (in the spoon) his "tempests" are tame, his "fire" is tame, and his "fever fussy" is tame. But it is only there, in the reflection of the masque,[23] and not in the masque itself, that his problems seem insignificant compared to the fall of Christ or of the angels. The poem ends as deceptively as it began. Upon first reading, it sounds as if the poet is telling himself that, in reality, he is exaggerating both the significance and consequences of his problems. But the poem only seems to sound this note; it does not actually stop on it. The phrasing acts to hide the deeper, more profound meaning while revealing an apparent surface meaning. This simultaneous hiding and revealing ends the poem with a similar tension that resulted from the ambiguity of its the first lines.

The poet can draw slight comfort that only in a reflection does his life lose its agonizing edge. The spoons that bring to his body the food that creates the excreta of which he is ashamed and that lead to infection that sickens him until he must take medicine in those same spoons also become, sadly and ironically, a source of comfort in their illusory powers, just as his poems, throughout his life, had provided him with relief, even if a false and temporary relief, by reflecting and, perhaps, refracting certain elements in his life and the world.[24]

2

"The shepherd's brow" is, by any measure, an intensely personal poem, as are most of Hopkins' major works. In intensity it matches the "Terrible Sonnets" written four years earlier. In its own way, this sonnet too is "terrible": it offers its reader no resolution of the tension created through its metaphorical structure and its language.[25] This structure represents only the façade of the plentiful concerns that Hopkins attempted to deal with in his Dublin years and, even more so, in the months prior to his death. As with most of his other poems, his prose works — both letters and private notes — act as guides.[26]

While key words exist more in critical readings than in a poem, there are in this poem four words whose placement, sound, and meaning provide the base for the poetic construction. Each word occurs as the final utterance in its poetic unit (i.e., quatrain and tercet), and each acts as a synopsis of sorts for what has been said in the immediately preceding lines. They are "groans," "tones," "hussy," and "fussy," all words that in or out of context bear negative connotations and elicit negative responses in the reader. "Groans" are the angelic complaints that establish the first part of the metaphor of complaint and provide the basis for comparison of these majestic exhalations to the pitiful "tones" that man is capable of; "hussy" is the degrading epithet attached to the physical/sexual side of man's existence, in contrast to the purer elemental existence of the angelic creatures of the first quatrain, and "fussy" is Hopkins' self-appraisal. These four words exhibit the structural unity and dictional consistency of the poem as well as the source of tension both within the poem and in the poet's mind at the time of composition. Man's complaints are nothing compared to the truly tragic nature of the first falls, and man's physical existence is disgusting and — as manifested by Hopkins himself — temperamental.

But such thoughts are by no means original to Hopkins, nor should they present insurmountable obstacles in the path of a religious who has devoted his life to the cause of God and His Church. Yet, in Hopkins' case, they do, and some of his private meditation notes reveal why. In fact, just as Hopkins' journals provided a poetic outlet during his silence from 1866–1875 and were later mined for images and words when he broke that silence, his devotional writings often anticipate poetic expression of the same concerns or, in some cases, the same language structures. Hopkins' thoughts on "The Principle or Foundation," written probably after 1885 (*Sermons*, pp. 238–241), is a virtual gloss on "The shepherd's brow."

"The Principle" is concerned with — in extremity — the glorifications of God by his creatures, both brute and human. In fact, "glory" (or some form of the word) occurs 29 times within the few pages of this meditation, sometimes repeated to the point of near parody.

Even more striking, however, is the juxtaposition of other tenets next to the call to glorify the Creator. The exercise begins with God's creative power and his work in infinity compared to man's labor in temporal and spatial bonds. Hopkins observes: "MAN CANNOT CREATE a single speck, God creates all that is besides himself" (p. 238). Like "The shepherd's brow," this meditation begins by establishing divine magnitude as the basis for the comparison that follows. This structural similarity extends even to the beginning of the third paragraph with: "But MEN OF GENIUS ARE SAID TO CREATE." The second stanza of the poem begins: "But man — we." In both poem and meditation Hopkins focuses on man's limitations after delineating the infinite might of the divine. Men are said to create, he says, but they create "from themselves, from their own minds." And immediately the poet observes: "And they themselves, their minds and all, are creatures of God" (p. 238). The paradox — rooted in linguistic and semantic vagueness as well as Christianity's basic teachings — Hopkins is close to expressing here can be phrased thus: All things emanate from God — things such as human beings, brute animals, oceans, iron ore, the sun, the rain, poems, hussies, and faeces. The "Glory be to God for dappled things" of 1877 has by now become a confusion of good and bad, enhancing and diminishing, and dichotomous irreconciliation.

At least in the meditation Hopkins attempts to resurrect his now-faded ability to take joy from Nature. He turns to the size of the world, the vastness of the universe, and the speed of light, only to end his homily with this self-deprecating note: "So that the greatest of all works in the world, nay the world itself, was easier made than the least little thing that man or any other creature makes in the world" (p. 238). Hopkins is galled in his reverence, almost choked by his praise. All his "undertakings miscarry"; he is but a "straining eunuch" (*Sermons*, p. 262), "Time's eunuch" (*Poems*, p. 107), whose straining to produce yields only an absurd image: an emasculated creature vainly fornicating with an amused muse. Significantly, in "The shepherd's brow," Hopkins excluded himself from the category of mated (hence fornicating) man presented in the first tercet. Hopkins knows no ease — or success — in creating.

The meditation then asks why God created His works in the first place, and this question frees Hopkins to gain some comfort by repeating to himself the reason: "*to give him* [God] *glory,*" "to yield him glory," "to shew him glory," "to pay him glory," "to rise to his glory," "to sacrifice to his glory," and (again and again) "to give him glory."[27] (Remember that "glory" was the only word not inverted in the second line of the poem.) God does not need this glory, but He takes it. Brute creation does not think of glorifying God, but it does, even if this is but "poor praise, faint reverence, slight service, dull glory" (p. 239). Hopkins grapples with this thought, reaches for its consequences, and couples together two creatures who occupy prominent places in the poem: "But AMIDST THEM ALL IS MAN, man and the angels." "Man was made to give, and mean to give, God glory" (p. 239). Hopkins can easily join all creation in having been created to give God glory and in having done so simply by living out his created existence, but the qualification — that man must mean (and, we assume, therefore try) to give God glory — creates a tension that makes its way into the poem as well as the remainder of this exercise.

At this point in the exercise, Hopkins gets personal (as he does in the poem): "I WAS MADE FOR THIS, each one of us was made for this. Does man then do it? Never mind others now nor the race of man: DO I DO IT? — If I sin I do not: how can I dishonour God and honour him?" (p. 239). Hopkins establishes the category of man, observes it from a distance, then shortens the distance to allow himself to enter; he can then turn almost exclusively upon himself as a member of the category, thus sharing the traits he has been discussing, and weigh himself on the scale of virtue. In the exercise, that scale reveals an interesting turn in Hopkins' mind. He knows why he was created; he asks if he is living up to the ideals of the Creator, but his answer contains its own corollary, both sides, of course, being theologically "true," but both sides not admitting discussion at this crucial juncture, both sides, in other words, straining to pull apart rather than to unite the mind that poses them. True, if Hopkins commits sin he is not giving glory to God (one does not uphold a law by breaking it), but the question Hopkins has running through his mind — the question that controls so much of this exercise — but that he cannot bring himself to formulate is: Do I sin if I do not give glory to God?[28] If I willfully fail to honor him, do I dishonor him by denying my human birthright and joining the brute in mere automatic actions? That is the question that flows just beneath the surface of this exercise, and that is the question that also controls much of the texture and tension in "The shepherd's brow." If, says Hopkins, my bones are brittle, my breath is short, my voiding is shameful, and my sexual nature is brutish, how can I give glory to God?[29] Even more so, if I am a poet who once sang the praises of the Creator and His Creation, who actively controlled words in the service of God, can I give glory to Him by griping about my "fever fussy" in a paltry sonnet?

The poem is the answer to these asked but unuttered questions. The poet who before could utter: "I feel thy finger," "I did say yes," "I whirled out wings," "I kiss my hand," "I remember a house," "I say more," "I plod wondering," "I walk, I lift up, I lift up heart," "I caught," "I can," "I wake," "I cast for comfort" — that same poet can now end a poem with only an interrupted "I that" clause; he is now not the active agent; he is merely "[I] / That . . . in smooth spoons spy life's masque mirrored." The poem literally leaves the poet in the middle of one of his ever-shortening breaths, struggling to ascertain what and who he is but more importantly what it is that he does (or can do) that will glorify God.

The meditation is one attempt to raise himself to a level of offering such praise, but it fails and falls back on repetition as its main instrument, as if to say over and over, "You are healthy," to a sick person could make that person well. The meditation fails, and in failing records the minds that years later would express the same thoughts in the poem.[30] Even much of the imagery in the exercise reappears in the poem. For example, "Are we his glass to look in? we are deep in dust or our silver gone or we are broken or, worst of all, we misshape his face and make God's image hideous" (p. 240) becomes the distorting instrument of reflection in the poem: the spoon. "Are we his censer? we breathe stench and now sweetness" becomes the breath that "is our *memento mori*." And: "Smiting on an anvil, sawing a beam, whitewashing a wall, driving horses, sweeping, scouring, everything gives God some glory if being in his grace you do it as your duty. To go to communion worthily gives God great glory, but to take food in thankfulness and temperance gives him glory too. To lift up the hands in prayer gives God glory, but a man with a dungfork in his hand, a woman with a sloppail, give him glory too" (pp. 240–241) becomes the ugly image of man living hand to mouth and voiding with shame, his mate a hussy (with sloppail in hand?).

It would be too easy to look at the exercise and the poem and say simply that both show that Hopkins' fastidiousness and "anality" were still strong up to his death. On the other hand, it would be hard to deny such an assertion. The poem is certainly anal in its imagery and theme;[31] the exercise insists on jamming together images of taking in food and giving glory to God for such sustenance with images of breathing stench, dungforks, and sloppails. The exercise, interestingly, catalogues activities of cleaning-up as especially exemplary of ways to give God glory: whitewashing a wall, sweeping, and scouring.[32] But these two works reveal much more of Hopkins' state of mind during his final years and final weeks than merely his fixation on cleanliness and his preoccupation with bodily discharge.

They show a man whose sense of failure extends not only into his art but also into his spiritual core, that part of him he had always been able to count on as ascetically pure. His quest for aesthetic purity had produced some of his loveliest lyrics, when his body was physically able to allow joy to be felt and his mind was not tormenting itself with doubts. That aesthetic purity had yielded to the reality expressed in the "Terrible Sonnets," where the poet could not turn his attentions away from the ugly inner-scape to the lovely outer-scape. Certainly, the "Terrible Sonnets" were relatively fresh reminders to Hopkins of the movement of his life, from the beauty of Wales, the beauty of children, the beauty of his Maker, and the beauty of himself, to the sordid existence in Dublin, amid hostile and ugly people, away from his dear native land, and removed from his Maker's comfort — and, thereby, according to Hopkins' theology, removed from his Maker.[33] "The shepherd's brow" records the poet's recognition of this removal as he enters and leaves the categories he creates within the poem, confusingly making himself human, too-human, and sub-human, only to drop the effort in mid-thought.

The meditation attempts to bring the poet out of his spiritual stupor. He extols himself: "This [to give God glory] is a thing to live for. Then make haste so to live" (p. 240). A few years later he records: "I wish then for death" (Sermons, p. 262). In between these thoughts occurred a process that might be called Hopkins' "humanization": his carnal nature refused to yield to his spiritual, no matter how hard he struggled, no matter how much he prayed, no matter how many examinations he marked, and no matter how many poems he was able to compose — or unable to complete. The physical torment fed the spiritual and dined from it as well. This cycle of anguish was one of the few things in his life that was complete, and as he looked back at his life and his achievements — as he noticed that, according to all the philosophy and theology he embraced, he should have been walking in joy in the grace of God but he was more crawling in the gutter of darkness—he was drawn to one of his first—and most abiding—loves: language, especially poetic language. Even so close to his death-bed as he was, he could still compose, he could still structure language, even though that language could only mirror—like the spoon—the internal struggle. That language can only reflect "life's masque" is a fact that a reluctant Hopkins has to admit in "The shepherd's brow"; that his language would not completely carry to Bridges (and whatever audience God decreed) what he was almost desperate to say, he also has to admit. The language of "The shepherd's brow" is just that admission—admitting and revealing simultaneously.

3

The language of the poem is symmetrical, as nearly perfect as the poet could make it. The symmetry acts twofold: it serves as a kind of soothing for his tormented mind, and it is, in its balance, the medium for the dichotomous contrast that runs throughout the poem.

The language is also economical: there are only 117 words in the poem, and of these 44 are pronouns, conjunctions, articles, and prepositions, leaving only 73 primary words to convey the essential ideas of the poem. These essential ideas are paired off, for either contrast or complement.[34] Here is a list of the primary words, divided into their parts of speech:

verbs:	owns (perceives)—spy	
	breathe—gasp	
	lives—die	
	feed—void	
	is—are	
	fall—(only unmatched verb)	
participles:	fronting—forked	
	blazoned—mirrored	
nouns:	glory—shame	tones—bass
	tower—scaffold	mate—hussy
	story—masque	babyhood—age
	hand—mouth	angels—man
	groans—breath	*memento mori*—deaths
	tempests—havoc	name—Man Jack
	lightning—flame	spoons—viol
	fire—fever	

Doubtless, other pairings could be made and justified by either semantic or linguistic or poetic rationale, but this listing does reveal the poet's quest for symmetry in the restricted realm of the sonnet form as well as, perhaps, his inability to perceive and express the world in any way but by "pairing" phenomena. Ironically, as his feelings of failure intensified and he viewed his own works and language in general as a faulty medium, his creative ability remained sharp, in this case giving a clear structure to the language of doubt and contest with one's Maker.

The words themselves carry the meaning, but they also mean by being in a certain place and by being in contrast or complement to other words within the poem and within Hopkins' life. Within the poem the words are, for Hopkins, especially clear, with only one compound— "groundlong"—which is apparent; the macaronic *memento mori* is a bit unusual in the late poems. It appears, then, that Hopkins was not intent upon extravagant linguistic experimentation in this penultimate composition, wishing rather to use the poetic vehicle to explain. Hopkins had earlier written to Bridges: "We should explain things, plainly state them, clear them up, explain them; explanation—except personal—is always pure good; without explanation people go on misunderstanding; being once explained they thenceforward understand things; therefore always explain: but I have the passion for explanation and you have not," (*Letters*, 1, 275). Hopkins' parenthetical exception is revealing. He probably remembered this (or some similar) injunction against too-personal explanation when he wrote and revised this poem, for the poem, in spite of itself, explains to Bridges the cycle of defiance, despair, and resignation that so dominated Hopkins' entire personal and religious life.[35] The poem encapsulates that cycle, infuses the language with defiance (fronting), despair (groans) and resignation (tame), but retains in its structuring one of the last acts of confession and contrition that Hopkins could bring himself to offer both his Maker and Bridges. Hopkins paired off words, hoping his reader would understand the words and the act behind them and their meaning in contrast, and would comprehend the consequences of both. Significantly—and again the poem reveals so much more than its literal meaning can—the poet left unpaired the verb "fall." The angels do fall, the poet tells us, but he then goes on to convey the idea that man's fall does not compare with the former in scale or effect. In fact, as a follower of Scotus, Hopkins "did not see God the Son's descent into creation merely or primarily as the reparation for sin. He saw it as an act of love which would have taken place in one form or another whether or not there had been any sin," for, as Scotus says, "The Fall was not the reason for Christ's predestination. Even if no angel had fallen, nor any man, Christ would still have been predestined—yes, even if no others were to have been created save only Christ" (*Sermons*, p. 109). This paradox is also at the heart of the tension in the poem and also at the heart of the tension within the poet: Man's fall was not necessary to bring God's grace. The whole process—the brittle bones, the gasping breath, the meager existence, the fouling of the body, the need for fornication—summarized in the poem was not necessary, was and is pointless, and *that*—and not Hopkins' exaggerated sense of his own "fever fussy" — is what makes the poem cynical and, finally, defiant in its unresolved tension. Hopkins fell because man fell because Lucifer fell, but all these creatures did not have to fall — did not have to suffer with fever, diarrhea, examinations, doubts, and the process of composing poems — to gain God's grace. In the poem, with its economical and symmetrical language, the poet looks back on all life and lets the structuring of that language control his intense anger and his bitter antipathy. The language succeeds in that control, releasing little by little the mind and heart of the man who composed it a few months before his death of, ironically, a "fever fussy."

4

"The shepherd's brow" is one of Hopkins' last communications. In it, the poet retains the same creative impulse that led to the handful of poems for which he is most widely known and appreciated — his "Wreck" and his sonnets of natural beauty — as well as his record of spiritual despair: the "Terrible Sonnets." The poem has proven elusive to many readers: Bridges excluded it from the finished works, as did his other editors, Williams and Gardner. Even its sympathetic readers have balked at some of its ugly imagery and its "unfit" sentiment. However, the poem must be, like the "forked lightning," confronted on its own terms, terms that Hopkins was keen to have contained within the language of the poem itself. That language is rooted in struggles that the poet conducted throughout his entire life. Here is Hopkins in 1865:

> But what indeed is ask'd of me?
> Not this. Some spirits, it is told,
> Have will'd to be disparadised
> For love and greater glory of Christ.
> But I was ignorantly bold
> To dream I dared so much for thee.
> This was not ask'd but what instead?
> Waking I thought; and it sufficed:
> My hopes and my unworthiness,
> At once perceivèd, with excess
> Of burden came and bow'd my head.
> (*Poems*, pp. 161–162)

The Hopkins of 1889 and "The shepherd's brow" is essentially the same person, worn by age, struggle, and now by disease to a point of continuing but futile resistance to a creator whose will he was never able to grasp, whose workings he was never able to comprehend as they affected his personal life,[36] and whose glory he felt he was never able to give adequately. The poem is, then, a multiple discourse that uses language effectively to hide and to reveal. The dying Hopkins was no doubt aware of Bridges' response to his words, and, true to his love of all linguistic play, he packed this sonnet with more personal revelation than many of his more straightforwardly personal poems, including *The Wreck*. It is not enough to read this poem as merely one of Hopkins' final poems, nor as a "pietistic resignation" (Beyette, ["Hopkins Phenomenology of Art,"] p. 209), nor as "a prayer of humility" (Mariani, "Artistic and Tonal Integrity," p. 66), nor as "a deeply felt expectoration of disgust" (Boyle, ["*The Wreck*"] p. 105). Rather, it must be viewed holistically as the summary of Hopkins at that time and for all his time and as a plea for the understanding of a less-than-perfect poet and religious who spent his life trying in vain to fill what he perceived to be his Maker's dicta. The poem records the failure, but it succeeds as art in rendering the meaning of human fallenness. As with Hopkins and as with his other works, it succeeds in spite of its limitations and in spite of its judgments. Its reader must be careful, however, to allow it its full scope and to allow the Hopkins that emerges from within and between its lines to stand as a completely human and humane figure; if we deny the poet that right, we deny his penultimate poem its success.

Notes

1. In retreat notes written in January, 1888, Hopkins complained: "Outwardly I often think I am employed to do what is of little or no use" (*Sermons*, p. 261). Quotations from Hopkins' works are taken from the following volumes: Claude C. Abbott, ed., *The Letters of Gerard Manley Hopkins to Robert Bridges* (Oxford Univ. Press, 1955), Vol. I; Christopher Devlin, S.J., ed., *The Sermons and Devotional Writings of Gerard Manley Hopkins* (Oxford Univ. Press, 1959); Humphry House and Graham Storey, eds., *The Journals and Papers of Gerard Manley Hopkins* (Oxford Univ. Press, 1959); and W. H. Gardner and N. H. MacKenzie, eds., *The Poems of Gerard Manley Hopkins*, 4th ed. (Oxford Univ. Press, 1967).

2. As Hopkins had stated in a letter to Bridges dated August 21, 1877: "You are my public and I hope to convert you" (*Letters*, I, 46). A decade later this statement carried even greater weight. For an interesting discussion of Hopkins' concept of his audience—particularly in the "Terrible Sonnets" but with relevance here—see Daniel A. Harris, *Inspirations Unbidden: The "Terrible Sonnets" of Gerard Manley Hopkins* (Univ. of California Press, 1982), especially pp. 129-144. Harris' comments on p. 134, however, fail to recognize Hopkins' ability to alter, or even abandon, some of his long-held rhetorical practices and patterns.

3. Hopkins had always been fascinated by storms. His journals abound with brief notes of occurrences of bad weather and lengthy descriptions of storms and their aftermath (see, e.g., *Journals*, pp. 172, 186, 189, 201, 230, and 233).

4. In his journal for 1873 Hopkins had devoted much space to a description of a thunderstorm, including this statement with its emphatic use of "fork": "Several strong thrills of light followed the flash but a grey smother of darkness blotted the eyes if they had seen the fork" (*Journals*, pp. 233-234).

5. Peter Milward, S.J., *A Commentary on the Sonnets of G. M. Hopkins* (London, 1970), p. 141.

6. It is no coincidence, I think, that the poem manifests in its order of creatures—Christ, angels, man—the same order of creation Hopkins painstakingly established in his spiritual writings: "Christ is the firstborn among creatures" (*Sermons*, p. 196); "Also out of this same world or stead of things in which Christ lived before he became man I suppose to have been made the earthly paradise planted by God from the beginning, that is perhaps /

when the angelic world was brought into being, so that spirit and flesh started together, flesh being the name for a condition of matter" (*Sermons*, p. 171); "Christ then like a good shepherd led the way; but when Satan saw the mystery and the humiliation proposed he turned back and rebelled . . . and so he fell, with his following" (*Sermons*, pp. 197–198).

7. Alison G. Sulloway, *Gerard Manley Hopkins and the Victorian Temper* (Columbia Univ. Press, 1972), p. 172.

8. Milward, p. 141, and Robert B. Clark, S.J., "Hopkins's 'The shepherd's brow,' " *VN*, 28 (1965), 16–18.

9. Paul L. Mariani, *A Commentary on the Complete Poems of Gerard Manley Hopkins* (Cornell Univ. Press, 1970), p. 306.

10. L. van Noppen, "The Last Rub: An Explication of Hopkins' 'The shepherd's Brow,' " unpublished ms.

11. Robert Boyle, S.J., "*The Wreck* from the Perspective of 'The shepherd's brow,' in Peter Milward, S.J., and Raymond Schoder, S.J., eds., *Readings of* The Wreck (Loyola Univ. Press, 1976), p. 108.

12. Norman H. MacKenzie, *A Reader's Guide to Gerard Manley Hopkins* (Cornell Univ. Press, 1981), p. 204.

13. Robert Boyle, S.J., strongly disagrees with this reading: "As I can see it, Christ is nowhere present in this sonnet" (p. 106). In papers presented at the 1984 International Hopkins Association Conference in Dublin, both W. Bronzwaer and Lionel Adey reached the same conclusion regarding the identity of the shepherd as Christ. Bronzwaer draws on the "simplified and shortened version of the Chain of Being" in the poem as evidence of Christ as shepherd, while Adey relies on the image of Christ beholding Satan's fall from heaven as sufficient proof.

14. Hopkins referred to Christ as a good shepherd on at least three occasions: see *Sermons*, pp. 74, 197, and 249.

15. Not enough emphasis can be placed on the bridge made by the dash in this line. This is Hopkins' penultimate song; he is singing to his Maker and his fellow men, and what he wants — more than all other worldly goals at least — is contained within the space of this dash: identification with all his fellows. He has lamented the death of the farrier Felix Randal, praised the anatomy of Harry Ploughman, sympathized with St. Alphonsus Rodriguez, and empathized with Tom and Dick. He has always been attracted to his opposites: doers, makers, creators of tangibles. Now, in his approach to death, he wants to be among them, not apart from them. This line begins in the manner usual and typical, with the poet objectifying his own species; but it is the Catholic, the Jesuit, the Victorian poet who does this objectifying. After the dash, after the leap, it is the humanized Hopkins who proudly acquiesces and takes his weaknesses as almost defiances of God and His "grandeur." The movement is present in Hopkins, and all the critical neglect of decades will not remove it. "The shepherd's brow" is, I think, as crucial a work to understanding this complex man as is "The Windhover" or "The Wreck of the Deutschland."

16. The closeness of "story" and "scaffold" anticipates "masque" in the thirteenth line. Hopkins seems to be creating a "micro-masque" within the poem, the scaffold being its structure, the story being a summa of history.

17. Mariani sees this movement as Hopkins' "isolat[ing] himself above the Jacks to plead his own particular case, his own sake, his intensely personal agony" ("The Artistic and Tonal Integrity of Hopkins' 'The shepherd's brow,' " *VP*, 6 [1968], 65). Bronzwaer (in the paper read at the Dublin conference) makes some very interesting comments on the categories created by these personal pronouns, seeing in them Hopkins' attempt to place himself outside the Chain of Being.

18. In a very interesting reading of this word, Norman White contends that "void" should be taken to mean "withdraws himself" (OED), i.e., simply dies, and should not be

associated with bowel movements (unpublished ms from a forthcoming book on Hopkins' Dublin sonnets; used with kind permission of Dr. White). White further contends that " 'Lives and voids' is preferred, because of its superior alliteration and its lower associations, to the simpler first thought 'lives and dies.' " I hold, however, that Hopkins is using the word in its excretory sense. In the mss, he carefully introduced the comma between "lives" and "voids" in the final two versions after writing three drafts with no comma. Without the comma, the association with "lives and dies" would be strong; with the comma, however, Hopkins demands a pause and seems to imply a causal relationship, namely, in order to live one must void with shame. Further, the almost-immediate reference to man's mate implies reference to sexual functions.

19. Barely beneath the surface of these lines—the "underthought of them," to use Hopkins' own phrase—is the scotching of one of Hopkins' dear ideas, namely that the blazoning of a poet's name is crucial if that poet, in this case Bridges, is to have a greater and more beneficial influence upon the Empire. Here is Hopkins in a letter to Bridges: "By the bye, I say it deliberately and before God, I would have you and Canon Dixon and all true poets remember that fame, the being known, though in itself one of the most dangerous things to man, is nevertheless the true and appointed air, element, and setting of genius and its works. . . . To produce then is of little use unless what we produce is known, if known widely known, the wider known the better, for it is by being known it works, it influences, it does its duty, it does good" (*Letters*, I, 231).

20. It is possible that Hopkins uses these conjunctive beginnings as analogues for the poet's gasping for breath, just as speakers short of breath will often use such words to enable them to draw in more air.

21. For discussion of this image see Sister Mary Hugh Campbell, "The Silent Sonnet: Hopkins' 'Shepherd's brow,' " *Renascence*, 15 (1963), 133–142; Mariani, "Artistic and Tonal Integrity," pp. 66–68; Thomas K. Beyette, "Hopkins' Phenomenology of Art in 'The shepherd's brow,' " *VP*, 11 (1973), 211–213; and White, unpublished ms, for a reading of the image as anamorphic.

22. Robert Boyle, S.J., writes: "I recall my own experience in Jesuit dining halls, waiting with downcast eyes while the faculty and other head-table officials filed past my table, and watching their black forms reflected in the large and small spoons on the table" (p. 109).

23. "Masque" reminds the reader of "tragic" (for contrast) and "story," whose positive and negative values have been discussed above. The obvious masque/mask pun needs little comment. While not essentially about art, this poem reveals a preoccupation with that subject that certainly was subconscious in Hopkins at this time and likely even surfaced to become one more of the numerous concerns that plagued him in his last years. For discussions of his poems—specifically his late ones—as centrally about writing/art, see Beyette, pp. 207–213, and Michael Sprinker, "*A Counterpoint of Dissonance*": *The Aesthetics and Poetry of Gerard Manley Hopkins* (Johns Hopkins Univ. Press, 1980), pp. 121–145.

24. Beyette is certainly justified in his reading of these spoons as Hopkins' sonnets (p. 211).

25. Boyle provides an adequate summary of the various and varying interpretations of what this poem really is. Whether or not there is any such tension as I am attempting to show seems a subject of some critical disagreement.

26. For one discussion of this relationship see John Ferns, "Activity in Silence: G. M. Hopkins' *Journal*, 1866–1875," *HQ*, 2 (1976), 163–174.

27. Hopkins sometimes (perhaps too often) easily slipped into exaggerated discussions or "epic" calls to duty, relying on hyperbole as much as catalogues. As one example only, see *Sermons*, pp. 50–53. It appears that Hopkins was too eager to be his own severest critic and harshest judge, setting standards humanly—and Catholically—impossible to reach.

28. Hopkins comes close to posing this question toward the end of the meditation, but its phrasing betrays his continuing attempt to categorize and understand his place on the scale of virtue: "*When a man is in God's grace and free from moral sin,* then everything that he does, *so long as there is no sin in it,* gives God glory and what does not give him glory has some, *however little,* sin in it" (p. 240). I have italicized the qualifications to emphasize how incredibly weak the assertion really is when it finally receives expression.

29. Harris' discussion of "Nature and the Human Body" in the "Terrible Sonnets" (pp. 19-71) offers further insight into Hopkins' preoccupation with bodily functions at this stage of his life. Harris charts Hopkins' growing inability to take joy from the earth—now "a confused and incoherent chaos, nearly emptied of God" (p. 21)—and his equally increasing disenchantment with his own physicality.

30. That Hopkins just before his death either read or remembered these notes seems more likely if an image from his meditation on hell, which immediately follows "The Principle or Foundation," is compared to lines from his final sonnet: "You have seen a glassblower breathe on a flame; at once it darts out into a jet taper as a lance-head and as piercing too" (*Sermons*, p. 242); "The fine delight that fathers thought; the strong / Spur, live and lancing like the blowpipe flame" (*Poems*, p. 108). As Alan Heuser has pointed out (*The Shaping Vision of Gerard Manley Hopkins* [Oxford Univ. Press, 1958], p. 80), Hopkins was trained in the faculty of memory as were many Jesuits. His ability to retain words and images for decades is attested throughout his works.

31. For a discussion of Hopkins' "anality" and its expression in many of his writings, see Robert Rogers, "Hopkins' Carrion Comfort," *HQ*, 7 (1981), 143-165.

32. There may be a very logical explanation for this: see Norman White's article on the "Irish row" created by Hopkins' appointment to University College and the appalling—and unhealthy—physical surroundings that greeted the poet on his arrival in Dublin (*HQ*, 9 [1982], 91-107).

33. Beyette has aptly observed the apparent lack of "God's grace or strength" in this poem (p. 209).

34. Hopkins' keenness for pairing words can be seen in, of course, the etymological entries in his diaries, but also in many of his spiritual writings (e.g., *Sermons*, pp. 129 and 133). The following schema may, in fact, be an illustration of what Hillis Miller calls one of Hopkins' "three apparently incompatible theories of poetry" ("The Linguistic Moment in 'The Wreck of the Deutschland,'" in Thomas D. Young, ed., *The New Criticism and After* [Univ. Press of Virginia, 1976], pp. 47-48). According to Miller, "Poetry may be the representation of the interlocked chiming of created things in their relation to the Creation"; "Poetry may explore or express the solitary adventures of the self in its wrestles with God or in its fall into the abyss outside God"; and "Poetry may explore the intricate relationships among words." The schema lends weight to the final theory, offering an example of Hopkins' attempts to delineate linguistic "chiming" (in hope of restoring the "chiming" among created things and Creation?). Indeed, the whole of "The shepherd's brow" is a superb text for illustrating Miller's notions.

35. For a discussion of the patterns and cycles in Hopkins' life—biological and spiritual—see Donald Walhout, *Send My Roots Rain: A Study of Religious Experience in the Poetry of Gerard Manley Hopkins* (Ohio Univ. Press, 1981), especially pp. 97-122.

36. In his spiritual notes Hopkins observed: "And my life is determined by the Incarnation down to most of the details of the day" (*Sermons*, p. 263). Hopkins always felt—even in the "Terrible Sonnets"—that his life was somehow controlled by God, as if he were on a leash. He felt also, however, too much slackness or tautness in that leash, rarely sensing the ideal tension.

The Sound of Oneself Breathing   Paul Mariani*

The critical act of attention in this century tends to be eye-centered, with the reader, like the poet, zeroing in on the image, the metaphor, the symbol, the icon. Beyond that is an attention to the sound of the poem: to chimings picked up by the ear—assonance, consonance, rhyme, aural parallelisms. But there is something more, which the reader can sometimes pick up or at least feel is present somewhere just off the screen of consciousness. This ghostly presence suggests the sort of dynamic metaphor felt somewhere along the reader's marrow. It is an image or icon that suggests an activity with its own independence and life. It is a kind of metaphor, really, that goes deeper, goes beyond the radiant stasis of even the most pervasive theologically centered icon to partake of the very act of the poet's utterance. And more, it does in fact transform the poet's utterance, giving that utterance an unmistakable authenticity. Admittedly this is a difficult topic about which to write convincingly, but it is a subject that has shimmered on the fringes of much avant-garde criticism I have seen in the past few years, and it is something to which I should like to address my attention now.

Consider the difficult example of Gerard Manley Hopkins. A good critic of Hopkins (like Robert Boyle, James Cotter, J. Hillis Miller, Elisabeth Schneider, or half a dozen others) could demonstrate convincingly the nearly constant presence in Hopkins's poetry of a dimension of theological iconography acting as a kind of underthought or second voice grounding and underpinning the paraphraseable content of the poem. Two examples of the kind of thing I am talking about may suffice here. Addressing his attention to the sestet of "As kingfishers catch fire," Boyle draws our attention to the homophonic pun on "I/eye," a chiming with very serious theological overtones, instressing as the lines do the activity of the Trinity in the acts of the just man.[1] Here are the lines:

> I say more: the just man justices;
>   Keeps gráce: thát keeps all his goings graces;
> Acts in God's eye what in God's eye he is—
>   Chríst. For Christ plays in ten thousand places,
> Lovely in limbs, and lovely in eyes not his
>   To the Father through the features of men's faces.

What Boyle does with these lines is to point not only to the "I/eye" identity, where the just man "acts in God's eye and in God's I what there he *is*—the 'I' of Christ as well as his own," but to Hopkins's seriously playful recapitulation of the three persons in the Trinity, where the just man, acting as Christ's eye/I, plays before the Father in God's eye/I, lovely in all

*From *A Usable Past: Essays on Modern & Contemporary Poetry* (Amherst: University of Massachusetts Press, 1984), 142–50, 263.

those eyes/I's not his, ten thousand specific personalities reflecting through the Spirit the faces of the Son in his attention to the Father. That metaphoric yield is significant.

And so is this, an example taken from Cotter.[2] At the close of Hopkins's great caudated sonnet, "That Nature is a Heraclitean Fire," there is the extraordinary incremental chiming catalogue which suggests in its own protean lexical shifts the profound theological idea of death, sacrifice, and transformation, but a transformation that raises the self of self to a radically new cleave of being. Much has been done with this line, and quite ably; but what Cotter adds is the deeper significance of the term "matchwood" in the marvelous close of the poem, where the *I am* embedded in "diamond" is carried to the forefront of the poem:

> This Jack, joke poor potsherd, ' patch, matchwood, immortal diamond,
> Is immortal diamond.

That matchwood, Cotter sees, is more than merely the kindling that will be transformed phoenixlike into diamond: it is a lexical signature for the Great Sacrifice itself, as this Jack's wood (cross) is made to match his Master's in death. Dying in Christ, he comes to live in Christ. Cotter, especially, has made it abundantly clear to many of us that Christ's inscaped love—in Hopkins's reading of the world—underlies many of Hopkins's poems, which would seem to have their energies focused on some natural image, some land, water, or treescape. A more careful meditation on the poems, however, reveals a level of linguistic resonance, hinting at a traditional corpus of images associated by long use with the Great Sacrifice. Christ's last words, the lance, the gall, wood, nails, the oustretched arms and buckling body: all point toward the right reading of all that Hopkins sees in the fact of creation about him. And nearly all this imagery works by way of visual or linguistic chiming: *these* scenes in nature or these packed phrasal units, as with the poetics of the Ignatian meditation, suggesting the primal theological drama of sacrifice.

What I should like to examine more specifically here, though, is the authenticity of the aural/visual metaphoric complex of breath and inspiration, especially as this informs—literally—the texture, the saying, of the last two sonnets Hopkins wrote: "The shepherd's brow" and "To R. B." There is in these last-breath utterances the encoding of a kind of psychological and religious resolution which comes to one only slowly and by degrees. Read aright, they signify not failure but victory. But the critics know, of course, that they are speaking to readers of widely divergent backgrounds, and so must try their best to ground their "findings" in a critical vocabulary that can be understood and perhaps shared.

For me, Hopkins's last two poems form the two halves of a diptych concerned, apparently, with the problematics of human weakness, the loss of inspiration, and the laughable yet titanic struggle to accept or at least acknowledge failure. What hinges these two poems together (poems composed less than three weeks apart) is the complex natural metaphor of human breath. Human breath, that is, as the poet's awareness at some level of the presence of divine inspiration or inbreathing—the Spirit's indwelling—and human breath as the sine qua non for all poetic utterance. For Hopkins, as for Milton, the utterance should be the child of *both* indwelling activities: the human, the divine. That is, even beyond the pictorial or iconographic traces of metaphor in the poem is an authenticity of utterance which marks and validates the distinctive presence of the very inspiration that Hopkins has made the subject of these last poems.

But first, by way of contrast, consider the sounds of oneself breathing in an earlier poem that also uses the breath/air/spirit/inspiration lexical complex: the opening and closing sections of "The Wreck of the Deutschland." "Thou mastering me / God! giver of breath and bread." Hopkins initiates that ode, announcing thus dramatically the alpha and groundswell of his inspiration. And, having followed the procession of the word out, the ode rounds on itself, calling at its dramatic climax on the Spirit and on the Sacrificed Word to reveal to the poet what it was the nun meant by her last, frantically repeated utterance before the sea stilled that breath forever. "Breathe, arch and original Breath," Hopkins cries, summoning like Milton before him the Creating Spirit. And then again: "Breathe, body of lovely Death," the repetition driving home the urgency of Hopkins's beseeching. So the nun breathes in Christ's "all-fire glances" and utters the word "outright," signaling with her last breath a sign to "The-last-breath penitent spirits." There has been an intense inspiration, flamelike, devouring, and there has been a complementary expiration with the woman's last breath. It is the kind of parallel that the imagination finds at some level aesthetically satisfying.

Margaret Clitheroe, too, pressed to death, catches, in Hopkins's telling, the crying out of God, "The Utterer, Uttered, Uttering," a superb metaphor for the three distinctive activities of the Trinity: for the Self who utters eternally, for the Self who is eternally uttered, and for the eternal act of that *in*-spiration that coevally partakes of that divine selving, the Self that proceeds from the wellspring of that aeonion Verb. Intent only on that divine cry, intent only on imitating Christ's final yes, Margaret's response is reduced by the extremity of her situation to a counter cry ending like the nun's, in a primal "choke of woe." No matter what glottal, dental, or sibilant, that final expiration is for Hopkins the all-important signature. Still, in both these examples, the metaphor of breath remains largely a linguistic strategy of the logocentric poet, whose distinctive register here is an enthusiasm (in its radical sense of divine indwelling) born of deep meditation, employing the Ignatian exercises as prelude to uttering the word.

As a reading of the corpus will tell us, Hopkins is a distinctively air-centered poet whose tactile imagination is self-reflectively aware of the very air he breathes in, breathes out. Take, for example, the fine metaphysical conceit of "The Blessed Virgin compared to the Air we Breathe," which Hopkins composed in May 1883, while at Stonyhurst. "Wild air," he exclaims:

> Wild air, world-mothering air,
> Nestling me everywhere,
> That each eyelash or hair
> Girdles. . . .

It is this very air, as pervasive as grace itself,

> which, by life's law,
> My lung must draw and draw
> Now but to breathe its praise.

The Incarnation itself, Hopkins suggests, was initiated by the fiat of Mary; by this she was impregnated with the Word; by *this* inspiration, this indwelling, she could in time deliver *that* Word, distinctive, a fleshing-forth of that *yes*. In the forward riding of time, moreover, Hopkins suggests that that indwelling, that inspiration, becomes available to others, since the facticity of the Incarnation continues to touch people even more closely than the very air we consciously or unconsciously keep breathing in. So we take in air that we may breathe out airs, as breath is transformed into air, melody, song, word.

Hopkins's use of the air/breath metaphor appears both early and late in his sermons, letters, journals, retreat notes, as well as in his poems. But it undergoes a subtle and important alteration in those last two sonnets. In the first of these, "The shepherd's brow," Hopkins stresses, instresses, the nature of the aeonian fall from grace—Satan's narcissistic insistence on indwelling on his own beauty—comparing those "just, majestical, and giant groans" to Man Jack's (and his own) poor gasps. Hopkins, sick, diarrhetic, suffering from migraine headaches, in fact dying in the spring of 1889, hears now the sputter and sucking sounds of his own raspings, each breath a painful recollection of his absolute dependence of air, that sound serving as signature of his own poor mortality, and sees that his feverish body is feeding carrionlike off its own bone-fire. Over and over again, those sick lungs must suck in the very air that will be expelled as complaint, until, at poem's close, the poet prays that his comic, overly dramatic "tempests" may be tamed. He prays too that his fever, the only fire he is capable of self-generating, may be quieted. The last lines, following the pause, the hiatus, of the Miltonic rhotomontade, capture quite marvelously the quintessence of utterance diminished to gasp, the poet reduced to little more than a sputtering blowpipe hissing out its barely directed flame: ". . . in smooth spoons spy life's masque mirrored: tame / My tempests there, my fire and fever fussy." The emphasis, then, is on the repetitive nature of the rhythm of breathing, and the linguistic counters register that emphasis, moving through an arc that begins with the *groans* of the mighty fallen, proceeding out in a kind of inversion of the aeonian De Processu, the Word returning to its Source, drawing to its own lexical swerve the terms *breathe, gasp, breath, tones, voids,* and terminating at last mockingly, to the poet's own self-inflated *tempests.*

"To R. B.," however, considers the whole question of inspiration (and, in its encoding, fame) not from the human perspective this time, but rather from the divine side. And the marvelous control, the absence of that anxiety so characteristic of Hopkins's extraordinarily powerful dark sonnets of 1885, testify to this other dimension. True poetic inspiration is for Hopkins, as for Milton (whose lines Hopkins seems to have been mulling over frequently in the winter and spring of 1889), from the Holy Spirit. Rather than a constant inbreathing, however, such an inspiration strikes the mind with the force of achieved sexual ecstasy, impregnating the womb of the very self with the force of an actual, sensible impress. Such tremors, we know from experience, of course will not stay. That "fine delight" breathes when and as it will, often, as Hopkins once told Bridges, coming "unbidden," unsummoned, even unasked for. But the mind *will* harbor that insight, *will* continue to direct it, though in fact the inspiration already contains the dynamics and potential for its own inner development. And though it may take years before the word is finally realized, the Word was already there, waiting.

If by late 1880s Hopkins scarcely breathes his raptures now, it is because the Spirit seldom moves him sensibly. But in fact his winter world can and does — paradoxically — yield, give up, produce — an explanation that is, finally, not only his but the Spirit's as well. For this sonnet is *their* explanation, and it has produced this final child, this last utterance, this last magnificent poem. Like "The shepherd's brow," this poem also ends on a string of strong sibilants. But these *s* sounds have quite another effect upon the reader, the effect here of a quiet and profound surrendering, as of a woman remembering her lover's embraces now she has come to term.

In discussing "The Wreck of the Deutschland" through the lens of "The shepherd's brow," Fr. Boyle astutely sees Hopkins as giving over, finally, any illusions of being a Catholic Milton for his time, as mocking himself for having tried in his great ode to "justify the ways of God to men." That seems to me a satisfying way of speaking about the problem of anxiety over the colossus of the tradition. If, as I pointed out some years ago, *Paradise Lost* and George Eliot's remarks about Milton in *Middlemarch* provide several key images for "The shepherd's brow," *Lycidas* seems in its own way to have informed "To R. B." That echoes of *Lycidas* should float just beneath the surface of this poem reveals in fact part of the poem's underlying tension and resolution. Milton, of course, is a subject that occurs frequently in Hopkins's letters to Bridges and, we may assume, in Bridges's lost letters to Hopkins. Bridges's essay on Milton's prosody, which grew eventually into his important monograph on that subject, was of course well known to Hopkins from its manuscript inception in 1886.

Hopkins referred to it frequently, spoke highly of it, showed it to potential readers in and around Dublin, even offered Bridges suggestions on it. In fact, the only extant letter we have from Bridges to Hopkins, dated May 18, 1889 – when Hopkins lay dying in the Jesuit infirmary at St. Stephen's Green – is a little note meant to cheer Hopkins up, and mentions having sent Hopkins "a budget of notes on Milton's prosody."[3]

In fact, Milton and Bridges and the whole subject of fame and inspiration seem locked into the linguistic grid of "To R. B." And *spur*, a word that appears only once in all Hopkins's poetry, seems to provide a key. "When I spoke of fame," Hopkins had written to Canon Dixon ten years before, "I was not thinking of the harm it does to men as artists: it may do them harm, as you say, but so, I think, may the want of it, if 'Fame is the spur that the clear spirit doth raise To shun delights and live laborious days' – a spur very hard to find a substitute for or to do without."[4] Of course Hopkins had given over trying to publish his own poems, though it must have rankled deeply, not for the sake of fame, but for what he there called "the loss of recognition belonging to the work itself."[5] Had he not in fact upset Bridges in the very same letter in which he enclosed the sonnet to Bridges by laughing at his friend for desiring fame even as he was publishing his poems in a limited edition of twenty-four copies?[6]

> But the fair guerdon when we hope to find,
> And think to burst out into sudden blaze,
> Comes the blind Fury with abhorrèd shears,
> And slits the thin-spun life.

The blowpipe flame, in Hopkins's laboratory image of the Bunson burner, needs breathe only once to impregnate the imagination. And then what is needed is the leisure, the period of slow ripening. But now, cutting off the chance for any further development: those abhorrèd shears, the fact of death. The corrective to all of that, of course, is the "perfect witness of all-judging Jove," who pronounces lastly on each deed. "The only just judge," so Hopkins's apparent gloss on these lines would go, "the only just literary critic is Christ, who prizes, is proud of, and admires, more than any man, more than the receiver himself can, the gifts of his own making."

What the last poem tells us, then, is that Hopkins has come to accept his very human condition. We might corroborate this from his last letters to Bridges and to his parents; for the first time he no longer seems anxious about unfinished work, about the stacks of examination papers to be graded, about the political tensions in Ireland which had made his five years there such a difficult experience. Instead, he seems to have accepted in the very lay of the syllables of his last poem the historic condition – Jowett's Star of Balliol teaching classics in provincial Dublin – to which his call to duty had brought him. Now, he says (and the word is uttered three times here), *now* his winter world can yield up not *his* explanation only, but the Spirit's as well. Ironically, for the first (and last) time in the poetry, the density of anxious fretting in the introspective sonnets has lifted. One senses that Hopkins has come to accept himself, the apparent failure signaled by his long poetic silences, but the movement of the Spirit operating as well within the poet. Affective and elective wills have for once meshed. The voice in this song is aware of the cost of silence to one's poetic reputation, aware, but willing without anxiousness for once to pay the price. For once, then: something. For once, the poet's breath, haggard and diminished though it is, has responded fully to that "arch and original Breath," as authentic expiration answers, now, as best it can, to authentic inspiration.

Notes

1. In Father Boyle's "Time and Grace in Hopkins' Imagination," presented at the 1976 MLA seminar on Hopkins.

2. In conversation with James Finn Cotter. See also Cotter's seminal *Inscape: The Christology and Poetry of Gerard Manley Hopkins* (Pittsburgh: University of Pittsburgh Press, 1972), passim.

3. *Further Letters of Gerard Manley Hopkins*, ed. Claude Colleer Abbott (London: Oxford University Press, 1956), p. 433.

4. Letter of June 13, 1878, in *The Correspondence of Gerard Manley Hopkins and Richard Watson Dixon*, ed. Claude Colleer Abbott (London: Oxford University Press, 1935), p. 6.

5. Ibid.

6. Cf. Hopkins's letters to Bridges of March 20 and April 29, 1889 in *The Letters of Gerard Manley Hopkins to Robert Bridges*, ed. Claude Colleer Abbott (London: Oxford University Press, 1955), pp. 301-6.

Hopkins as Jesuit Poet

Poet of Nature

Jerome Bump*

The sacramental concept of poetry implied in *The Wreck of the Deutschland* is related, as we have seen, to the Oxford Movement's concept of a "type" which could become an "instrument" as well as a sign of "real things unseen." If "Rosa Mystica," the source of the rose imagery in *The Wreck*, is a good example of how Hopkins applied biblical typological principles to traditional images in his poetry, "The Windhover" is the paradigm of how he adapted the hermeneutics of the Book of Nature developed by Keble and by his own father and uncle in their *Pietas Metrica*.

The question of how to assimilate the multidimensional, polysemantic character of Hopkins's art, first posed by *The Wreck*, is raised again by "The Windhover" because, as Marshall McLuhan put it, "there is no other poem of comparable length in English, or perhaps in any language, which surpasses its richness and intensity, or realized artistic organization."[1] Indeed, there are so many different interpretations of this poem that readers are tempted to quit trying to sort them out and simply retreat into pure subjectivism and relativism. Thus it could be argued that "The Windhover" is not only the best illustration of Hopkins's poetics — for the concentration of parallelism and multivalence is higher than in any of his other poems — but is the ultimate test of one's ability to explicate a poem.

One way of assimilating all the diverse, contradictory readings of this, the most explicated poem of its length in the language, is to apply the techniques of biblical hermeneutics we discussed in our reading of "Rosa Mystica" and the related sections of *The Wreck*. A return to some of the principles of this, the first literary criticism (if we may call it that), the interpretation of the Book of western civilization, can help us organize our responses to "The Windhover." The four levels of medieval biblical interpretation which Dante applied to the *Divine Comedy* are particularly valuable for discussing multivalent works such as "The Windhover" because they assimilate complexity and ambiguity of meaning yet resist

*From *Gerard Manley Hopkins* (Boston: Twayne, 1982), 129–66, 206–7. Reprinted by permission of G. K. Hall.

tendencies to solopsism and relativism both by insisting on the primary reality of things over words and by affirming the existence of the primal unity from which Hopkins's apparently endless permutations emanate.

THE LITERAL LEVEL

The best antidote to pure subjectivity in interpretation may in fact be a reemphasis on the first of the four levels of medieval hermeneutics: the literal. The literal level has always been essential in the Christian interpretation of the Incarnation, for it was a bulwark against the assertion of Manicheism that Jesus had no physical reality, only a phantasy body, an assertion which reduced the Incarnation to a fiction. For a poem to be interpreted typologically in the biblical sense, therefore, rather than merely allegorically, we must be conscious of a level of literal truth. Hence the famous typological problem in *The Divine Comedy:* defining what is literally true, that is, Dante's own conversion experience.

Hopkins was far more explicit about this literal level than Dante, however. He wrote to Bridges about *The Wreck*, for instance: "I may add for your greater interest and edification that what refers to myself in the poem is all strictly and literally true, and did all occur; nothing is added for poetical padding" (*B*, 47). The literal level is especially important for Hopkins's poetry because most of his poems are lyrics, a genre even more dependent than the ode or the epic on conceiving of poetry as autobiographical.

In the tradition of lyric poetry, moreover, romantic lyrics place unusual stress on a literal interpretation of the poet's self in the poem. Heavily influenced by medieval hermeneutics,[2] romantic imagery is almost by definition typological in that it implies not merely a comparison but one in which there is a discernible relation between the image and reality, at least the reality or personal experience of the speaker. In romantic nature lyrics in the tradition of Wordsworth especially, such as those Hopkins composed in 1877, the emphasis on literal reality extends to nature as well as to the speaker. Wordsworth was "well pleased to recognize / In nature and the language of sense / The anchor of my purest thoughts" ("Tintern Abbey," ll. 108–9). The anchor was William Tyndale's metaphor for the role of the literal sense in biblical criticism. This sense of "thingness," the physical presence of nature, is important not only for readers familiar with biblical typology but for all modern readers influenced by science and its basic assumption that nature does have an existence independent of ourselves and our symbols.

The neglect of this literal level in our reading of Hopkins's own poetry is epitomized by the absence of notes in texts of the poem to explain adequately the physical reality upon which "The Windhover" is based: the unique flight patterns of this particular bird. The word "riding" in "The Windhover" refers specifically to the famous flight pattern for which the bird is named: by rapidly beating its wings it seems to hang stationary in one spot like a helicopter rather than circling or gliding like other birds of prey.[3]

This is what Hopkins "caught" sight of that morning. This falcon, itself dappled like the dawn, was drawn forth by the dappled dawn to hunt. Hopkins saw it hovering over one spot as if drawn or painted against the background of the rising sun, much as the "flake leaves light" in Hopkins's "Epithalamion," "painted on the air, / Hang as still as hawk or hawkmoth." Hopkins was fascinated by his hovering, his "riding of the rolling level underneath him steady air," his "striding high there," that is, astride of, straddling the wind, "reining" or controlling it with his undulating, "wimpling" wings. The windhover "rung" upon his wings much as a bell ringer pulls up and down on the bell ropes or the rider of a horse "undulates" his belled reins.

On certain occasions windhovers have also been known to fly in rings or semicircles: the male has been known to fly in circles above the female in courtship and sometimes the bird takes a circular path to a new hunting location. Thus the secondary senses of "ring" here, as a term in falconry meaning to rise upward in spirals, and as an equestrian term denoting the training of a horse to run in circles with a long rein, are not entirely inappropriate.

In any case, after catching sight of the hovering, Hopkins then sees the windhover move off to a new location, either by hurling itself down and then suddenly "gliding" up to a new spot, or else by hurling itself horizontally into the wind and then gliding in a "bow-bend" pattern until it reaches a new spot. In either instance, it manages to "beat back" the wind once again, the root meaning of "rebuff." The "achieve" and "mastery" of the bird in the maneuver are like that of a skater approaching along one side of a bow-shaped bend at high speed and then gliding swiftly around it, as ice hockey players often do behind the goal.

As we move from the octet to the sestet, there is an abrupt change in the rhythm. The striking initial double stress on "Brute beauty" imitates the new movement of the bird climaxed by the word "Buckle." The bird buckles its wings together and falls from the sky, as if it were wounded or buckling under, collapsing, crumpling under pressure, but in fact it is buckling to, buckling down, preparing for action, getting ready to come to grips with its prey. In this dive all its features, all its "brute beauty," "valour," "act," "air, pride, plume," come together, are buckled together. The fiery flash of light that breaks from it as it dives with the rising sun behind it is far "lovelier," for the sight of a diving windhover is even more rare than that of a hovering one, and it is obviously far more "dangerous" when it dives down upon its prey.

With the pause between tercets, the attention shifts from the heavens to the earth to which the falcon has descended. The V-shape made by the windhover in its dive (its wings are more pointed than those of the

American kestrel) is that of the ploughshare, that of the furrow a plough makes when it buckles up the earth, and the shape of embers collapsing or buckling through a gate.[4] The blue-gray color of the upper part of the bird, moreover, corresponds to the blue-bleak color of both the embers and the ploughshare, while the russet color on the lower part of the bird recalls both the shining on the ploughshare after ploughing and the fire breaking through the bottom of the buckling ember. Thus the colors as well as the shape of the diving windhover resemble both a ploughshare ploughing through the air and a falling ember.

The sense of "fire" breaking from the bird is caused by the fiery flashes of the colors of the diving bird as well as the effect of the rising sun, directly behind the bird as it dives. The result is a "shining" like that of the bursting ember, the gleaming surface of the ploughshare being polished by use, the shine of the moist, new sillion (the strip between the furrows), the sparks produced when the ploughshare strikes the blue-bleak rocks, and the colors revealed by shearing them open. The implication is that if even the "sheer plod" of ploughing can produce such a "shining," there should be "no wonder" that a handsome bird of prey can.

THE METAPHORICAL LEVEL

Of course the bird does not literally catch on "fire," nor is it really a "dauphin" or horse-rider. The second level of interpretation is a more systematic exploration of the metaphors which deny merely literal explanation. We soon discover that many of the metaphors in this poem are connected, moreover, especially the chivalric and fire images, suggesting the possibility of a consistent "underthought" in the poem, to use Hopkins's term (F, 253).

The key "underthought" is suggested by the subtitle, "To Christ our Lord," added six years later as a dedication and/or a way of addressing the entire poem to Christ. The subtitle thus reminds us that Hopkins dedicated all of his life and art to Christ and emphasizes that in this poem as in biblical typology the most consistent "underthought" is Christological, that is, most of the metaphors point to Christ.

The first obvious metaphors are "minion," meaning loved one and servant of the monarch, among other things, and "dauphin," a royal son and heir apparent, terms that also fit Jesus as the Son of God. This particular "dauphin" is the heir apparent to the "kingdom of daylight," moreover, echoing the recurrent stress in the New Testament on the "kingdom of heaven," Hopkins's emphasis on the "daylight divine" in "Rosa Mystica," and the close association of dawn imagery with God throughout his poetry, especially in "Barnfloor and Winepress," "Easter," "God's Grandeur," and the chivalric imagery concluding *The Wreck of the Deutschland.*

Accompanying this symbolism of Jesus as the Son of God is the related undercurrent of imagery of Christ the King, especially important to Hopkins because of the pervasive emphasis on the Kingdom of Christ and on chivalric imagery in the Society of Jesus. It has been suggested that Hopkins's splitting of "king" and "dom," for instance, reminds us that "dom" is a shortened form of "dominus" or "Lord," and thus an echo of the dedication to Christ, "our Lord." The rest of the chivalric imagery of minion, kingdom, and dauphin is then developed in the riding, striding, and rein imagery in the octet. Most of this imagery echoes the speech in Shakespeare's *Henry V* in which the dauphin praises his flying horse: "When I bestride him, I soar, I am a hawk. He trots the air, the earth sings when he touches it. [He is a] beast for Perseus. He is pure air and fire. . . . His neigh is like the bidding of a monarch, and his countenance enforces homage . . . for a sovereigns' sovereign to ride on, and for the world, familiar to us and unknown, to lay apart their particular functions and wonder at him. I once writ a sonnet on his pride and began thus: 'Wonder of nature—' " (III, vii, 11–42).

Hopkins reverses the negative connotations Shakespeare gives this speech by replacing the French dauphin with a more obviously Christian rider for his Pegasus, the flying steed traditionally symbolizing poetry. In his "St. Thecla" Hopkins had already suggested St. Paul as the proper rider for Pegasus and in "Andromeda" it is Christ himself who, like the windhover, "Pillowy air he treads a time and hangs." The metaphor of "riding" itself recalls Jesus who "on wings dost ride" in Hopkins's "Halfway House" and the striding, hurling, gliding, mastery, and pride imagery all echo *The Wreck of the Deutschland*, especially the representation of "The Master, / *Ipse*, the only one, Christ, King" who can "ride, her pride, in his triumph" (st. 28), yet also "with a love glides / Lower than death and dark" (st. 33).

Moreover, when the undercurrent of the chivalric imagery culminates in the "valour," "plume," and "pride" of the sestet of "The Windhover," it is clearly the chivalric imagery of Christ the King of the conclusion of *The Wreck*. This constellation of images is epitomized in "Buckle!" which evokes not only the "buckler" of medieval armor but also "buckling," a word for the combat of knights in Shakespeare's *Henry VI* plays. The fire breaking from their lances hitting the armor is clearly more "dangerous" an activity than merely riding, because it results in "gashing" and "galling," in this context meaning "abrasion."

This is the imagery of the "hero all the world wants" described in Hopkins's sermons: Christ as a "warrior and a conqueror," a "king" who "was feared when he chose," who "took a whip and singlehanded cleared the temple." "I should have feared him," Hopkins makes clear. Yet "in his Passion all this strength was spent," all "this beauty wrecked, this majesty beaten down" (S, 34–38). For Hopkins, Christ's triumph was inherently paradoxical: "doomed to succeed by failure; his plans were baffled, his hopes dashed, and his work was done by being broken off undone" (D,

138). "Poor was his station, laborious his life, bitter his ending; through poverty, through labour, through crucifixion his majesty of nature more shines" (S, 37).

The essence of Christianity for Hopkins, as we saw in *The Wreck*, was the concept of the sacrificial Incarnation, here postfigured in the dive of the windhover from the heavens to the earth. In this view, Christ could have remained about the earth, but he chose to swoop down, not to destroy but to save his prey, the hearts of men, to restore them to the kingdom of heaven. To this end he, rather than his prey, suffered the insult of the "gall" offered him to drink and the "gash" of the spear. When His "valour" and "act" were buckled together in the "brute beauty" of the Crucifixion, it was an apparent collapse or buckling under which was actually the preparation, the "buckling to" of the warrior for the victory of the Resurrection and the triumph of Christianity throughout the Western world. The V-shape of the diving windhover prefigured the collapse of Christ's pinioned arms "when his body buckled under its own weight," yet the result was the release of grace for "billions" of souls.[5]

The "fire that breaks from" Christ then, the fire lit on the cross ("I have come to bring fire to the earth," Luke 12:49), is the fire of love, the fire of God Himself: "For love is strong as Death. . . . The flash of it is a flash of fire, / A flame of Yahweh himself" (Song of Sol. 8:6). This flash of fire from the cross is "a billion / Times told lovelier" and more "dangerous" to the prey, men's hearts, because it demands complete commitment. This is the purging Pentecostal fire of the Holy Spirit (Luke 3:17) and the fire of the God of Psalm 18 who soared on the wings of the wind and came down from the heavens and kindled live embers with his consuming fire.

The "danger" is that of Christ the Master who preys on men's hearts, claims them totally, tears them away from their families, becoming their "sword / strife," as Hopkins put it in "To seem the stranger." This "dangerous" call to die unto the old self is reinforced by the plough imagery: "Once the hand is laid on the plough, no one looks back who is fit for the kingdom of God" (Luke 9:62), a phrase which haunted Hopkins throughout his life. The "sheer plod" that must follow putting one's hand to the plough may be a bleak life but, like the buckling ember, it can burst into the "lovelier" fire if the ploughman deliberately imitates the type of Christ's sacrifice, evoked by the final gold and vermilion imagery, the traditional colors of the Crucifixion in art.

The conclusion thus seems far removed from the initial chivalric imagery of the falcon—a contrast developed in Hopkins's "St. Alphonsus Rodriguez" (1888)—but the windhover is actually an appropriate type of one who was valiant though his "station was poor" for, according to the medieval hierarchy of falconry, it was "at the bottom of the social ladder, reserved for knaves, servants, children."[6] Thus the basic paradox of Christianity is present from the beginning in the poem, the paradox so well expressed in the conclusion of "That Nature is a Heraclitean Fire":

I am all at once what Christ is, since he was what I am, and
This Jack, joke, poor potsherd, patch, matchwood, immortal diamond,
      Is immortal diamond.

THE MORAL LEVEL

In quadrivalent biblical typology the third level is as closely related to the second and first as they were to each other. The assumption is that if a reader makes a genuinely Christological interpretation he will be changed as a result; he will "turn," the root meaning of "trope," hence the label *tropologia* for this level. Hopkins's hero, Origen, emphasized this level, the most popular one in the Middle Ages, though Jerome was the first to restrict the term to this meaning.

For Hopkins the Book of Nature as well as the Bible demanded a tropological reading, a moral application to the self: "This world then is word, expression, news of God," he wrote; "it is a book he has written . . . a poem of beauty: what is it about? His praise, the reverence due to him, the way to serve him. . . . Do men then do it? Never mind others now nor the race of man: DO I DO IT?" (*S*, 129, 239).

Hopkins's attempt to answer that question, it could be argued, is the most literal meaning of "The Windhover," just as Dante's own conversion is the literal meaning of *The Divine Comedy*, and Christ's fulfillment of the Law is the literal meaning of Old Testament types in Luther's theology. The sense of a dialectic between Hopkins's own history and that of Christ, whether perceived in the Bible or the Book of Nature, is in fact evident in the very shape of Hopkins's poems. His sonnets, like *The Wreck*, are divided into two parts, with the second answering the first, like the New Testament answering the Old, with the pause before the sestet signaling a shift from one level of interpretation to another.

The initial "I" of "The Windhover" foreshadows this shift because it stresses the experience of the self as the literal meaning of the poem. The obvious tropological application of the lesson of the Book of Nature to the self begins with "My heart in hiding / Stirred for a bird" at the conclusion of the octet. The most literal meaning is that his heart was not visible, that he was trying to avoid being seen by the falcon, but one does not need to hide to observe windhovers, and in any case the bird could not see "his heart." To discover what his heart is hiding from the reader is again forced to another level of interpretation.

One biographical answer is that he was hiding from fulfilling his ambitions to be a great painter and poet. Instead of ostentatiously pursuing fame in that way, wearing his heart on his sleeve, he had chosen to be the "hidden man of the heart" (1 Pet. 3:4) quietly pursuing the *imitatio Christi*. As Hopkins put it, Christ's "hidden life at Nazareth is the great help to faith for us who must live more or less an obscure, constrained, and unsuccessful life" (*S*, 176).

Hopkins did live such a life, but the windhover reminded him of Jesus' great achievements after Nazareth. The windhover "stirred" his desire to become a great knight of faith, one of those who imitate not only the constraint but also the "achieve of, the mastery of" this great chevalier. The fluttering wings of the falcon are an image of zeal in the *Paradiso* (19: 34–36) and its "ecstasy" recalls Hopkins's initial desire in "Il Mystico" to be lifted up on "Spirit's wings" so "that I may drink that ecstacy / Which to pure souls alone may be" (ll. 141–42). Ultimately, Hopkins became aware that he had been hiding from the emotional risks of total commitment to becoming a "pure" soul. The phrase "in hiding" thus means not only hiding from the world, or from worldly ambition, but also hiding from God, the meaning it has in Hopkins's "Thee God, I come from": "Once I turned from thee and hid, / Bound on what thou hadst forbid; / Sow the wind I would; I sinned."

This is the basic predicament of stanza 2 of *The Wreck*. The "hurl and gliding" of the windhover recall how once before his heart swooned before the "sweep and hurl" of God. The solution in "The Windhover" is the same as that of stanza three of *The Wreck*, a renewed conversion to Christ, again conveyed by heart and flight imagery. The "mastery" that "stirred" his heart in "The Windhover," therefore, was ultimately that of the "mastering me / God" of *The Wreck* (st. 1), the "Master" who could "ride" down our "pride," convert "at a crash Paul," and "master" Augustine.

The words "here / Buckle!" thus mean "here in my heart," as well as here in the bird and here in Jesus. Hopkins's heart in hiding, Christ's prey, now senses him diving down to seize it for his own. Just as the bird buckled its wings together and thereby buckled its brute beauty and valour and capacity to act; so the speaker responds by buckling together all his considerable talents. He renews his commitment to the *imitatio Christi*, deciding anew that "his truth shall be thy shield and buckler" (Ps. 91). Like Spenser's Redcrosse knight, he buckles on all the chivalric imagery of Eph. 6 in order to buckle down, buckle to, in serious preparation for the combat, the grappling, the buckling with the enemy. As Paul said, "Put on the whole armour of God, that ye may be able to stand against the wiles of the Devil."

Hopkins wrote this poem only a few months before his ordination as a Jesuit priest, the ultimate commitment to sacrifice his worldly ambitions. Just as Jesus' paradoxical triumph was his buckling under, his apparent collapse; so the knight of faith must be prepared for the same buckling under or collapse of his pride, for a life of "sheer plod" and "blue-bleak" self-sacrifice, if need be. Nevertheless, the knight of faith has the promise that a fire will break from his heart then — galled, gashed, and crucified in imitation of Christ. The fire will be "a billion times told lovelier" than that of his "heart in hiding," and far more "dangerous," both to his old self (for the fire is all-consuming) and his enemy, Evil.

In Hopkins's case the fire also became far more "dangerous" to his worldly poetic ambitions. "The Windhover" also represents Hopkins's Pegasus, the classical flying steed of poetry. The collapse of his own poetic self is implied in this imagery, for Pegasus threw off Bellerophon because of Bellerophon's pride. Fearing his pride in his own poetry, Hopkins burned his poems upon entering the Society of Jesus, believing that poetry always had to give way, buckle under, to the "greater cause" of his religion. As a result, there was a very real danger that his poems would never reach the public they deserved, that he would have to sacrifice all the worldly fame promised him as "the star of Balliol" for a life of "sheer plod." "Plod," echoing "on you plod" in his "Soliloquy of One of the Spies left in the Wilderness," evokes the dreary lot of the Israelites crossing the wilderness from Egypt to the Promised Land, the standard *typos* of conversion among the Victorians.

Yet the Israelites did reach the Promised Land and the "plod" makes the plough "shine" in "The Windhover." The plough scratching the field was in fact also a common medieval metaphor for the writer's pen scratching across the paper, the furrows corresponding to the rows of letters. Hopkins's paradoxical triumph as a poet is that, although his poems were created out of that life of sheer plod and remained as obscure as blue-bleak embers to most of his contemporaries, now that they have found an audience to appreciate them they have burst into fire, shining like multifaceted diamonds.

Hopkins's new self, in short, was able to mount Pegasus again, transforming the classical flying steed into a Christian symbol of poetry as Dante had (*Paradiso*, 18:81). In this very poem in fact the steed carries him, its chevalier, to fame.

In other words, "The Windhover" is, among other things, as Michael Sprinker has shown, an allegory of Hopkins's rediscovery and renewal of his poetic vocation.[7] "I caught" thus not only means "I caught sight of," I grasped with my senses and my mind, I attained full possession or knowledge of an object, coming upon it unexpectedly or by surprise, "catching it in the act," as we say. "I caught" also means here "I was caught by" the windhover, that is, the "dapple-dawn-drawn Falcon" caught my eye and drew me forth, drew me out of myself that dawn, drew a poem out of me, summoned my lyrical voice to an act of creation. The result is quite properly dedicated to "Christ our Lord," for like the nun in *The Wreck of the Deutschland* this speaker, looking at nature, is "wording it how but by him that present and past, / Heaven and earth are word of, worded by" (st. 29). The result is a "catch," in still another sense: a canonical, rhythmically intricate composition for several voices.

One of those voices, though only one, is the voice of a poet attempting to find himself again as a poet. The bird's "mastery" of its environment inspires him to attempt a poetic "mastery" of the symbols of the Judeo-Christian tradition to which he had dedicated his life. Consequently,

Hopkins constructed, or "achieved," not only an extraordinarily successful mimesis of the bird's "achieve," and a brilliant conversion of the bird's hovering and dive into a symbol of Christ's Incarnation, but also simultaneously a symbol of his own plunging into poetry, his own incarnation as a Christian poet.

The "buckling" of the bird and the crucifixion imagery of the sestet represent the poet's askesis as well as the terrible askesis of Christ's Passion. One could argue that the secret of Hopkins's eventual success was indeed his sacrifice of his early poems and his willingness to spend seven years in a hidden life, like Jesus' at Nazareth, waiting for the right occasion to write again; in other words, that it was Hopkins's ascetic restraint that made his poems so compressed, so rare, so much like diamonds.

Hopkins's application of the moral sense of the Book of Nature to himself is only the beginning of the tropological interpretation of "The Windhover," however. The primary moral application is to you, the reader. Hopkins's aim is clearly to call upon you to effect a similar change in your life. By virtue of his approaching ordination as a priest, Hopkins felt a special urgency about communicating this need for change to others. His poetry thus resembles the biblical tradition of typology in that "by its very nature," it "fastens on an event of conversion with the aim of effecting another . . . with a call to a radical re-alignment, with a challenge to change your mind, your way of life, your allegiances."[8]

THE ANAGOGICAL LEVEL

The fourth level is related to the third level in biblical criticism in that it too focuses on the life of grace in the soul — Dante's example is the soul leaving sin for a life of sanctity and freedom — but the fourth level is ultimately the "mystical" level that teaches "ineffable mysteries" according to Origen. In *Contra Celsum* he used the word now translated as anagogical, meaning "leading up," to distinguish this from the literal or historical senses. The most common "ineffable mystery" associated with this level is that of "eternal things" or the "future life," especially heaven and the Second Coming. In the Middle Ages, however, an equally, if not more important "ineffable mystery" was the discovery that the Creation and the Incarnation were being constantly reenacted in a "kind of continuous present."[9] The anagogical level was thus basically a breakthrough to alternative conceptions of human time.

Following Rom. 1:20 ("For the invisible things of Him . . . are clearly seen, being understood by the things that are made") some medieval theologians believed that the anagogical level could be attained by reading the Book of Nature as well as the Bible. For them nature became the universal symbolism of the Incarnate Word, eventually conceived of as equal to the Bible and to the liturgy in which the two converged. As Hugh of St. Victor put it, types could be discovered *per creaturam*, in creatures, as well as *per doctrinam*, in doctrine. Thus there was a double book for a double universe.[10] Because of the Fall, the Book of Nature had become obscure, hiding God, but it could still reveal Him to readers who reached the anagogical level. According to the theory of universal symbolism in Aquinas's *Summa*, this belief is based on the inclusion of material things, as well as Old Testament prefigurations of Jesus, in the category of "symbols of sacred things which are sacred in themselves."[11]

The romantics revived this tradition of discovering types of eternity in nature. Wordsworth, for instance, discovered that the features of nature

> Were all alike workings of one mind, the features
> Of the same face, blossoms upon one tree;
> Characters of the great Apocalypse,
> The types and symbols of Eternity,
> Of first, and last, and midst, without end.
>   (*The Prelude*, 6:636–40)

The influence of Wordsworth, therefore, as well as the medieval poets and critics, is evident in Hopkins's response to the Aurora Borealis: "This busy working of nature wholly independent of the earth and seeming to go on in a strain of time not reckoned by our reckoning of days and years but simpler and as if correcting the preoccupation of the world by being preoccupied with and appealing to and dated to the day of judgment was like a new witness to God and filled me with delightful fear" (*J*, 200). *The Wreck of the Deutschland* and a number of his other poems express not only his sense of the providential ordering of human time but also the delightful fear inspired by this discovery of Apocalyptic time in nature.[12]

Most of his nature poems suggest not so much that sense of the end of the world common in Protestant anagogical typology, however, as his experience of the beginning of the world. Nature could lead him back as well as forward in time. When he contemplated the sacramental quality of St. Winefred's Well in Wales, for instance, he wrote: "The strong unfailing flow of the water and the chain of cures from year to year all these centuries took hold of my mind with wonder at the bounty of God in one of His saints, the sensible thing so naturally and gracefully uttering the spiritual reason of its being (which is all in true keeping with the story of St. Winefred's death and recovery) and the spring in time to its spring in eternity: even now the stress and buoyancy and abundance of the water is before my eyes" (*J*, 262).

Nature was thus a corridor through time, giving the viewer access to the very beginnings of the world, to Eden itself. The "ecstasy" of the windhover is that of the creatures in Hopkins's "Spring" (1877) — "What is all this juice and all this joy? / A strain of the earth's sweet being in the beginning / In Eden garden" — and of Tennyson's "Wild bird, whose warble, liquid sweet, / Rings Eden through the budding quicks" (*In Memoriam*, no. 88). The windhover's "ecstasy" was also a taste of that second Eden, the Incarnation, that "ecstasy all through mothering earth" which "Tells Mary her mirth till Christ's birth" ("The May Magnificat").

Such a breakthrough to Edenic time was not as rare as we might think. Even as late as the nineteenth century, thousands of miles from Wales, for instance, during the same years Hopkins was describing nature's "ecstasy" in "The Windhover" and "The May Magnificat," Dosteovski was focusing the climax of part 2 of *The Brothers Karamazov* on Father Zosima. Zosima's doctrine of the worship of sinless nature was based on a sense that "Christ has been with [the creatures] before us," a feeling that "every leaf is striving to the Word," that "paradise" is at hand. Hopkins's "ecstasy" in "The Windhover" almost seems to be a response to Father Zosima's injunction: "pray to the birds too, consumed by an all-embracing love, in a sort of transport, and pray that they too forgive you your sin. Treasure this ecstasy, however senseless it may seem to others."

The "fire" that breaks from the windhover when it dives, then, is the fire of the Word becoming incarnate, the revelation of the spark of divinity in each and every creature, the fire of "God's Grandeur" and "As kingfishers catch fire." As McLuhan says, "familiarity with Hopkins soon reveals that each of his poems includes all the rest."[13] "As kingfishers" opens with virtually the same image as "The windhover." Like windhovers, kingfishers usually hang stationary (in their case on a branch) overlooking their prey before descending. The invitation to compare them with Christ is even more obvious because Christ the King was known as a fisher of men. The meaning of the octet of "As kingfishers catch fire" is simpler and more direct, however: "Each mortal thing does one thing and the same: / Deals out that being indoors each one dwells."

The "being" that dwells "indoors," the "fire" within all mortal things which can be "dealt out," is the fire of "God's Grandeur," to turn to still another sonnet, one composed just before "The Windhover." "God's Grandeur" is also dominated by an image of a bright winged bird suspended over the world at dawn. It too states simply, "The world is charged with the grandeur of God. / It will flame out. . . ." The dearest freshness "deep down" in things which will "flame out," in the windhover, then, as well as any other creature, is nothing less than the grandeur of God.

Thus, as Hopkins put it in "As kingfishers catch fire," "Christ plays in ten thousand places," not only in "just men," the immediate subject of the sestet of that poem, but in all things; "All things therefore are charged with love," he wrote in his commentary on Ignatius, "are charged with God and if we knew how to touch them give off sparks and take fire . . . ring and tell of him" (*S*, 195). Hopkins found support for this idea, as we have seen, in Scotus's concept of the Incarnation continuing in nature, that is, in the idea of nature as the mystical body of Christ. This world is charged with God's grandeur because it too is part of His mystical body. When the speaker in "Hurrahing in Harvest," another sonnet of 1877, discovers that "hills are his world-wielding shoulder," his heart is snatched up, as if by a bird of prey, and it "rears wings bold and bolder / And hurls for him, O half hurls earth for him off under his feet." There should be "No wonder of it," "The Windhover" reminds us, for the symbolism of the Incarnate Word is a universal symbolism, including ploughs and coals as well as hawks and hills.

Inner meanings of the text such as these are revealed only to those who seek them, however, according to Clement of Alexandria, the founder of the multivalent school of biblical hermeneutics. This is particularly true of the Book of Nature, for the creatures of nature, from the medieval perspective, were not descriptive symbols like words, that is, mere signs, but rather interpretive symbols which have an obvious meaning but "at the same time they contain, in their capacity as signs, a hidden meaning which will be revealed only to the one who knows how to interpret it . . . the one who allows himself time for meditating upon created things."[14] Origen felt that only those who were endowed with a special "grace" could achieve the highest spiritual level, the anagogical: "the more beautiful the soul, the more divine beauty it can perceive in things."[15] This idea recurs in Hopkins's theory of perception of inscape, as we shall see, and especially in stanza 5 of *The Wreck of the Deutschland* which emphasizes how rare and mysterious is the discovery of divine beauty in nature: "For I greet him the days I meet him, and bless when I understand."

WELSH EDEN

In *The Wreck*, "The Windhover," and his other sonnets of 1877, Hopkins clearly did attain the highest "spirituality," the mystical sense, the "anagogical" interpretation of the Book of Nature. In other words, if we look back to some of the melancholy poems of the 1860s, he moved from *acedia* to "ecstasy." Because the inner way sometimes resulted only in a discovery of that inner emptiness and ennui that Pascal defined, many religious before Hopkins had turned to the outer way to find a unity in the external world that would lead them to God. Thus, these poems represent another movement in the ongoing dialectic Hopkins experiences between the two ways.

Indeed, his great outburst of nature poetry in the late 1870s may be represented as a natural reaction against the *acedia* which often accompanied his overemphasis on the inward way. Dante defined *acedia* as a joylessness most conspicuous in the victim's inability to appreciate God's creation, a sense of *acedia* also relevant to the romantic melancholy of Goethe's Werther, Senancour's Obermann, and Coleridge's "Dejection" ode. A traditional way to escape *acedia*, therefore, from St. John Chrysostom on, was to love God's creation. Even the primarily inner-directed

Spiritual Exercises of Saint Ignatius include "The Contemplation for Obtaining Love" in which "The second point is to consider how God dwells in His creatures. . . . The third point is to consider how God works and labors for me in all created things on the face of the earth, that is, He conducts Himself as one who labours; in the heavens, the elements, plants, fruits, flocks, etc. He gives them being, preserves them."[16] Hopkins uses the same verb, "dwells in," in "As kingfishers catch fire."

As we have seen, as early as "Half-way House" Hopkins felt a need to approach God in this way: "I must o'ertake Thee at once and under heaven / If I shall overtake Thee at last above." As "The Windhover" and Hopkins's other sonnets of 1877 reveal, Hopkins found such a halfway house not only in the communion bread and wine but also in the Vale of Clwyd and the rest of the countryside around St. Beuno's College, Wales, where he studied theology from 1874 to 1877. His swing from *acedia* to enthusiasm is evident in his earliest letters from there (*F*, 124–27). Wales provided the occasion for his greatest experience of nature, as it had for Wordsworth (at Mt. Snowdon and Tintern Abbey), John Dyer (at Grongar Hill), and Henry Vaughan.

Hopkins's awakening to an unfallen world of nature in Wales is recounted in "Moonrise" (1876) and in his Welsh poem, "Cywydd" (1876), in which he asserted that the appearance of the earth shows an eternal share of virtue; only the human element is defective, man alone is backward. For Hopkins nature seemed not only unfallen, but in a sense eternal due to God's presence and protection: because the Holy Ghost broods over it, "nature is never spent" ("God's Grandeur").

Some of the most luminous symbols of that presence in Hopkins's Welsh poetry are the sunrises and the "sea-sunsets which give such splendour to the vale of Clwyd," as Wordsworth put it in his preface to "Descriptive Sketches." Such sights were distilled in Hopkins's nature poetry in his imagery of sunlight which "sidled like dewdrops, like dandled diamonds" ("The furl of fresh-leaved dogrose down," 1879). Everything from ploughed furrows to clouds to their reflections in pools is shining and gleaming. Even night reveals a world of strangely translucent moonshine or of stars that gleam like "bright boroughs" or "diamond delves" or "quickgold" in grey lawns; all of nature was perceived as a "piece-bright paling" that was Christ's "home," as Hopkins put it in "The Starlight Night":

> Look at the stars! look, look up at the skies!
>   O look at all the fire-folk sitting in the air!
>   The bright boroughs, the circle-citadels there!
> Down in dim woods the diamond delves! the elves'-eyes!
> The grey lawns cold where gold, where quickgold lies!
>   Wind-beat whitebeam! airy abeles set on a flare!
>   Flake-doves sent floating forth at a farmyard scare! —
> Ah well! it is all a purchase, all is a prize.

Buy then! bid then! — What? — Prayer, patience, alms, vows.
Look, look: a May-mess, like on orchard boughs!
   Look! March-bloom, like on mealed-with-yellow sallows!
These are indeed the barn; withindoors house
The shocks. This piece-bright paling shuts the spouse
   Christ home, Christ and his mother and all his hallows.

Hopkins clearly found in the Vale of Clwyd what the Pre-Raphaelite painters were seeking: "They chased, as it were, all the year round over the bright valleys of the earth, their ideals of luminosity; from the backcloth of bright earth and sky they cut out, as if with sharp knives, square panels of eternal paint; they gave to material phases of nature a relative permanency, a comparative immortal life."[17]

Pre-Raphaelite color and brightness convey immortal life in a poem such as "The May Magnificat": Hopkins's "strawberry-breasted" thrush, "bugle-blue" eggs, "drop-of-blood-and-foam-dapple" bloom, and "azuring-over" greybell, all shades of crimson and blue, relate the Incarnation to nature; "crimson and pure blues seemed to me," Hopkins recalled, "spiritual and heavenly sights fit to draw tears once" (B, 283). The painter's eye is also evident in the lush colorful landscape of wheat and flowers in "The Woodlark." Its painterly terminology — "The sky is two and two / With white strokes of blue" — recalls not only the bright colors of many Pre-Raphaelite paintings, but the heavy emphasis on actual strokes of paint in such impressionist paintings of the next decade as Van Gogh's *Wheat Field with Lark.*

Hopkins anticipates Van Gogh specifically in "Mirror surgentem" (undated) which focuses on Orion, the constellation used to represent the transcendent God in *The Wreck of the Deutschland.* In the Latin poem Hopkins wonders how Orion rises in the sky and flashes its fire which a force not its own makes brilliant in the heavens. Its soft luster comes and goes, he says, giving the impression that the wind could whirl its seven star-points round and round. The most appropriate analogue for this particular vision is not so much the Ruskinese search for the evidence of an underlying force in recurrent forms, or the Pre-Raphaelite ideal of luminosity, as it is the dramatized vision of nature in such impressionist paintings as Van Gogh's *Starry Night.* In Hopkins's "The Starlight Night" the stars are indeed animated in Van Gogh's fashion. They seem to be fire-folk and elves-eyes revealing sudden flashes of movement, like leaves of whitebeam or abeles when they are dramatically flipped over by sudden gusts of wind and flash the whiteness of their undersides, or like doves suddenly flying into the sky "at a farmyard scare."

As the primary symbol of nature's energy and God's grandeur, fire dominated Hopkins's imagery. The poppy buds in "The Woodlark" and "flame-rash rudred," "aflash" with the colors of fire. "Fire" breaks from the falcon and embers reveal the fire within in "The Windhover." Chestnuts are fresh "firecoals" and finches' wings flash the colors of fire in "Pied

Beauty." Kingfishers "catch fire" and dragonflies "draw flame" in "As kingfishers catch fire." God's grandeur "will flame out" ("God's Grandeur"). Once again Hopkins seems to prepare the way for Van Gogh, especially Van Gogh's flamelike plants such as the cypresses in *Road with Cypresses and Stars.*

Both artists use fire imagery to convey their sense of the great forces molding and shaping nature. Hopkins's use of the word "vital" in his description of an internal fire, a "vital" candle in the heart in "The Candle Indoors" (1879), moreover, suggests affinities between his conception of nature and the "vitalism" of Carlyle, Browning, and Van Gogh, among others. When Hopkins translated Parmenides' Being as an "ethery flame of fire, comforting the heart" he added, "he is thinking of it perhaps as a vital principle" (*J*, 130).

Hopkins's vital principle, his sense of a divine spark within all creatures, was an explicitly Christian one, however, based on the idea of the Incarnation. In *The Wreck* we perceive God not only as a transcendent Orion of light in heaven but also in the thundering storm itself, but one instance of that presence of God in the world invoked in the fifth stanza of that poem. The first signs of the extension of the sacramentalism suggested in that stanza are found in Hopkins's poems about St. Winefred's Well, a spring in the town of Holywell not far from St. Beuno's reputed to have the power of curing the sick and the lame. As we have seen, Hopkins discovered in this well an accepted example of sacramental nature, a holy "sensible thing" (*J*, 261) which offered in itself a sacred opportunity for worship. His poem "On St. Winefred" (undated) closely identifies the activity of the spring with St. Winefred herself: "she lends, in aid of work and will, / Her hand from heaven to turn a mill." In "In S. Winefridam" (undated) Hopkins suggests that if he followed "the traces of the ancient deed" properly, they would still be "full of holy power." In his Welsh "Cywydd" Hopkins extended this sense of the sacramental quality of St. Winefred's Well to other springs and streams near St. Beuno's, which he also described as "a holy remnant kept for us by Beuno and Winefred." Having moved from a sense of the sacramental quality of one fountain to a sense of the sacramental quality of many fountains and streams, it was but one step further to the conception of all of nature as a sacrament, offering sacred opportunities for worship everywhere.

That Hopkins took that step is nowhere more obvious than in the line, "and the azurous hung hills are his world-wielding shoulder," in "Hurrahing in Harvest," words which fulfill Ruskin's injunction to give up mere realism and treat "the pure and holy hills" as "a link between heaven and earth" (3:449). Following that advice, Hopkins obviously went beyond purely transcendental religious views which allow admiration for nature solely as a source of analogies, a pale reflection of God's beauty. He even surpasses some of the mystics and prophets who conceived of nature as the garment, the time-vesture of God. As we have seen, for Hopkins nature was more than a veil for a transcendent God: it actually shared in the presence, the Being of God.

God is immanent in nature, moreover, not only in the general sense that the earth is part of the mystical Body of Christ but, more particularly, He dwells inside of creatures in nature such as the windhover and is expressed in the action of each one in its own way, as Hopkins suggests in "As kingfishers catch fire":

> As kingfishers catch fire, dragonflies draw flame;
>   As tumbled over rim in roundy wells
>   Stones ring; like each tucked string tells, each hung bell's
> Bow swung finds tongue to fling out broad its name;
> Each mortal thing does one thing and the same:
>   Deals out that being indoors each one dwells. . . .
>
> (ll. 1–6)

This is not to say that God dwells in other creatures in the same way He dwells in the "just" man discussed in the sestet. The being of each creature participates in the Being of God according to its capacities; the capacity of men to imitate Christ being greater, their potential for sharing in the Being of God is greater. Nevertheless, as Hopkins makes clear in his Welsh "Cywydd," nature has one very significant advantage: it is not subject to sin, it is not fallen. The being of any one of its creatures participates fully from its conception in God's Being according to its capacity, whereas man must strain to achieve this potential level of participation and rarely succeeds. Thus the evidence of God's Being is much greater in nature than in mankind because, as Hopkins says in "Ribblesdale," nature "canst but only be, but dost that long— / Thou canst but be, but that thou well dost. . . ."

This sense of God's presence within creatures and their acts can be seen even in those poems of 1877 to 1879 which seem devoted to a transcendental conception of God. The Holy Spirit is brooding over the world at the conclusion of "God's Grandeur," but the entire world, everything in nature is also "charged," filled to the brim with God's splendor, not as a vague aura about the earth, but as an eternal freshness "deep down" in each thing in nature, something that "will flame out" from within each one:

> The world is charged with the grandeur of God,
>   It will flame out, like shining from shook foil;
>   It gathers to a greatness, like the ooze of oil
> Crushed. Why do men then now not reck his rod?
>
> And for all this, nature is never spent;
>   There lives the dearest freshness deep down things;
> And through the last lights off the black West went

> Oh morning, at the brown brink eastward, springs —
> Because the Holy Ghost over the bent
> World broods with warm breast and with ah! bright wings.
>
> (ll. 1–4, 9–14)

Even in an apparently conventional, transcendental poem such as "The Starlight Night" there is the suggestion of the presence of Christ "within-doors," "shut home" in the stars of the night and in more earthly stars: flowers on bushes and trees, "flake" doves scattered into flight, leaves of trees turned and flashed by the wind.

THE POETRY OF RECONCILIATION

In such poems Hopkins was trying to convey both the transcendent and the immanent aspects of God. In general, his attempt to resolve any one of the tensions in his nature poetry of this period necessarily involved the reconciliation of other intimately related oppositions, a continuation of that revolt against dualism which we traced in his poetry and prose of the sixties. Just as the attempt to integrate the destructive and benevolent aspects of God and nature made *The Wreck of the Deutschland* a great poem, attempts to reconcile such opposing ideas as the transcendent and the immanent aspects of God, the beautiful and the sublime, unity and variety, formal order and formless change lend greatness to many of the poems after *The Wreck.*

For instance, as we have seen, Hopkins could embody the orthodox view of God above nature, transcending it, as well as dwelling within it, in such lines as "thou art above, thou Orion of light" in *The Wreck* (st. 21). This traditional conception of God is also evident in poems written after *The Wreck* such as "Miror surgentem," which includes an image of God's provident hand stretched out everywhere to nature. Although He extends a special protection and aid, God is clearly conceived anthropomorphically and apart from nature. Similarly, although protecting and cherishing the earth, the Holy Spirit in "God's Grandeur" is separate from and above nature, like a mother dove over her egg or Milton's Holy Spirit which "with mighty wings outspread / Dove-like satst brooding on the vast Abys / And mad'st it pregnant" (*Paradise Lost*, 1:20–22). Likewise in "The Starlight Night" heaven seems to be represented in the conventional sense as a place just above or behind the stars. The basically transcendental approach of this poem and the representation of the moon as a "paring of paradisaical fruit" in "Moonrise" a year before recalls such poems as "For a Picture of St. Dorothea" and the many poems of Christina Rossetti in which ecstatic contemplation of ascension into a starry heaven is the reward for ascetic withdrawal from the things of this world.

Besides balancing these transcendent aspects of God with the evidence of His immanence in his 1877 sonnets, Hopkins assimilated both the beautiful and the sublime moods of nature. "God's Grandeur," for instance, uses the Italian sonnet structure and the inclusiveness of the word "grandeur" to suggest God's presence in both the sublime and beautiful aspects of nature. As we have seen, Hopkins explained that he chose to illustrate the idea "it will flame out" by the metaphor of "shining from shook foil" because it evokes images of both sheet and forked lightning (B, 169), images recalling the "lightning and lashed rod" and the chastising "lightning of fire hard-hurled" in *The Wreck* (sts. 2, 34). The sense of a fire that "will flame out" also recalls other instruments of the blacksmith God's forging fire in *The Wreck* such as Death's "flame" and the "white-fiery" snow. The violence of "shook" and "crushed" in "God's Grandeur" supports this sense of a great power, a threatening "rod" that must be reckoned with by man. Thus the "grandeur" of God expressed in the octet can be seen as the awesome majesty of infinite power associated with the dynamic sublime and the Old Testament God.

Yet the word "grandeur" can also mean the splendor of a great display of beauty. Even "lightning" can have this connotation, as in "Spring" where it is the vehicle for the union of the beautiful and the sublime in a single image: a thrush "Through the echoing timber does so rinse and wring / the ear it strikes like lightnings to hear him sing." If the octet represents the awesome "grandeur" of God, the sestet of "God's Grandeur," especially the concluding image of a sunrise revealing the bright-winged Holy Spirit brooding over the world, conveys this other meaning of the word.

The fusion of the sublime and the beautiful in a single creature in "The Windhover" represents another stage in Hopkins's revolt against dualism. The striking opening of the sestet, "Brute beauty," emphasizes through consonance, assonance, and a double stress the unity of these opposites. What is admired is both the beauty of the bird's flight patterns and its "dangerous" brute force. Likewise, in "Hurrahing in Harvest" God's grandeur in both the hills and the stallion is seen as beauty as well as strength: "And the azurous hung hills are his world-wielding shoulder / Majestic — as a stallion stalwart, very-violet-sweet! — " (ll. 9–10). The hills are "azurous-hung" like a painting as well as "world-wielding," and the stallion is "very-violet-sweet" as well as an image of God's "stalwart" power.

Hopkins went on to reconcile nature's unity and variety as well as its sublimity and beauty, moreover, a continuation of the effort begun in his definition of "inscape" in his prose. The fairly single-minded quest for unity in his search for inscapes in nature is reconciled with a delight in nature's variety, motion, and changefulness in "Pied Beauty," for instance:[18]

> Glory be to God for dappled things —
>   For skies of couple-colour as a brinded cow;
>   For rose-moles all in stipple upon trout that swim;
>   Fresh-firecoal chestnut-falls; finches' wings;

> Landscape plotted and pieced — fold, fallow, and plough;
> And áll trádes, their gear and tackle and trim.
>
> All things counter, original, spare, strange;
> Whatever is fickle, freckled (who knows how?)
> With swift, slow; sweet, sour; adazzle, dim;
> He fathers-forth whose beauty is past change:
> Praise him.

Hopkins's representations of the landscape as "plotted and pieced" implies the kind of recurrence and regularity he discovered when "the lines of the fields, level over level, are striking like threads in a loom" (*J*, 23). In "Pied Beauty," however, he also focuses on individual piedness, variegation, and change, as well as on those manifestations of a fixed pattern of unity so painstakingly collected in his journals.

The individuality of each thing that constitutes the variety of "All things" is stressed in lines 7 and 8. Each thing is "original," "counter" to all other things, "spare" in the sense of being not abundant, not repeated, and hence "strange," not known before, new. In other words, the speaker does not automatically categorize things as most adults do. Seeing some fallen chestnuts he does not simply classify them under the noun "chestnuts" and pass on, but pauses to recognize that these chestnuts are not exactly like all previous chestnuts, that to some extent they have an individuality that evades our linguistic categories, an original strangeness which ordinary language levels.

Wishing to resurrect the wonder that the counterness and spareness of all things created in us as children ("who knows how?"), Hopkins often created new words such as "unleaving," "wanwood," and "leafmeal," which he used in a poem such as "Spring and Fall" to recreate a child's wonder at the fall of leaves. In "Pied Beauty" we see his simpler method of making one linguistic unit, "fresh-firecoal chestnut-falls," out of adjective, noun, and verb, in order to suggest that what he saw could not be simply classified, that some of its individuality resided in the intersections of our categories. The cumulative effect of this recurrent perception of the individuality, the original counterness of "All things," is a sense of the infinitely rich variety of nature.

Yet, simultaneously there is a sense of unity. In one place a trout is marked by a rose-mole and in another it is not; at one moment it is swimming swiftly and is "adazzle" and at another it is resting and appears "dim." Nevertheless, throughout all these spatial and temporal changes it is the same trout. Each dappled thing unifies its own variety. The use of plurals and collectives in the poem also emphasizes the larger unity of the class: all trout are "fickle, freckled," but they are unified by certain common characteristics which place them in the species, trout. The great variety of the different species is in turn unified by the poet's most powerful tool, metaphor — the demonstration of unexpected unity between things thought to be unrelated such as trout and roses, skies and cows, chestnuts and coals. Finally, imitating the cyclical structure of nature, the poem ends where it began, with the focus on the word for the ultimate unity, "God."

In this short poem, encompassing both earth and sky and the traditional four elements of earth, water, air, and fire, the oneness of the biosphere can be heard as well as seen. The sound structure of the poem reinforces the reader's sense of a complex unity in the midst of all the counterness and spareness. Alliteration in line 4, for instance, unites the "fresh firecoals," the "falls" of chestnuts, and the "finches"; in line 9 it suggests the presence of an underlying unity between the apparent opposites. Throughout the poem, assonance, consonance, rhyme, and rhythm all work to create an intricate model of how unity and variety depend upon and sustain each other.

Yet instead of the quiet beauty of a stable, unifying order, nature in "Pied Beauty" is in constant flux. Hopkins's emphasis on action and change in the poems of the late 1870s resulted in representations of nature in which a wild willfulness of forms displaced regular patterns, and loveliness consisted not only in the forms but also in the behavior of objects such as the clouds in "Hurrahing in Harvest": "up above, what wind walks! what lovely behavior / Of silk-sack clouds! has wilder, wilful-waiver / Meal-drift moulded ever and melted across skies?" Nature is being represented here not as it was in the journals but as it was in *The Wreck of the Deutschland:* as a world of great activity. Hopkins proceeded in his subsequent poems to include both the formless dynamic energy and change of nature that he had embodied in that poem and the opposite sense of nature's unchanging stable order and formal unity that he had so laboriously cultivated in his journals.

"Pied Beauty" also reveals Hopkins's conception of the relationship between God and this world of variety and change: God "fathered-forth" this world but, paradoxically, was Himself "past change." This dual conception of God as removed from the world of mutability and yet at the same time the Progenitor of that world was an ancient paradox, of course, but Hopkins felt the necessity of a new reconciliation of the idea of nature as a world of regularly recurrent patterns of unity, reflecting a transcendent Oneness, with a concept of nature as full of variety and change being continually created by a God who was very closely identified with, actually immanent in that process.

One of his reconciliations is the representation of the recurring act, the inscape of change. The "rash-fresh" yet "re-winded" sounds of the skylark in "The Sea and the Skylark," for instance, represent ageless patterns. What Hopkins admires is the "resumption by the lark of his song, which by turns he gives over and takes up again all day long, and this goes on, the sonnet says, through all time without ever losing its first freshness, being a thing both old and new" (B, 164). The skylark's song is both a pattern of sound which recurs throughout the day and throughout all time, typifying and thereby uniting the species, and yet a song that seems to be new, an original utterance of one individual, unique creature. Thus the song is an instance of both unity of recurrence and diversity of original expression, immutability and mutability, stability and change.

Hopkins's most successful reconciliations in his next set of nature sonnets, in 1879, were often achieved by limiting his search in this way to individual objects, acts, or scenes which had a formal unity, thereby revealing the force within them to be both a diversifying and a unifying power. The landscape of "Binsey Poplars," for instance, the first of his pair of elegies for the countryside around Oxford in 1879, combines specialness with recurrent regularity. Part of the attraction of the Binsey poplars for Hopkins was the regularity of their form, their "following folded rank." This regularity contrasted with the willful variation of the "river and wind-wandering / Weed-winding bank," phrases which echo the "wind-walks" and "wilful-waiver" clouds of "Hurrahing in Harvest." This balance of regularity and variety constituted the "sweet especial scene," an expression or "selving" of the tender "being" of the country. When the "following folded rank" of the poplars was cut down, the entire scene was "unselved."

"Duns Scotus's Oxford" enlarges the focus to all of the landscape surrounding the university town, and considers the special balance between town and country. The city had its man-made towers, for instance, but it was also "branchy between towers"; it was swarming with bells, but also with cuckoos, larks, rooks, and shepherds. The result was "rural keeping." "Keeping," according to Webster's, means among other things "the harmony or correspondence between the different parts of a work of art," as in "the foreground of this painting is not in keeping." In Hopkins's notes on painting in 1874 he uses the term "inscape of composition" in a similar way to define the qualities of correspondence, regularity, and often internal recurrence necessary in an individual painting to give it "keeping" in this sense, that genuine unity which he so admired (J, 248).

Hopkins's interest in the "special" scenes of "Duns Scotus's Oxford" and "Binsey Poplars" reveals the same painterly interest in an unusual harmony and balance, a special unity destroyed by the addition of any foreign element or the removal of any part. The harmony between the "coped and poised" powers of Oxford and its rural surroundings, for instance, was destroyed by the new "graceless growth" of brick suburbs. Similarly, the balance between the regularity of the "following folded rank" of the Binsey poplars and the variety of the "wind-wandering weed-winding" river upon which their shadows swam was destroyed when the poplars were chopped down. (Incidentally, poplar shadows upon a stream is the same image of harmony as that of several Monet landscapes.) The result in both cases was an "unselving," the destruction of a special unity. A striking manifestation of the tender "being" of the "country" disappeared from both scenes. Evidence of the immanent unifying and diversifying force was lost to all "after-comers."

Hopkins's attraction to that force is also embodied in the celebration of the "forged feature," the rehearsal "Of own, of abrupt self" in "Henry Purcell" in 1879. Hopkins clearly intended to praise individuality and the special case in this poem. Yet, "beyond that," he admired Purcell because, as he said in his preface to the poem, Purcell "uttered in notes the very make and species of man as created both in him and in all men generally." The analogy to the great stormfowl in the poem works in the same way: "the seabird opening his wings with a whiff of wind in your face means the whirr of motion, but also unaware gives you a whiff of knowledge about his plumage, the marking of which stamps his species" (B, 83). Hopkins is fascinated by both the unique individual and that pattern in the plumage which, recurring throughout the plumage of all birds of that species, unifies the species and thus reveals the evidence of an integrating force in nature.

THE TRAGIC VISION

Hopkins believed that if other people could see this unifying force in nature as he did, they could be brought closer to God. The chief difficulty with this idea of nature as a mediator between man and God, however, has always been that even a poet cannot effectively communicate a sensitivity to his environment if his community is not ready for it. The Psalms suggest how old this problem is: "The heavens are telling the glory of God; and the firmament proclaims his handiwork. Day to day pours forth speech, and night to night declares knowledge. There is no speech, nor are there words; their voice is not heard; yet their voice goes out through all the earth and their words to the end of the world" (19:1-4). This is the Psalm echoed in "Where Are the Nine?" in *Pietas Metrica*. This lament for man's inability to appreciate and respect nature increasingly dominated nineteenth-century literature as industrialization and urbanization spread. Wordsworth and Coleridge had already registered their complaints when Thoreau wrote of how "The morning wind forever blows, the poem of creation is uninterrupted; but few are the ears that hear it."[19] Eventually Hopkins came to a similar conclusion, realizing how sadly "beauty of inscape was unknown and buried away from simple people and yet how near at hand it was if they had eyes to see it and it could be called out everywhere again" (J, 221). Yet it was not only simple people who lacked the requisite vision: the eyes of the vast majority of people, then as now, had not been trained to see the beauty of inscape, the beauty of the intricate unity intrinsic in nature's richest variety. As Origen observed centuries before, a "special grace" was needed to reach the "anagogical" level.

Hopkins was more isolated than most poets, moreover, because, though nature still testified to him of God's presence and offered meditation, for many of his contemporaries who also responded to nature God was a transcendent deity who did not live in the world or had disappeared altogether. In either case, for most of his contemporaries, nature existed only to be exploited. As Hopkins put it in "God's Grandeur," the shod feet of modern men "have trod, have trod, have trod; / And all is seared with trade; bleared, smeared with toil; / And wears man's smudge and shares man's smell. . . ."

The anguish that Hopkins and other nineteenth-century writers felt because industrial man not only failed to respond to the forms of nature, but in fact seemed dedicated to their annihilation should not be underestimated. One of Hopkins's journal entries reads, "The ashtree growing in the corner of the garden was felled. It was lopped first: I heard the sound and looking out and seeing it maimed there came at that moment a great pang and I wished to die and not see the inscapes of the world destroyed any more" (*J*, 230).

The pervasiveness of this unusual sensitivity to the environment and the tragic vision it produced in the nineteenth century may be suggested by Hardy's ascription of the "weakness of character," ultimately even the death wish, of his nineteenth-century man, Jude, to a similar sensitivity: "He could scarcely bear to see trees cut down or lopped, from a fancy that it hurt them; and late pruning, when the sap was up and the tree bled profusely, had been a positive grief to him in his infancy" (*Jude the Obscure*, pt. 1, chap. 2). Earlier, Thoreau had written, "Sympathy with the fluttering alder and poplar leaves almost takes away my breath . . . if any part of the forest was burned . . . I grieved with a grief that lasted longer and was more inconsolable than that of the proprietors. . . . I would that our farmers when they cut down a forest felt some of that awe which the old Romans did when they came to thin, or let in the light to, a consecrated grove (*locum conlucare*) that is, would believe that it is sacred to some god."[20] It was both the immediate loss, and the fact that the "After-comers cannot guess the beauty been" ("Binsey Poplars") that led Hopkins to plead in "Inversnaid" (1881), "What would the world be, once bereft / Of wet and of wildness? Let them be left, / O let them be left, wildness and wet; / Long live the weeds and the wilderness yet."

Industrialization continued to consume the wilderness as it still does, however; whole landscapes like those around Oxford were destroyed by what Hopkins called "base and brickish" suburbs. Finally in 1882 he wrote of the Ribble river valley:

> . . . strong
> Thy plea with him who dealt, nay does now deal,
> They lovely dale down thus and thus bids reel
> Thy river, and o'er gives all to rack or wrong.
>
> "Ribblesdale"

Though in 1882 Hopkins felt that nature's plea was still strong with God, that nature was still somehow "never spent," in this poem he at first puts God's rule over the river in the past tense—"dealt"—and concludes the octet replacing the image of God brooding protectively over nature ("God's Grandeur") with a new image of God giving all of nature over to "rack or wrong."

The source of this wrong being done to nature was, as the sestet reveals, the egoism of the stewards of the earth:

> And what is Earth's eye, tongue, or heart else, where
> Else, but in dear and dogged man?—Ah, the heir
> To his selfbent so bound, so tied to his turn,
> To thriftless reave our rich round world bare
> And none reck of world after. . . .

Hopkins discovered anew the aptness of the motto that Ruskin chose for the title page of *Modern Painters:* a citation from Wordsworth on how Nature and Truth revolt "offended at the ways of man" who

> prizes
> This soul, and the transcendent universe
> No more than as a mirror that reflects
> To proud Self-love her own intelligence.

A chief cause of this proud self-love according to Wordsworth was increasing urbanization. In *The Prelude* Wordsworth focused on the dangerously narcissistic introversion of city life, where the self is "Debarr'd from nature's living images. / Compelled to be a life unto itself" (6:313–14). Hence it is not surprising that it was in Hopkins's first extended comparison of the city and the country, "The Sea and the Skylark" (1877), that his tragic vision of environmental degradation received its first full expression. Hopkins tried to suggest that an Edenic purity was there, just outside the cities and towns, that other men also could feel how the cleansing song of the thrush could "rinse and wring" the ear ("Spring"). He admired the sea and the skylark because they had "the cheer and charm of earth's past prime," they were as "rash-fresh" and "pure" as if they were still in Eden.

But when he turned from this "freshness deep down" in nature to urban civilization symbolized by the nearby town of Rhyl, he felt the vulnerability of man and nature to each other. The town seemed "frail" both because its temporal existence seemed so negligible beside the apparent immortality of nature itself, and because the seemingly infinite power of the sea that roared around its edges could crush it. Yet man also posed a serious threat to nature's frailty: Hopkins's "Our make and making break, are breaking, down" suggests not only that man's basic structure, his make, is disintegrating, but even his attempts at construction, his making, is itself a breaking. This paradox is defined more fully in "Binsey Poplars":

> Since country is so tender
> To touch, her being só slender,
> That, like this sleek and seeing ball
> But a prick will make no eye at all,
> Where we, even where we mean
> To mend her we end her

For Ruskin in "The Two Paths" it was the names "of great painters" that were "like passing bells" of decaying civilizations (16:342). For Hopkins it was the sounds of the sea and the skylark that ushered out like bells at the end of the year his own "sordid turbid time." Hopkins's representation of this "sordid turbid" time breaking down to man's last "dust," draining fast toward man's first "slime," recalls similar accounts of dust, slime, and pollution in the works of Tennyson, Dickens, Ruskin, and others.[21]

Not long after he completed "The Sea and the Skylark" Hopkins was assigned to Chesterfield. From this time until his death the pollution of the industrial cities to which he was assigned took a mounting toll of his energies and his spirit. Of his life in Chesterfield in 1878 he wrote, "Life here is as dank as ditch-water. . . . My muse turned utterly sullen in the Sheffield smoke-ridden air" (B, 47–48). After a brief sojourn at Oxford he was sent in 1879 to Bedford Leigh, near Manchester, which he described as "very gloomy . . . there are a dozen mills or so, and coalpits also; the air charged with smoke as well as damp" (D, 29, B, 90). In 1880 Liverpool was his assignment: there "the river was coated with dirty yellow ice from shore to shore" (B, 116). Sent to Glasgow in 1881, Hopkins wrote, "My Liverpool and Glasgow experience laid upon my mind a conviction, a truly crushing conviction, of the misery of town life . . . of the degradation even of our race, of the hollowness of this century's civilisation: it made even life a burden to me to have daily thrust upon me the things I saw" (D, 97). Finally, in 1884, after teaching at Stonyhurst for two years, Hopkins was sent to Dublin, "a joyless place and I think in my heart as smoky as London is" (B, 190).

Throughout the whole of his career in the Victorian cities a remarkably modern concern for pollution weighed heavily upon him: "our whole civilisation is dirty, yea filthy, and especially in the north; for is it not dirty, yea filthy, to pollute the air as Blackburn and Widnes and St. Helen's are polluted and the water as the Clyde and the Irwell are polluted? The ancients with their immense public baths would have thought even our cleanest towns dirty" (B, 299). From this sense of physical pollution Hopkins moved to a sense of the general pollution of the human race: "the filthy, as the scripture says, are filthy still: human nature is so inveterate. Would that I had seen the last of it" (B, 110). Such connections between physical and moral pollution were not uncommon in Victorian writers. Dickens's Dombey and Son (1848), Ruskin's "The Stormcloud of the Nineteenth-Century" (1884), and other Victorian works anticipated many recent findings in the human sciences about the relations between environmental and human deterioration.

Eventually, Hopkins "saw the last of it." He died in Dublin at the age of forty-four of typhoid fever, apparently caused by the polluted urban water supply. The continuing attraction of nature for him even toward the end, however, his desire to snatch brief moments of light and joy in nature before the night overwhelmed all, is evident in his last nature poem, the fragment "Epithalamion" (1888). It was intended as an ode on the occasion of his brother's marriage but the result is a tale of one man's encounter with nature which anticipates some of the nature poetry to follow Hopkins.

The direct personal voice and the primary action, a man swimming alone in nature, anticipates Lawrence's "Wild Common," for instance, and the diction and syntax sound often like that of another lover of Wales, Dylan Thomas:

> Hark, hearer, hear what I do; lend a thought now, make believe
> We are leafwhelmed somewhere with the hood
> Of some branchy bunchy bushybowered wood,
> Southern dean or Lancashire clough or Devon cleave,
> That leans along the loins of hills, where a candycoloured, where a
>   gluegold-brown
> Marbled river, boisterously beautiful, between
> Roots and rocks is danced and dandled, all in froth and water-
>   blowballs, down.
>
> (ll. 1–8)

"Epithalamion" also summarized Hopkins's own experience of nature:

> Till walk the world he can with bare his feet
> And comes where lies a coffer, burly all of blocks
> Built of chancequarrièd, selfquainèd, hoar-huskèd rocks
> And the water warbles over into/filtered/with glassy grassy quicksilvery
>   shivès and shoots
> And with heavenfallen freshness down from moorland still brims,
> Dark or daylight on and on. Here he will then, here he will the fleet
> Flintry kindcold element let break across his limbs
> Long. Where we leave him, froliclavish, while he looks about him,
>   laughs, swims.
>
> (ll. 35–42)

Hopkins obviously had discovered the applicability of Wordsworth's preface to *The Excursion*:

> Paradise and groves
> Elysian, Fortunate Fields, like those of old
> Sought in the Atlantic Main — why should they be
> A history only of departed things,
> Or a mere fiction that never was?
> For the discerning intellect of Man

When wedded to this goodly universe
In love and holy passion, shall find these
A simple produce of the common day.

Hopkins's poetry, wedded to the universe in love and holy passion, is a
modern record of Eden found — and lost. To retrace the final result of that
marriage, the increasing sense of man's destruction of nature and the
desire to enjoy some fleeting moments with her before it is too late, is to
define what is essentially our own relationship with nature.

EVALUATION

Our evaluation of Hopkins as a poet of nature often depends to a
great extent on how well we think he relates to the "scientific" response to
nature, however. Aldous Huxley, for instance, felt that he had to reject a
poem such as "The Starlight Night" because it was so out of touch with the
scientific forefront of thought that it was "not at all legitimate," "simply
inadmissable."[22] Admittedly, this and many of Hopkins's other nature
poems challenge our basic assumption that art must mirror "our sense of
the age," as Robert Langbaum put it. Langbaum argues that our age is
mirrored in "the new nature poetry" of Marianne Moore, D. H. Lawrence, Wallace Stevens, Ted Hughes, and others who extend Ruskin's
attack on personification as "pathetic fallacy," rejecting even the vestigial
anthropomorphism of Swinburne and Hardy in order to focus on the true
"mindlessness of nature, its nonhuman otherness."[23]

It is true that a poem such as Wallace Stevens's "The Course of a
Particular," with its fierce rejection of any trace of personification of
nature, is more of a midwife to our new scientific world. Hopkins's "The
Starlight Night" and his other nature poems seem to breathe life into the
old world, the age of faith in the "pathetic fallacy," in the personification
of God and nature, and the verbal imagination generally. Yet this
apparent opposition between science and the ancient traditions of personification in religion and the humanities is simplistic, for metaphor is the
scientist's as well as the poet's most powerful tool.[24]

A creative scientist recognizes the value and validity of any and all
metaphors which provide access to important dimensions of reality,
whether or not they happen to operate in his own field of specialization.
Hence he should have little difficulty perceiving that one of the most
powerful and meaningful of all the dominant metaphors of Western
civilization is the personification of nature — the assertion of some sense of
identity between man and nature. This is one of the languages that puts
man in the landscape and the landscape in man. It has been abused more
than most theoretical models in science, of course, but it can still be made
responsible to feedback and remains congruent with significant aspects of
reality.

Yet Huxley rejects Hopkins's metaphors of stars as "fire-folk sitting in the air" as anachronistic in an age of science, and presumably on the same grounds, Hopkins's imagery of "elves' eyes," the "piece-bright paling" which "shuts Christ home, Christ and his mother and all his hallows." Admittedly these are not the metaphors of science. Why should they be? Hopkins no more thought of his discipline as a mirror of popular science than a scientist thinks of his as a mirror of popular poetry. A creative scientist and a poet can each respect the other's work because they are both interested not in mirroring but in modeling and changing our conception of reality, and to this end the more powerful the metaphor the better.

Thus, refusing to limit himself to the models fashionable in Victorian science, Hopkins resurrected a sense of a universe animated by powerful cosmic forces, employing metaphors at once more precise and suggestive than those of his contemporaries, metaphors which enabled him to fill and satisfy our imagination as a great nature poet must. Compare Hopkins's nature poetry with Matthew Arnold's in this respect, for instance. Afraid of committing the "pathetic fallacy," Arnold's representation of a thrush is tentative, an admission of ignorance: "Sometimes a thrush flit overhead / Deep in her unknown day's employ" ("Lines Written in Kensington Gardens"). Sure of the presence of God in this world, Hopkins's representation of a thrush is an enthusiastic celebration of communion: "Thrush's eggs look little low heavens, and thrush / Through the echoing timber does so rinse and wring / The ear, it strikes like lightnings to hear him sing" ("Spring").

Hopkins achieves what other nature poets of his day could not partly because he recognized the importance of personification; in his case the significance of the ultimate personification: the cosmic Christ. Unlike most of his contemporaries, imagining God in the flowers and waters Hopkins approached them with a belief that they were alive, and thus kept his poetry free of the debilitating shame, hesitation, and alienation which plague the "modern" view of nature according to Ruskin (5:231). Because Hopkins rediscovered part of what Arnold called the great medieval "Sea of Faith," especially the belief in the verbal imagination and the vitality of tradition, as we have seen, Hopkins could resurrect Hebraic pastoral even in the age of science: "What is all this juice and all this joy? / A strain of earth's sweet being in the beginning / In Eden's garden" ("Spring").

Unlike the speaker in Wallace Stevens's "The Course of a Particular," Hopkins does not merely hear the cry of a bird, therefore; he makes a real attempt to see it as "part of everything," as a "cry of divine attention" concerning everyone rather than "no one at all," as Stevens puts it.[25] Compared with Stevens's poem and a surprising number of Arnold's and Wordsworth's poems, moreover, Hopkins's poems seem fiercely reactionary in their insistence on richness of image and sound as perceptible emblems of order and splendor in the world, flashes of the grandeur with which the world is "charged." Ironically, this supposedly archaic, anthropomorphic attitude toward the universe produced poems such as "Binsey Poplars" and

"Ribblesdale" which place Hopkins in the forefront of the current struggle in the environmental sciences to overcome the anthropocentrism threatening our environment. Hopkins thus shares a common cause as well as a common language (metaphor) with innovative scientists and, as Robert Lowell has suggested, should still be considered "Probably the finest of English poets of nature."[26]

Notes

1. Herbert Marshal McLuhan, "The Analogical Mirrors," in *Gerard Manley Hopkins: "The Windhover*," ed. John Pick (Columbus, 1969), p. 24.

2. See Abrams, pp. 239–41.

3. M. L. Grossman and J. Hamlet, *Birds of Prey of the World* (New York: C. N. Potter, 1964), p. 407.

4. Paul Mariani, *A Commentary on the Complete Poems of Gerard Manley Hopkins* (Ithaca, 1970), p. 111.

5. Ibid., p. 112; see also David J. DeLaura, "Hopkins and Carlyle: My Hero, My Chevalier," *Hopkins Quarterly* 2, no. 2 (1975): 67–76.

6. Grossman and Hamlet, p. 79.

7. Michael Sprinker, *"A Counterpoint of Dissonance"; The Aesthetics and Poetry of Gerard Manley Hopkins* (Baltimore, 1980), pp. 12–13.

8. A. C. Charity, *Events and Their Afterlife* (Cambridge: Cambridge University Press, 1966), p. 168.

9. See D. W. Robertson, *A Preface to Chaucer* (Princeton: Princeton University Press, 1962), pp. 301–2; Claude Tresmontant in William E. Lynch, *Christ and Apollo* (New York: Sheed and Ward, 1960), pp. 219–20; and Georges Poulet, *Studies in Human Time*, trans. E. Coleman (Baltimore: Johns Hopkins University Press, 1956), pp. 6–7.

10. Henry de Lubac, *Exégèse Médiévale*, vol. 4 (Paris: Aubier, 1964), pp. 172–77.

11. John Chydenius, *The Theory of Medieval Symbolism* (Helsingfors: Societas Scientiarum Fennica, 1960), pp. 19, 29.

12. See Sulloway, *Gerard Manley Hopkins and the Victorian Temper*, pp. 158–95. For a parallel with Wordsworth see M. H. Abrams, *Natural Supernaturalism: Tradition and Revolution in Romantic Literature* (New York: W. W. Norton, 1971).

13. McLuhan, p. 23.

14. Chydenius, pp. 13, 15.

15. Stephen Manning, "Scriptural Exegesis and the Literary Critic," in *Typology and Early American Literature*, ed. Sacvan Bercovitch (Amherst: University of Massachusetts Press, 1972), p. 64.

16. *The Spiritual Exercises of St. Ignatius*, trans. A. Mottola (New York: Doubleday, 1964), p. 104.

17. Ford Madox Hueffer [Ford], *The Pre-Raphaelite Brotherhood* (London: Duckworth, 1907), p. 164.

18. See Miller, *The Disappearance of God*, pp. 298–305.

19. Henry D. Thoreau, *Walden and Civil Disobedience*, ed. Owen Thomas (New York: W. W. Norton, 1966), p. 57.

20. Ibid., pp. 87, 166.

21. See Jerome Bump, "Hopkins, the Humanities and the Environment," *Georgia Review* 28, no. 2 (1974):238–39.

22. Aldous Huxley, *Literature and Science* (New York: Harper and Row, 1963), pp. 53–54.

23. Robert Langbaum, *The Modern Spirit* (New York: Oxford University Press, 1970), pp. 109, 102–3.

24. See Jerome Bump, "Science, Religion, and Personification in Poetry," *Cahiers Victoriens & Edouardiens*, no. 7 (1978):123–37; and Max Black, *Models and Metaphors* (Ithaca: Cornell University Press, 1962).

25. See Sigurd Burkhardt, "Poetry and the Language of Communion," in *Hopkins*, ed. Hartman, pp. 160–67, and Jerome Bump, "Stevens and Lawrence: The poetry of Nature and the Spirit of the Age," *Southern Review* 18, no. 1 (1982):44–61.

26. See "Preface," note 1.

The First Apocalypse: "The hour of fulfilment" in G. M. Hopkins

David Anthony Downes*

Among Gerard M. Hopkins's first sermons is an Advent sermon on a text from Saint Paul to the Romans: "In all this remember how critical the moment is. It is time for you to wake out of sleep, for deliverance is nearer to us now than it was when first we believed. It is far on in the night; day is near."[1] Hopkins reiterates Paul to his parish congregation in these words: "Mark these two things: every minute true, for it is at any minute true to say our life has gone on some time since Christ's first coming and made some approach to his second; and also every minute truer for every minute we and the world are older, every minute our death and the world's end are nearer than before. For life and time are always losing."[2] Hopkins then advises his congregation "to walk honestly, that is honourably," to make every minute true.

Hopkins was, of course, dutifully addressing a touchstone of Christianity at an appropriate time of the liturgical year. But, as we know from Hopkins's life and writings, the Apocalypse was more than an item in his Christian consciousness. It is accurate to say that along with the Incarnation, the Apocalypse was the most imposing force in Hopkins's religious personality and hence a central theme in all of his thinking and writing.

The general apocalyptic temper of Hopkins's religious sensibility has been sharply clarified by Alison G. Sulloway in her book, *Gerard Manley Hopkins and the Victorian Temper*. In the last chapter she describes the general calamitarian mood of the Victorian age and notes the number of important Victorian personalities who in one way or another stressed the symptoms of the times as compelling evidence of at least a world calamity and

*This essay was written specifically for this volume and is published here for the first time by the permission of the author.

maybe a coming end of the world as symbolically depicted in Saint John's Revelation. After her list of citations, encompassing an impressive number of Victorian sages, Sulloway then fits Hopkins into this calamitarian mood, showing how he, too, in his writings, expressed a deeply felt sense of time's ending. Of course, he viewed this possible eventuality in Christian terms as Sulloway ably demonstrates in explicating his first great religious ode, *The Wreck of the Deutschland*, the only major Victorian work, she observes, that draws its matter and form directly from the Apocalypse.[3]

The other explicitly apocalyptic poem in Hopkins's canon is "That Nature is a Heraclitean Fire and of the comfort of the Resurrection." This sonnet is perhaps his last great religious poem, as *The Wreck* was his first. James Finn Cotter has explicated this poem[4] in terms of its apocalyptic levels which reveal how Hopkins saw the Incarnation as the transforming event in the calamity of time and history. Cotter located in the sonnet numerous representations of the "inscape of Christ" which Hopkins saw as the center of John's Revelation.

Together, Sulloway and Cotter make clear how profound the apocalyptic mood was in Hopkins's poetic consciousness. Their critical readings, however, focus upon what Northrop Frye calls the "panoramic" apocalypse,[5] that theater of overwhelming events, calamitous and marvelous, which in the near future and at the end of time will take place according to John's Revelation. But I want to discuss the other apocalypse in Hopkins, that "personal apocalypse" that he referred to in his sermon, "our life has made some way on, our death has made some approach." What did Hopkins understand about what John's Revelation said and its relationship to every Christian's apocalypse, and how did he express his understanding in his poetry?

Let me pose the answers to these questions by going straight to some poems and looking for the way the answers got expressed in Hopkins's religious poetic consciousness. In "God's Grandeur"[6] Hopkins devotes the whole sonnet to exclaiming that God's luminous Presence is everywhere yet goes unheeded in the here and now. Why? In "The Starlight Night"[7] he exhorts us to look at the heavens, not just to see stars and skies, but to see Christ—home. The whole exhortative spirit of the poem implies that we are not paying attention. Why? In "Spring"[8] the poet rhapsodizes on the beauties of the show of spring and then asks us to consider whose show it really is. Again there is the exhortation to see spring for what it really is—Christ's epiphany—implying that we do not see correctly. Why?

Or take some poems that depict what happens when we do see. "Pied Beauty,"[9] for example, celebrates seeing as much as the eyes can see as the "fathering forth" of God. What change in consciousness brings forth this doxology? "The May Magnificat"[10] inquires about why we associate the month of May with Mary. The poet alters our awareness of May from "mothering earth" to one of remembering and exulting in Mary's mothering. What change in perspective does the poet imply? Even more dramatic is "Hurrahing in Harvest."[11] Spring has come and gone, and so has summer. Does fall offer a vision of anything higher than its "barbarous beauty"? The poet tells us with great excitement that when he walked an autumn path, he felt lifted up to some ecstatic scene showing the Presence of Christ, a Christ that greeted him, and called forth from him a powerful sense of kinship, love, and affirmation. The poet tells us that the experience made him feel he was about to fly from the earth. What is the transformation that the poet is talking about?

Or let us take some poems that describe the consequences of failing to escape our subjective selves at moments when we view the objective world. In "The Sea and the Skylark,"[12] Hopkins tells us of portents of human doom in the song of the bird and the roar of the water: "Our make and making break, are breaking, down / To man's last dust, drain fast towards man's first slime." What are we "making break"? In "The Caged Skylark"[13] the poet depicts humanity like a bird in a cage unable to fly freely, unable to sing the song of true and lasting fulfillment. Thus we droop or rage, encumbered. What has happened to us? Or take what perhaps is Hopkins's harshest poem about the predicament of humanity, "Spelt from Sibyl's Leaves."[14] In this sonnet he tells us that the meaning of the patterns of natural time and space reveal a process of "Disremembering"; whether we know it or not, we are being sorted out by what we see and do not see, by what we do and do not do. The normal condition of human consciousness in this life is "thoughts against thoughts in groans grind." Is there no surcease for this ravaging internal battle?

These poems are really about a consciousness of what can be called a personal apocalypse. An understanding of this unusual spiritual state requires that we consider it within the context of Christianity. As biblical prophecy Christianity is a deeper vision of Divinity: whereas the prophecies of the Old Testament are about the coming of the Messiah, the New Testament offers a prophetic vision of the Messiah who has come. And what are the touchstones of this gospel vision? There are two levels. The first is that of the descent of Christ into time and history wherein the dilemma of original human identity is resolved. God took His creatures back with a promise of ultimate recovery — the Promised Land. This is the level of the Incarnation in time. On the level of time "resurrected," there is the transcendent vision of a return to a beatific identity where all people and all things are restored to what the prophet John calls heaven. Both compose the Apocalypse, the first directed towards the transformation of human nature here and now, and the last directed towards the ultimate consequences of the Incarnation for all the world and for every individual human being.

This new and deeper biblical prophecy in the Gospels, which Jesus calls the "Kingdom of God," does not in and of itself inspirit each human heart. To many — sometimes it seems to most of humanity — the vision is merely one among many religious doctrines that form the corpus of human religion. But to those who become true Christian believers, the vision in some unknown manner enters into their consciousness with a kind of basic transforming power so that their lives, their times, nature, therefore history and destiny, are radically altered. It is not too much to say that this new way of life takes one into a new human community, a new society in which members feel an enlarged vision of life, a new openness, a new freedom, a new fulfillment.

It is this state of grace, as Christians call it, in which one feels a correspondence with some Divine wish that makes the biggest difference between the old prophecy and the new prophecy in the Bible. In the old vision, the focus is on observance of the law; in the new, the focus is on a radical change of heart. Prodigality in the old is alienation, in the new, forgiveness. Another way of saying this is that in the old vision of the human situation, the issue is wisdom; in the new, the issue is sin and grace. Jesus' "Kingdom of God" acknowledges the pertinence of the old law with its implications of hell and death as human destiny on this earth, but He brought forth an original vision that proclaims the opening of a new consciousness, one that involves a transformation of awareness, an altered way of looking at everything, thereby inaugurating the beginnings of a new human emancipation from the legalistic torment of the old law and its punitive alienation — an eye for an eye and a tooth for a tooth. And even more crucial, this vision inspirits the soul in the here and now. Northrop Frye expressed the momentous moment in Jesus' vision this way: "In the 'kingdom' the eternal and the infinite are not time and space made endless (they *are* endless already) but are the now and the here made real, an actual present and an actual presence. Time vanishes in Jesus' 'Before Abraham was, I am' (John 8:56); space vanishes when we are told, in an aphorism . . . that the Kingdom is *entos hymon* (Luke 17:21), which may mean among you or in you, but in either case means here, not there."[15]

In sum, then, the gospel of Jesus is about the making of a new human being through a new union of God and mankind, with the result that the old fallen nature can now become a kind of phase of the reappearance of a new, higher life and ultimately a totally transformed life, a recovery of the innocence before the first calamity and a reprieve before the next. Now each visionary, that is, each Christian believer, has the human power to act in God's name through His divine power which transcends time and space. The old Mosaic law of legalized behavior becomes through Christ the commandments of love, or to put it another way, the new prophecy of an emancipation from sin.

The implications of this emancipation through grace (acting through, by, and with God's participation) are transfiguring. Through the Incarnation, the old fallen order of mankind and nature becomes a phase in the re-creation of the new human being — the Christ person — human nature joined in a new union with God. Saint Paul put it: "For all who are moved by the spirit of God are sons of God."[16] Hopkins put it in a poem titled, "As kingfishers catch fire":[17]

> Each mortal thing does one thing and the same:
> Deals out that being indoor each one dwells;
> Selves—goes its self; *myself* it speaks and spells,
> Crying *What I do is me: for that I came.*
> I say more: the just man justices;
> Keeps grace: that keeps his goings graces;
> Acts in God's eye what in God's eye he is—Christ.

The ultimate implication of this re-creation of a new self is a vision of faith that empowers a destiny that transcends space and time. This brings us back to the Apocalypse.

The Revelation of John expresses two prophetic visions. One is what might be called the outward apocryphal representation of the end of the world and the Second Coming of Christ. This end-of-the-world vision is the apocalypse that believers usually focus upon when they contemplate the revelation of things to come in the hereafter. In this vision the heathen worlds will be dismantled and the people of God raised to enter His kingdom. The prophet stresses the sayings and wonders that will portend the coming of this momentous event. John put forth one level of sacral history, namely, the order of events which will lead to a new heaven and a new earth; the revelation "was given to him so that he might show his servants what must shortly happen." But at the level of preaching the prophecy to every man, woman, and child, John was restating the Gospel of Jesus, that the "Kingdom of God" is now, that His Word is the inspiriting of a new consciousness that will radically change the spiritual awareness of every believer in his or her present life. Indeed, unless this happens soon in every life, it will be too late. Human beings will remain captured by the old order of time and history which is and remains a slow or fast agony of "Disremembering, dismembering all now," as Hopkins expressed it.[18] John's Revelation, then, is at one and the same time a summary of the spiritual vision in the Bible, a powerful representation of the destructiveness of the old order, and an exhortation to all readers to open their hearts to what all the scriptures proclaim—hear the Word of God in Jesus and heed Him, for time is short: "Happy is the man who reads, and happy those who listen to the words of this prophecy and heed what is written in it. For the hour of fulfilment is near."

It is this personal apocalypse in John's Revelation that I wish to stress in looking at Hopkins's religious poetry, the apocalypse that destroys the old, personal way of looking at human and natural order, and looks to a new beginning, an apocalypse that envisions life beyond the tension and terrors of thesis and antithesis, subject and object, law and freedom, humanity and divinity—in a phrase, the making of the new heart of the Holy Spirit. As John wrote, "Then he who sat on the throne said, 'Behold!

I am making all things new.' "[19] In the making of the new transcendent personality, what is often overlooked in our encounter with John's panoramic apocalypse is the individual apocalypse of faith in Jesus, indeed, the first apocalypse, the lifting of the veil to higher life that gives and makes the second apocalypse human destiny; John quotes the Lord in his prophecy: " 'I am the Alpha and the Omega' says the Lord God, who is and who was and who is to come, the sovereign Lord of all."[20] When Hopkins described this illuminative moment as one of "glee," yet filled with the terror that the "dismembering" of the old unredeemed self necessarily inflicts, he is confronting the first apocalypse, the apocalypse of individual personality, like the heroic nun on the *Deutschland* calling on Christ to come quickly, "unteachably after evil, but uttering truth."[21]

2

In the final analysis, then, Hopkins thought that Christianity is about personalities — his and Christ's. How every human self is connected with Christ is the elemental issue of Christian faith. We get no closer in scripture to this archetypal mystery of Christian faith than Saint Paul's explanation: "In Christ he chose us before the world was founded, to be dedicated, to be without blemish in his sight, to be full of love; and he destined us — such was his will and pleasure — to be accepted as his sons through Jesus Christ, in order that the glory of his gracious gift, so graciously bestowed on us in his Beloved, might redound to his praise. For in Christ our release is secured and our sins are forgiven through the shedding of his blood. Therein lies the richness of God's free grace lavished upon us, imparting full wisdom and insight."[22] The great illumination, then, in every believing person's life is that mysterious moment when the believer internalizes the reality of the Incarnation "imparting full wisdom and insight."

This great moment in Hopkins's own life is depicted in Part the First of *The Wreck of the Deutschland*, in stanzas 2–5, beginning, "I did say yes . . ."[23] Characteristically, those passages in Hopkins that depict his own apocalypse of faith are in the first person and dramatize a kind of colloquy between his own self and Christ, the talk being utterances of bonding love between his self and Christ. The colloquy reveals what might generally be called joyous submission to awesome power perceived, yet sweet tenderness received. In Hopkins's depiction we are given as well that thrust of transcendence such an illumination brings ("I whirled out wings . . ."), which suggests the re-creation of a new heart, a new vision, a new personality. Stanza 4, beginning "I am soft sift," stresses connection to Christ, "roped with, always, all the way down . . . ," for now the poet tells us an "at-one-ment" has taken place, a union with God here and now, the first apocalypse made real. Stanza 5, beginning "I kiss my hand / To the stars, lovely-asunder / Starlight, wafting him out of it . . ." is a hymn of celebration of both God and the human person, God for His gracious gifts, the person for his new personality.

This wonderful poetic moment depicts, it seems very likely, what was a glorious apocalyptic event in Hopkins's own life, and thus represents, in his lifetime both as a priest and a poet, the momentous occasion of his life. "No wonder of it" when he received his new realization that he was "roped . . . always" to the Incarnation, that he imaginatively envisioned the tall nun on the *Deutschland* as having a similar apocalyptic experience of realizing, with the deepest and most permeating intensity, Christ's Presence in her heart. Hopkins is careful in his depiction, for in stanzas 24–35,[24] he narrates the nun's predicament and its possible religious meaning in a mode that always reminds us that it is his own person telling, wondering, hoping, praying that her heroic last call to Christ was heard in her heart by a realization of Christ's Presence, and in faithful hope that her fate, and those of her companions, indeed, all on the death ship would receive what Paul called "his hidden purpose." This is the first of those great apocalyptic moments in Hopkins's poetry — which I have called the personal apocalypse — that manifest the first prophetic intention of John in his Revelation.

The apocalyptic focus in "The Wreck" fits nicely with the panoramic apocalypse that Sulloway delineates so clearly in her discussion of the ode. Looking back, we can now see that the poems which I surveyed for posing the question of the missing mysterious element that might effect a spiritual metamorphosis is the personal election of Christ, that alteration of the consciousness in which the meaning of the Incarnation begins to be unveiled — the first personal apocalypse.

The apocalyptic impetus in *The Wreck* carried over to the great religious sonnets. The second example of a great apocalyptic moment in Hopkins surely would be the intensification of Christ-consciousness expressed in Hopkins's famous sonnet, "The Windhover."[25] Here, the spiritual focus is set by an apocalyptic passage from *The Wreck*. In the climactic joy in Christ that Hopkins expressed in stanza 5, he added three lines to explain the event characterizing these apocalyptic renewals: "Since, though he is under the world's splendour and wonder, / His mystery must be instressed, stressed; / For I greet him the days I meet him, and bless when I understand." This passage opens up a new facet of the new Christian personality: in it the poet notes that the Christ connection must be maintained through spiritual effort. "Instress," that special word Hopkins coined for, among other things, the human power to realize deeply the being-energy in each existing thing, in this poetic context means trying to comprehend the spiritual energy of the Incarnation, a task, as we have seen, that can be begun only through the efficacious gifts of Christ's own being. Still, the poet says, he must keep himself open, be ready, respond when he realizes some gift of renewed awareness. And when some new insight happens, again he feels the charge of new spiritual life. The implication, then, is one of watching, waiting, yet keeping prepared, wearing the "armour of light," as Hopkins put it in his sermon on the Apocalypse, echoing the call to be alert that occurs in Revelation.

This element of holy perseverance is given powerful expression in "The Windhover." The octave depicts a fresh, new apocalyptic moment in which the poet "catches" his heart connecting to a falcon whose dramatic flight raises the poet's spiritual consciousness to the "instress" of Christ in Creation and in himself. But there is more on the poet's mind than a renewal of his radicalized Christian consciousness. He spends words in the sestet telling us how the apocalyptic moment enters human time and space, namely, how it lives in his personality in the situation of his human predicament. He turns to that difficult passage that bridges the glee of the birth of Jesus and His wondrous ascension — the Passion. Unfortunately, the apocalypse of Jesus was not just the teaching of Himself as the inspiriting way of the enlightenment, but also involved a martyrdom, a descent into a terrible death. Thus the Incarnation also means struggle, rejection, hatred, violence, and death.

Northrop Frye described this revolutionary aspect latent in the historical situation of the Incarnation as more than enlightenment: "Man has to fight his way out of history and not simply awaken from it."[26] It is this existential, secular fight that Hopkins addresses in the last section of this sonnet, the fighting with self and society to persevere "for the hour of fulfilment." The poet tells us such a fight is indeed worth it. When done in and through the sufferings of Jesus, the apocalyptic enlightenment of Christ is made all the more profound, for such a battle brings forth the grace of participation in the Resurrection of Christ: "Fall, gall themselves, and gash gold vermillion." This is the paradoxical part of the mystery that Hopkins described in *The Wreck* that must be "instressed, stressed."

Christ "instressed" in one's daily life means opening up a far greater participation of the Christ-self in the individual personality than in the bird, for in tapping into the energy of the Passion through receiving the Eucharist, the sacramental Presence of Jesus' Good Friday death on the cross, there results the release of true individuality of the personality, a union of Christ and the person, one on one. Frye, in commenting on this insight derived from Saint Paul by Simone Weil, wrote, "The swallowed Christ, eaten, divided, and drunk, in the phrase of Eliot's 'Gerontion,' is one with the potential individual buried in the tomb of the ego during the Sabbath of time and history, where it is the only thing that rests. When this individual awakens and we pass to resurrection and Easter, the community with which he is identical is no longer a whole of which he is part, but another aspect of himself, or, in the traditional metonymic language, another person of his substance."[27] The language in the sonnet which expresses this notion is in the famous first three lines of the sestet, centered on the word "Buckle," about which critics have exercised so much ingenuity. There is little doubt, however, that the poet is telling us that the "buckling" process that the bird-watcher undergoes will produce something far more wonderful, more meaningful, than the hero-like falcon — "a billion/Times." The underthought here can surely be traced to Saint Paul: "I have been crucified with Christ: the life I now live is not my life, but the life which Christ lives in me, and my present bodily life is lived by faith in the Son of God, who loved me and gave himself up for me."[28] Like Hopkins, Paul is describing the re-creation of the new Christ self—an essential phase of the first great apocalypse of the Christian faith.

It is in the context of the personal apocalypse of the passion of the Incarnation that we should approach those last poems of Hopkins called "the dark sonnets." It is hard to accept the spiritual violence that Jesus' vision of "The Kingdom of God" entails. The spiritual ideals of Christianity call for genuine identity between the self's self and Christ, "the Kingdom of God," but in the Christian perspective the world is mainly made up of the egoism of sin, suffering, and death, that path of pain mankind treads that is called history. The personal apocalypse of Christ calls for the death of what today is named ego, thereby effecting the re-creation, here and now, of a new personality that can achieve a truly self-fulfilling, transcendent vision. All secular circumstances are against this change because to Christians the world means power-ridden egos determining what is right and wrong. The secular personality is driven by the desire for self-enhancing success, namely, making nature and society so far as possible into its own image. The secular mind-set attempts to find ways to affirm the vision of the self glorified. As a collectivity, secular personalities comprise a society built on the basis of power and penalty through which the greater egos rule over the lesser. In this society somebody's heaven is another's hell. It has always been thus, so Christian readers of history affirm.

The Christian apocalypse challenges this perception of self and experience as a form of Hell which can only be altered through a *metanoia*, a change of outlook so radical that the secular world abhors the possibility. Anyone who dares to sponsor a "different kingdom" based upon the denial of ego in the name of a new "enlightenment of self-giving" is at war with the world. It is sobering to realize that Jesus would have been martyred by any society he entered at any time in the whole history of the world because of the prophecy he embodied. According to Christians, the apocalypse of Jesus is the only truly revolutionary prophecy ever promulgated in human history because it confronts the most vital principle of secular society — getting and spending the self selfishly. So threatening is the apocalypse to secular history and society, that the work of *metanoia* involves suffering and sacrifice, the psychomania of Christ, realized in the experiences of his martyrdom and descent into death, and reexpressed in the image, symbol, and reality of the Eucharist. To persevere in the Christian *metanoia*, the believer must fight, as Saint Paul stressed, fight against time and society, to break out of that ancient round of death and taxes that is human history. Many of Hopkins's last religious poems are about this battle-rage for Christ.

Turning to those poems of Hopkins called "dark" (I would include more poems than are usually grouped under this critical word in Hopkins criticism), we should not find them in any way atypical as Christian religious poems. The poet talks of the night battle in these poems in personal, priestly, and societal terms. In his priestly poems, like "Felix Randal,"[29] he depicts the fury of physical illness that fells a powerful man ("Sickness broke him"), and in the military poems, "The Bugler's First Communion"[30] and "The Soldier,"[31] he presents the recruits who fight this world's battles, and though he finds comfort in Christ's comforting them, what we remember most perhaps is the stanza in the first poem in which the poet-priest who, in giving the young bugler his first communion, reflects on his youthful innocence and his probable doom, now become an "instress" of Christ: "Nothing else is like it, no, not all so strains? / Us— fresh youth fretted in a bloomfalls all portending / That sweet's sweeter ending; / Realm both Christ is heir to and there reigns."[32] Hopkins identified soldiers and their battles with Christ. He made a similar association of struggle and strife and Christian duty in his sonnet, "In honour of St. Alphonsus Rodriguez." "Honour is flashed off exploit, so we say; . . . / and, on the fighter, forge his glorious day. / On Christ they do and on the martyr may."[33]

Now turning to what might be called Hopkins's societal "dark" poems, in "Harry Ploughman"[34] he drew a picture of the manly beauty of the lowly laboring class which in "Tom's Garland"[35] he showed to be suffering the fate of the dispossessed; "Undenizened, beyond bound / Of earth's glory, earth's ease, all. . . ." The poet's focus is again on suffering in the battle for survival, a fight that is more than a struggle for daily bread; Tom is fighting for his humanity without which he, and others like him, will slip into the degrading state of "Manwolf."

But it is the so-called terrible sonnets that Hopkins most trenchantly stated the night-battle of and for Christ, perhaps because he was talking about his own intense, personal fights. The subjects are not surprising because they are the personal ailments of the spirit that are universal human afflictions—estrangement, depression, self-hatred, sorrow, impatience, self-pity, suicide. In each sonnet there is a sense of ending as the only way to beginning anew: this way must be walked to find a way out— and you can get lost! It is in these poems that the implications of the personal, first apocalypse and the second universal begin to meet, the end of the beginning and the beginning of the end—"Jesus Christ sacrificed / On the cross . . . / Judge that comes to deal our doom." Much has been written about the violence, the struggle (physical and spiritual), and the despair in these poems, sometimes forgetting that they express exactly what the gospels tell us: Jesus' teaching of the apocalypse of faith involves a Passion and a Death, the Cross of Good Friday before the Crown of Easter Sunday.

I have always felt that the best gloss on these searing last poems of Hopkins is a series of notes he wrote during a retreat at Tullabeg in Ireland the year before he died, 1888: After writing a bitter assessment of his spiritual state on the first day of the year, what might be called his New Year's irresolution ("All my undertakings miscarry: I am like a straining eunuch. I wish then for death: yet if I died now I should die imperfect, no master of myself and that is the worse failure of all. O my God, look down on me"),[36] on 2 January he entered another comment during his morning meditation (an exercise in *The Spiritual Exercises* of St. Ignatius in which Ignatius calls for reflections on the sin of the angels, the sin of Adam and Eve, and the sins of all humanity including one's own):

> This morning I made the meditation on the Three Sins, with nothing to enter but loathing of my life and a barren submission to God's will. The body cannot rest when it is in pain nor the mind be at peace as long as something bitter distills in it and it aches. This may be at any time and is at many: how then can it be pretended there is for those who feel this anything worth calling happiness in this world? There is a happiness, hope, the anticipation of happiness hereafter: it is better than happiness, but it is not happiness now. It is as if one were dazzled by a spark or star in the dark, seeing it but not seeing it: we want a light shed on our way and a happiness spread over our life.[37]

Hopkins has here expressed the basic human dilemma, the hopeful yearning for happiness here and hereafter that every person yearns for, including Christians straddling the paradoxes of their faith, dazzled by a star in the dark, "seeing it but not seeing it." Out of these human spiritual puzzles arise the problem of pain and the dazzle of *metanoia*, the new freedom of Christ. These last great religious poems of Hopkins are about the passion that leads to enlightenment—"it is not happiness now."

I have suggested in this essay that John's Revelation is first addressed to the personal apocalypse of every reader of his prophecy, that gracious but awesome unveiling of the inspiriting of Jesus' word into the human heart. Gerard Manley Hopkins, the religious poet, found his own "sweet especial" ways to restate the personal apocalypse of the Word that so mysteriously, so suddenly, so triumphantly enters and reenters the individual soul: "In a flash, at a trumpet crash, / I am all at once what Christ is, since he was what I am." With John, Hopkins tells us, it is always "the hour of fulfilment."[38]

Notes

1. Rom. 13:11-14. All biblical citations are from *The New English Bible with the Apocrypha* (Oxford and Cambridge: Oxford University Press and Cambridge University Press, 1970).

2. *The Sermons and Devotional Writings of Gerard Manley Hopkins*, ed. Christopher Devlin, S.J. (London: Oxford University Press, 1967), 41. Hereafter *Sermons*.

3. Alison G. Sulloway, *Gerard Manley Hopkins and the Victorian Temper* (New York: Columbia University Press, 1972), 158–95.

4. James Finn Cotter, "Apocalyptic Imagery in Hopkins' 'That Nature is a Heraclitean Fire and the comfort of the Resurrection,' " *Victorian Poetry* 24 (Autumn 1986):261–75.

5. Northrop Frye, *The Great Code: The Bible and Literature* (New York: Harcourt Brace Jovanovich, 1982), 136.

6. *The Oxford Authors: Gerard Manley Hopkins*, ed. Catherine Phillips (New York: Oxford University Press, 1986), 128. Hereafter *Poems*.

7. Ibid.

8. Ibid., 130.

9. Ibid., 132.

10. Ibid., 139.

11. Ibid., 134.

12. Ibid., 131.

13. Ibid., 133.

14. Ibid., 173.

15. Frye, *The Great Code*, 130.

16. Rom. 8:14

17. *Poems*, 129.

18. Ibid., 175.

19. Rev. 21:5

20. Rev. 1:8

21. *Poems*, stanzas 17 and 18, p. 114.

22. Eph. 1:2–10.

23. *Poems*, stanzas 2–5, p. 110.

24. Ibid., 116–19.

25. Ibid., 132.

26. Frye, *The Great Code*, 133.

27. Ibid., 101.

28. Gal. 2:20.

29. *Poems*, 150.

30. Ibid., 146–47.

31. Ibid., 168.

32. Ibid., 147.

33. Ibid., 182.

34. Ibid., 177.

35. Ibid., 178.

36. *Sermons*, 261–62.

37. Ibid., 262.

38. Rev. 1:3.

"Man Jack the Man Is":
The Wreck from the Perspective
of "The shepherd's brow"

Robert Boyle, S.J.*

> The shepherd's brow, fronting forked lightning, owns
> The horror and the havoc and the glory
> Of it. Angels fall, they are towers, from heaven — a story
> Of just, majestical, and giant groans.
> But man — we, scaffold of score brittle bones;
> Who breathe, from ground long babyhood to hoary
> Age gasp; whose breath is our *memento mori* —
> What bass is *our* viol for tragic tones?
> He! Hand to mouth he lives, and voids with shame;
> And, blazoned in however bold the name,
> Man Jack the man is, just; his mate a hussy.
> And I that die these deaths, that feed this flame,
> That . . . in smooth spoons spy life's masque mirrored: tame
> My tempests there, my fire and fever fussy.[1]

When, on a soft Dublin day in early April of 1889, Hopkins, brooding over his poetic products of the last fourteen years, cast his mind's eye on his once beloved firstborn, *The Wreck of the Deutschland,* I believe he experienced a feeling of disgust and revulsion. Not with the poem, exactly, but with the posing, shrill-voiced young poet whose categories were so narrow ("O world wide of its good!"), whose condemnations were so sweeping ("beast of the waste wood"), and whose egoism could challenge omnipotence ("Thóu mastering mé"). With Shelleyan semigrandeur bidding him too, like the voice of "Epipsychidion," to "dare beacon the rocks on which high hearts are wrecked," and with pseudo-Pauline boasting bringing him to shout with humble pride to the world "I did say yes," he compared himself on his pastoral forehead of Wales, with safe shepherd's brow, to the tall German nun drowning in the Kentish waters, and found the two of them, quasi-martyrs for Christ, quite satisfactory. A decade and a half later, with the chill April mist invading his tiny room on the top floor of the building where James Joyce would discuss the language of the conqueror with another English Jesuit a few years later, that same poet spat out a disillusioned rejection of the inflated aspect of his younger self. The sonnet in which he did this, quoted above and the second-last he wrote, was despised and rejected by Bridges, but it has for me a special value, indicating, as I think it does, an underlying and particularly

*From *Readings of* The Wreck: *Essays in Commemoration of the Centenary of Gerard Manley Hopkins' The Wreck of the Deutschland,* ed. Peter Milward, S.J., and Raymond Shoder, S.J. (Chicago: Loyola University Press, 1976), 101-14. Reprinted by permission of Loyola University Press.

probing level operating below the deepest level I had previously found in Hopkins' powerful early ode.

In this light (or perhaps, this shadow), I propose to compare, in this anniversary tribute to Hopkins' beloved firstborn poem, the early ode and the almost final sonnet. Hopkins' heroism and profound theological grasp of his own and of the nun's situations have been plumbed often enough, by critics who, like Mariani, share a good deal of Hopkins' own vigor, insight, and expressiveness. But the ridiculous aspects of that somewhat fanatical little man's heroic challenging of divine power and of his faintly magnanimous free choice to assent instead of dissent, that Browningesque complacent bluster (without the partially chewed bread and cheese but not without the bravado) of his satisfaction in his victory over fear of cosmic threat, have received little sympathetic treatment, and this seems to me a good time to attempt some.

Hopkins, in the midst of his theological studies in drafty, rambling St. Beuno's in North Wales, took himself, in basic matters, very seriously. His humor was not Falstaffian but rather, insofar as it existed at all, Holofernian, expressing itself most obviously in whimsical letters, wry triolets, and in pedantic practical jokes. When it came to his relationship to Christ, he was not prepared to smile at all, but, like the Stephen Dedalus whose creator he came within a few years of teaching, he strained to see himself elevated (in Hopkins' case because of his real belief in the infinite power of his "opponent") to epic pinnacles, requiring for expression the imagery, diction, and rhythmic sweep of the poet he most admired, Milton.

Thus in the first stanza of his ode, God's finger searches him out and touches him at the division of body and spirit, in the center of his very heart, threatening his evidently significant existence. And the rod of infinite authority lashed out at him, the apparently destructive lightning came hurtling toward him, and he sees himself choosing to say the *yes* of acceptance rather than hurling back that *no* (which Stephen Dedalus chose), which, as Hopkins develops in those baroque retreat notes so closely allied to the retreat sermons in *Portrait of the Artist as a Young Man*, would have found the divine tempest a descending whirlwind of fiery torment. The young poet enjoys and dwells on his happy self through the next eight stanzas, celebrating the Word, indeed, but as a consequence presenting Christ also as a foil to the admirably affirmative poet. He concludes the first part of his Christmas ode as a tardy Magus bringing his valuable gift of adoration to the newborn king.

There is at least some justice in looking at the poem from this angle, especially since Hopkins himself did something like that, and even in wondering if the overingenious young Romantic is not at least tending to subordinate not only the cosmos but God too to his own almost frenetic "Serviam!" The bird image in stanza 3, with a glance at bird images in following poems, may give some perspective on this possible attitude. The dove image follows what I take to be the bird image in stanza 2, where I see a pentecostal hawk sweeping and hurling like the later windhover, and in this case treading the smaller bird, the swooning heart ("swooning" a word that Hopkins, like Joyce, knew from Skeat to be an Anglo-Saxon derivation quite at home in chivalric context). In stanza 3, although I am deeply interested in Eileen Kennedy's recent attractive suggestion, in *Victorian Poetry* (Vol II, 1973, pp. 247–51), that the dove is the symbol-bringing bird of Noah, I nevertheless still find the same bird who operates in "The Handsome Heart": "What the heart is! which, like carriers let fly— / Doff darkness, homing nature knows the rest. . . ." This one, in stanza 3, since its home is the heart of the Host, which leads into infinity, flashes and towers indefinitely.

When a divine rather than a created dove shows up a few months later, in "God's Grandeur," it has achieved cosmic size and reveals its Miltonic genealogy. Here the pentecostal hawk of stanza 2 becomes the creative dove allied to Milton's epic dovelike Spirit brooding on the vast abyss to make it pregnant. Hopkins in *The Wreck* sees both himself and the nun, like Mary (in a special sense) and Peter, Paul, Augustine, and all successful humans, made pregnant with Christ, and that special Pauline insight — "My dear children, with whom I am in labor again, until Christ is formed in you" (Galatians 4:19) — adds considerable depth to Hopkins' echo of Milton. Doves scatter flakes in the farmyard of "The Starlight Night," not unallied to the storm flakes of stanza 21, and thrushes strike the ear like loving lightning in "Spring." The mothering wing of "In the Valley of the Elwy" contrasts with the absent wing of stanza 12. The soul as "a dare-gale skylark" is limited and suppressed by the body, a bone-cage, while the skylark of "The Sea and the Skylark" foreshadows the kingfisher and the great bell to come in No. 57, ringing out the pure self which speaks and spells the Word. Then, mastering the equine wind and buckled in his knightly pride, the great bird of literature, if the smallest of hawks, the windhover, glides in, and as an Ignatian knight with ride and jar echoes the triumphal march of *The Wreck's* final syllables — though the speaker of the sonnet, like St. Alphonsus and like Christ, achieves that victory in a realm beyond human natural sight, in contrast to the suffering and death which human eyes can note.

And the birds get bigger. The winged heart of "Hurrahing in Harvest" can hurl the whole earth behind him, and is rivaled only by the symbol of the artist Purcell, that great storm fowl which, like God in No. 69, scatters a colossal smile into the purple darkness, revealing that self which is the Word.

A diminution appears in "Peace," where the dove is small and shy, and broods now over a much smaller cosmos, the war-torn heart — or, rather, it is small enough to enter the heart and coo again over fragile life that, the poem suggests, won't last long either. It will be destroyed by those winged gryphons, the "beakleaved boughs dragonish" of "Spelt from Sibyl's Leaves." And in his final three poems, concerned like the Purcell sonnet with artistic production, the busy little birds, like the lovely star-eyed strawberry-breasted throstle of "The May Magnificat," can build nests for new life, but the sterile speaker cannot build, he says. He manages to write three magnificent self-contemning sonnets (having for years had, as he tells Bridges on January 12, 1888, no jet of inspiration that will produce anything larger than a sonnet) to express his inability to write at all. The man who started out his mature career as a poet with the confident claim to be uttering prophetic truth, impelled to ring out from his own inspired breast, touched like the breast cavity of the nun by the finger of God and set into clangorous motion, the inexpressible reality of the Pauline "mystery hidden for ages in God" of Ephesians 3 — now, in "The shepherd's brow," that same man with altered view looks back at his efforts to be a hawklike Son of Thunder, gazing unblinking and unafraid at the blinding "glory bare" of the Word, a new and greater Milton justifying the ways of God to man, and sees all that activity as a mere "fussy" flutter of fretting wings. What brought about such a change?

Here I see the more mature and manly Hopkins condemning with a truly Browningesque honesty the measure of youthful pretentiousness of the earlier years with the contemptuous adjectives "tame" and, most detestable to a balanced and now more tolerant man, "fussy." But some do not find any change at all. Bridges did, and judging such cynicism unworthy and uncharacteristic, banished the penultimate sonnet to the fragments. Several recent critics, disagreeing with Bridges, have sought to rescue the sonnet. Some years ago, in *Renascence* (Spring 1963) Sister Mary Hugh Campbell objected to Bridges' judgment, and in a most intelligent and stimulating reading, brought out many of the sonnet's strong points. Two unfortunate readings, however, weaken her defense, as I see it. She finds the "voiding" image very ugly, and owing to not having seen the early drafts, she is able to take "tame" as a verb and to find Hopkins addressing a pious, patient prayer to the Holy Spirit in the final lines. She also takes the "He" of line 9 to be the shepherd, which strikes me as unlikely. She does read the spoon image with remarkable acuity, I judge: "On the surface his daily existence seems ordered and urbane and perfect, a life whose 'smooth spoons' symbolize the safe distance that keeps him from both the great trials of 'forked lightning' and the indignities of the shepherd's 'hand to mouth' existence." She further sees the effect on the speaker of seeing "his own distorted image reflected to him in upside-down fashion" and realizing that appearances deceive, that no person really comprehends another, that he is a subject only for amusing masque, not tragedy. But, I am afraid, her misreading of the "tame" leads her to emasculate this most healthy and virile poem.

Robert B. Clark, S.J., does the same thing in his generally perceptive and occasionally brilliant "Hopkins's 'The shepherd's brow,' " in *Victorian Newsletter* (Fall 1965). He sees the shepherd as Moses, because of "forked, horrifying, and glorious" lightning, a good possible reference to "that shepherd" of *Paradise Lost*, I, 8. He somehow arrives at the conclusion, however, that the poem is an endorsement of religious meditation.

Paul Mariani, with his usual insight, in "The Artistic and Tonal Integrity of Hopkins' 'The shepherd's brow,' " in *Victorian Poetry* (Spring 1968), sees Hopkins' face or "masque" comic in comparison with the noble forehead of Moses or the ravaged visage of Milton's Satan, ". . . and he ends his meditation with a prayer of humility, chiding himself for having thought his 'tempests' were other than the 'fire and fever fussy' of a precisionist." Maybe, but I incline to see the "tempest" as an echo of Lear's "the tempest in my mind" and the fussy fever from Macbeth's murderously cynical "fretful fever," and these both contrasted to the winds and flames of the pentecostal Spirit. The final lines sound to me not like a prayer but like a deeply felt expectoration of disgust. I cannot find the "deeply instressed heroism in this self-chiding patience" that Mariani does, perhaps because I've been reading too much Joyce. But I must say that it seems rather a relief to hear the somewhat inflated poser of *The Wreck* saying at last, in effect, "This human stink-hole, including me, does smell." He admits that he smells of mortality, that he has a defecating body, and that his epic stance has its ridiculous aspects. Like Lear, and with similar bitter vulgarity, he perceives that he is, in contrast to the majestic threatening forked lightning, "a poor, bare, forked animal."

Mariani finds Hopkins' spoon image strikingly similar to one of George Eliot's in *Middlemarch:* "I am not sure that the greatest man of his age, if ever that solitary superlative existed, could escape these unfavourable reflections of himself in various small mirrors; and even Milton, looking for his portrait in a spoon, must submit to have the facial angle of a bumpkin" (Book I, Chapter X). The discussion of Eliot's commentator in the rest of the paragraph — "what fading of hopes, or what deeper fixity of self-delusion" and "Mr. Casaubon, too, was the center of his own world; if he was liable to think that others *were* providentially made for him . . . this trait is not quite alien to us . . ." — also has relevance to Hopkins' thinking in his sonnet, as he looks back at that would-be Catholic Milton who could so confidently picture and express himself as the center of God's providential interest. This mature sonnet I see as a reaction to that indeed orthodox yet somewhat adolescent egotism.

Mariani does not see it so. He sees the sonnet as a further expression of the heroism he finds throughout Hopkins' work, and, up to a point, I have no quarrel with that. A true hero, as I conceive him, is also a realist. Shakespeare's Bottom happens to be one of my heroes (and, to my mind, one of Shakespeare's). Hopkins is all the more a hero to me when he faces, with disgust for his past self-deceit, the fact that he is a jackass. But I must reluctantly quarrel (reluctant because of my respect for Mariani's insight and because I have on more than one occasion discovered him being right where I had long been wrong) with his notion that this poem is a colloquy between Hopkins and Christ: "The mention of Milton, of his 'bumpkin' reflection in a spoon, of the inner conflicts and of the growing uneasiness with what is or is not found within us when we submit to an earnest self-examination, and perhaps even the unflattering figure of Casaubon himself have been transformed in the alembic of Hopkins' poetic imagination into a deeply instressed, personal colloquy between Hopkins and his Lord. George Eliot's wittily probing scrutiny of Casaubon contrasts with Hopkins' searing flame of intense self-examination." As I can see it, Christ is nowhere present in this sonnet. Hopkins is looking at a pretentious fool who set out to be a Catholic Milton, not only a "just" man in the scriptural sense of No. 57, but a "just" poet as well, an inspired spokesman for God, a justifier of God's ways; and he sees an ineffectual sonneteer whose tragic bass is expressed in water-closet noises.

In No. 57, Hopkins echoes Paul's "I live now, not I, but Christ lives in me" (Galatians 2:20) when he says that the "I," the divinized person, "says" a new self, a "just" self who is more than the righteous man of the Old Testament just man, more, for example, than Abraham and Joseph as "just" men. The "I" of whom Hopkins speaks is both the limited human person and the human-divine Christ, all at once in totally mysterious identity: "I *am* all at once what he *is*, since he *was* what I *am*," as Hopkins puts it in "Heraclitean Fire," far more aware than Joyce that "I am" is the sacred name of God. Thus when he says, "I say more: the just man justices," it is evident that the Pauline insight into "just" has lifted the word beyond merely rational levels. So when we see the word twice used in "The shepherd's brow," with its emphasis now not on the capacity for divinization but with the stress on the at least apparent unfitness of man for anything but animal functions, we get more of the force of Hopkins' realistic appraisal of his human situation. He is not cynically rejecting the divine; he is, like Bottom, though in more complex and somewhat bitter mood, ultimately still expressing the same wonder that God could embrace his human creature, but now an idealistic stress on the spirit with little attention to the body does not appear. In "The shepherd's brow" he is at the opposite horizon of faith, still believing but finding what he once accepted as an object of divine interest, the "I" of *The Wreck*, now as an asinine and self-deluded versifier. The "just" of line 4 of the sonnet refers to the effect of Milton's stern God's just punishments, but the "just" of line 11, while grammatically it conveys the sense of "precisely that and nothing more," expresses the vast expanses within a human being of having potentiality to be both a divinized "just man" and "just a man Jack." In a mood where he can concentrate on himself in that second class, in a background of having overstressed the first one, especially an authentic hero might well be bitterly disgusted.

If indeed Hopkins was recalling George Eliot's powerful passage — and I have no doubt of it — it would probably increase his bitterness, since he disapproved of her. His contempt, as well as his self-conscious effort to salvage Christian charity, appears in his remark to Bridges: "How admirable are Blackmore and Hardy! Their merits are much eclipsed by the overdone reputation of the Evans-Eliot-Lewis-Cross woman (poor creature! one ought not to speak slightingly, I know), half real power, half imposition" (L I, p. 239). A case cannot convincingly be made against Hopkins as antifeminist. His admirations for the Blessed Virgin might in some circles be considered irrelevant, but his praise and imitation of Christina Rossetti, even if misguided, would indicate that he could appreciate a woman's product. His admiration of the tall nun and of St. Winefred could, I suppose, be attributed to their Catholicism, and some, like whoever wrote the Hopkins material in *The Oxford Anthology of English Literature* in 1973, probably would consider that Hopkins was drawn by the masculinity of their wills. That writer, by the way, could find explanations for Hopkins' revulsion in "The shepherd's brow" that I do not find, since with what I consider critical irresponsibility he states as a fact that Hopkins was a homosexual — the "possibly homosexual" of his introduction modulates easily into "the latent homosexuality he shared with Whitman" in the notes — and goes so far as to find the "baffled or repressed sexual passion" breaking out in the suggestive coinage "gay-gangs," referring to those evidently lustful clouds roystering in the heavens of "Heraclitean Fire." Other more responsible critics have felt, indeed, often however without considering Hopkins' own efforts to be strictly faithful to a sacrificial celibacy, that Hopkins' observation of and fondness for some males and the infrequency of his expression of equal fondness for females might be based on homosexual attitudes. Obviously that may have been the case. But the perpetrator of the Hopkins section of the Oxford textbook, offered for sale to a generation or so of truth-seeking students, substitutes a firm act of subjective faith for objective certitude. He thus bridges the gap between possibility and fact, and makes clear to the unwary that Hopkins, like the Shakespeare of Wilde's *Portrait of Mr. W. H.*, shows forth his homosexuality in his gay adjectives. A difference to be noted is that Wilde was writing honest fiction.

I see no evidence that Hopkins disliked women. His dislike of Mary Anne Evans, although *Romola* he had in 1865 accepted as "great" (L III, p. 224), was no doubt prompted more by her offense to his own decidedly puritanical standards — how else could he have been led into the monstrous opinion that Shakespeare's Beatrice was not only vain but "impure minded" (L III, p. 309) — than by her femininity or her literary power. And the very fact that he was now deriving a Miltonic context and a specific crass image from the masterful work of a woman he had formerly condemned as pagan and lacking in understanding and personal morality might stress for him his own pedantic hypocrisy.

Since I see Hopkins' sonnet as concerned centrally with his own artistic aims and products, it may be useful to mention how I see this mirror image, so important to artists since St. Paul used it to express how darkly we in our present fallen state can barely distinguish shadowy realities; since Hamlet defined drama (and for many deceived critics literary art) as a mirror held up to nature (Shakespeare thus, according to Oscar Wilde, demonstrated Hamlet's madness, since, as Wilde well preached, art does not reflect but determines); and since the reputedly dull lecturer of mathematics, Charles Lutwidge Dodgson, had in the logical twistings of his imagination found it to be a measure of rationality and the deceptions therein. Before I ran into Mariani's happy perception of the Eliot passage (though I believe I saw the reference first in the note in the fourth edition of *The Poems*, and I am not clear who derived the discovery from whom), I had wondered whether or not Eliot had been influenced in her own image by the vivid reflections in Dickens' mirror in *Our Mutual Friend*, Chapter Two, where "The great looking-glass above the sideboard, reflects the tale and the company." Among those reflected is "charming old Lady Tippins on Veneering's right; with an immense obtuse drab oblong face, like a face in a tablespoon. . . ." The approaches of these three powerful Victorian artists to this same image strike me as expressive of characteristic attitudes: Dickens' vulgar but powerful spoon distorts faces which resemble the aristocratically distorted houyhnhnm face of Lady Tippins, a possibly implied emotional attitude of Dickens toward the forces operative in the ruling class; Eliot's spoon distorts the aristocratic and admirable face of Milton into the earthy, common features of a bumpkin, a comfortable acceptance of the superiority of the educated and talented; Hopkins' spoon reduces his fancied elegant masque-role to his own small bathroom wind and sickly fire, not Miltonic pentecost, implying an attitude of judgment reaching beneath social forces to the basic pretensions of a pitiable animal. I suspect that these three images point toward one reason why Hopkins seems to most critics in our time a more important artist than the first two, so famous and influential in their time.

I myself see the shepherd of the sonnet's line 1 as basically Hopkins himself, ironically conceived as an epic or elegiac creation of himself as the greatest of literary artists, just as Lycidas and Satan and Adam and Christ are basically Milton, who powerfully expresses their human experience out of his own. The sonnet is, as I read it, concerned with Hopkins' literary career, such as it was, and, from many of the things Hopkins said to Bridges and especially to Dixon about the loss to England's ear of the neglect accorded their poems, from Hopkins' own poetic complaints of being left with only a "lonely began," from his edifying but sometimes frustrating efforts to escape the dead letter office and reach, as the nun apparently did, the divine ears, I do gather than Hopkins could identify most readily with the frustrated Lycidas. Further, Lycidas, like the nun of Hopkins' "firstborn," fronted lightning and tempest and drowned and, like her too, shared in some analogy with the beams that flamed in the forehead of the morning sky, the crimson-cresseted east. Although Moses does seem in many striking ways to fit better into that shepherd's role, I am attracted to Lycidas both because he does fit and principally because I figure that Hopkins needs an elegy to go with the following epic of fallen angels (towers like the tall nun who towered in the tumult); with the somber Grecian treatment of Samson's vast strength yet liable, like Caradoc, to fall; with the low viol solemn music of the great religious Miltonic sonnets; and with the relatively trivial masque—all the forms which Milton brought to the peak of perfection and all of which Hopkins attempted, and most often, in the larger forms, failed. But not only Lycidas and Moses, but Adam and the Bethlehem shepherds will in some ways fit the background. And maybe the Good Shepherd would serve best, from his role both in Milton and in *The Wreck*, and from the fact that he can best be set off against the "He," the ephemeral man of bones and breath who follows, a species in which shepherds and poets both exist. But in any case I take Hopkins as once aspiring to create out of his own poetic being a heroic shepherd of a story, a superhuman angel, and mystic which would enclose all the tragic grief and transcendent glory that the human heart has known, and do it better even than Milton could.

Thomas K. Beyette sees things somewhat in that vein too, in his "Hopkins' Phenomenology of Art in 'The shepherd's brow,' " in *Victorian Poetry* (Vol. II, 1973, pp. 207–13). With fine insight he considers the last three sonnets as concerned with the writing of poetry, and adds perceptive and interesting points to the readings of his predecessors. He disagrees with them, as I do, in their finding the final lines Christlike and pious, and considers that Hopkins is speaking of the fact that, as he complained to Bridges, he had no inspiration greater than that which, like an ephemeral blowpipe flame, would produce merely a sonnet. The pentecostal fire so generously apparent in *The Wreck* and the flamboyant vigor sweeping upward the soaring "Windhover" has in this sonnet dwindled to a flickering fever, a disease, which can produce only complaining poems which Beyette sees as smooth spoons. In this I am forced to leave him, since, among other difficulties, I cannot form any Hopkinsian notion of spying life through poems (in this Hopkins is not like Stephen Dedalus), and I would be forced also, as I can see it now, to wonder, if the sonnets were smooth spoons, whether or not the epics might be corrugated soup ladles. In other words, I find nothing to impel me to consider the smooth spoons as anything other than literal spoons and distorting mirrors, since they work perfectly as such. I recall my own experience in Jesuit dining halls, waiting with downcast eyes while the faculty and other head-table officials filed past my table, and watching their black forms reflected in the large and small spoons on the table. Hopkins might have had some such experience in his own imagination, as well as his response to the practice of literary artists all around him using the image with power and genius. In Hopkins' sonnet the harmless and useful real spoons balance effectively with the opening threatening metaphorical forks, and the food they convey to him does quiet his mildly tempestuous appetites and sustain his fretful fever. They serve him as an animal, but distort and limit him as an artist, and reveal to him, as I see it, that he is no more fit to write sonnets than to create, as he attempted to do with Caradoc, another ravaged Satan.

The light, then, that "The shepherd's brow" throws on *The Wreck* is that in the sonnet Hopkins reveals his mature perception of some of those immaturities he was conscious of in his letter to Bridges in 1881: "I agree that the *Eurydice* shews more mastery in art, still I think the best lines in the *Deutschland* are better than the best in the other. One may be biased in favour of one's firstborn though. There are some immaturities in it I should never be guilty of now" (L I, p. 119). Those immaturities could be anything, extremes of rhythm or diction or imagery, but I suspect the principal one is the slightly paranoic willingness to accept himself — "I may add for your greater interest and edification that what refers to myself in the poem is all strictly and literally true and did all occur; nothing is added for poetical padding" (L I, p. 47) — as an object of heroic stature, a character, really, in the inspired epic of a Catholic Milton. He actually was of heroic stature, I myself believe, but I am only slightly less embarrassed at his own acceptance and expression of this notion than I am when a lesser hero like Shelley does the same thing. Had Shelley lived to be forty-four, he might too have revealed a ripening manliness in a "The shepherd's brow" of his own, to balance "Prometheus" and "Epipsychidion."

And Hopkins' mature balance helps to make *The Wreck* look better, at least to me, because I find the experience expressed in it based on something not yet expressed and deeper and solider than the slightly hectic projection of faith the poem reveals. "The shepherd's brow" suggests to me a profound spiritual adjustment at work in Hopkins' "subnesciousness" (to use Joyce's expressive word, deeper than subconsciousness). I seem to find some qualification of his overly intense discipleship of Scotus, of Milton, and of the narrower aspects of the Catholicism he found operative in his islands (vivid in the experience of Stephen Dedalus) when, as in this second-last sonnet, he faces up finally and without qualification to the tyranny of the Prufrockian life-measuring spoon. This late reaction suggests beneath *The Wreck* a human honesty that will realize fully one day that faith is not a flight from nor a negation of human animality, an illusion that the young Hopkins, like the young Stephen Dedalus, at least approached. "The shepherd's brow" indicates no great love for animality, indeed, but it does show an acceptance of it. And the final and in many ways the greatest of Hopkins' poems, "To R. B.," celebrates in a new and wholesome way the beauty and joy of sexual intercourse and the gestation of a new animal — not only a "Simon Peter of a soul," bound in by a cage of bones — as the perfect symbol of the conception and gestation of an immortal poem.

As I look back, then, toward *The Wreck* from the vantage point of

"The shepherd's brow," I realize better than I did before why I felt some slight discomfort with Hopkins' too self-conscious expression, especially in stanza 28, of his inability to put the nun's ineffable vision into human sentences. He did not admit, or perhaps realize, the whole reason for his necessary failure. Throughout *The Wreck*, I believe, his expression occasionally fell short of his powerful vision, owing to too romantic a reaction to the knightly imagery of *The Spiritual Exercises*, too narrow a view of the operation of Catholic faith, and above all an unwillingness to accept his own animality. He produced a powerful ode, but a flawed one. His success flowed from the power of his experience, his ability to listen to his heart beyond the limits of his brain, and his realization that the music, the counterpoint, of his responsive verse would best carry his feeling into the accepting, time-centered eardrums, as well as to the more objective, space-oriented retinas, of other humans. To the hearing, he could best express, better than eyes could see, the deepest mystery of the Word his brain could not comprehend but his heart could apprehend. He slipped into some measure of treachery to his heart and his poetic vision, I now judge, when he turned to the formulations of theology to express the cure for the nun's extremity. In "Heraclitean Fire" he would remain true to his heart by expressing what he believed and felt, not by expressing the obligation of all men to come to Christ's feet. In that overwhelming "sonnet" he remained a poet, not a theologian merely. But in *The Wreck*, as in a few other poems like "To what serves Mortal Beauty?" we see him at climactic moments bowing to a dogma which may or may not be operative for every human, rather than expressing the movement and the multileveled counterpoint of the heart, to which every human can respond. He falters as a poet, I judge, when with the confidence of a dogmatist he tries, with the mere meanings of human words, to break through rational bounds to boundless mystery.

As in stanza 28 he approaches the statement which should clarify what the nun meant, he experiences, owing to his turning from his heart to his brain, from his intuition to his reason, the unaccustomed frustration of his fancy. He attributes the breakdown of his fancy wholly to the havoc and glory of what the nun experienced, and adverts not at all to his own human asininity in making a direct assault on the adamantine limits of reason. He attempts precisely what Shakespeare, his other great master along with Milton, attempted in *A Midsummer Night's Dream*, the treatment of the artist's role in expressing ineffable mystery, the "strange and admirable," but Hopkins misses one point that Shakespeare, through the admirable ass Bottom, hit exactly. Shakespeare shows Bottom's acceptance of his "dream" and the breakdown of his effort to express it in human sentences, his turning to St. Paul for some kind of analogy for the embrace of a fairy queen, and his final resolve to get the literary artist, Peter Quince, to bring about the miracle of expression of the experience in black ink. Hopkins, aiming directly at expression of the nun's experience, suffers the same breakdown as does Bottom, uses the same Pauline text as does Shakespeare, and by calling on the mere names which symbolize all of Catholic tradition on the Mystical Body, the union of Christ and Christian, acts as if he had achieved his direct artistic aim. He has stepped outside of her experience and his own in order to complete his effort to express what the nun meant by her mysterious Johannine cry, and thus while his response is satisfactorily theological, it tends to limit and diminish an actually ineffable human experience. Hopkins does not fail, certainly, but neither, as I can now judge the matter, does he succeed as fully as he does succeed in some later, and particularly his three final, poems. Shakespeare succeeds totally by maintaining the basic ambivalence of a "dream," experienced by a human ass under the influence of forces he cannot comprehend. He accepts and works with human animality throughout, the very element the young Hopkins neglected.

When Bottom awakes from his "dream" of having been embraced by the fairy queen, he paraphrases St. Paul in his own effort to find expression for the ineffable: "The eye of man hath not heard, the ear of man hath not seen, man's hand is not able to taste, his tongue to conceive, nor his heart to report, what my dream was" (IV, 1). Paul in 1 Corinthians 2:9 had turned to Isaiah to find some poetic effort to express the ineffable, quoted here in a translation, from the Geneva Bible of 1560, which Shakespeare may have followed: "But as it is written, The things which eye hathe not sene, nether eare hathe heard, nether came into mans heart, are, which God hathe prepared for them that love him." Shakespeare thus effects an analogy between the deepest Pauline insight into mystery and the strange and admirable human experience of honest and open Bottom. Shakespeare proceeds to do something of special interest to literary artists, including Hopkins and especially James Joyce. Bottom, unable to express, not his thought, but a strange experience which transcended his reason and left his fancy paralyzed, can only stammer: "Methought I was—there is no man can tell what. Methought I was—and methought I had—but man is but a patched fool if he will offer to say what methought I had." This is precisely what happens to Hopkins in stanza 28:

> But how shall I . . . make me room there:
> Reach me a . . . Fancy, come faster—
> Strike you the sight of it? look at it loom there,
> Thing that she . . . There then!

Joyce in his own mysterious effort to breach the limits of consciousness and to broach what visions may lie in and beyond the subnesciousness, maybe foul but certainly unknown, willing to risk an experience of hell as Hopkins strove to point toward an experience of heaven, turns to ineffectual puns and riddles (and pins and needles) as other mature artists turn to ass's heads and distorted spoon reflections: "Helldsdend, whelldselse!

Lonedom's breach lay foulend up uncouth not be broached by punns and reedles" (*Finnegans Wake*, 239).

Bottom, having failed in his effort to express what he has apprehended (short of comprehension, or rather, far beyond that rational grasp so praised by Theseus at the opening of Act V), turns to the literary artist, his director, producer, and writer, the alter ego of Shakespeare himself: "I will get Peter Quince to write a ballad of this dream." The only chance for getting some expression of this suprarational mystery, lacking a prophet or an apostle, is to call on that creative imagination so contemned by the practical Theseus as lunacy. In *The Wreck* Hopkins gets the message from his heart, not from his brain, he does not comprehend it—"What can it be, this glee?"—and his faithful fancy breaks down in its effort to provide poetic expression to infinite mystery, and can only point with names at that most rare vision which escapes reason.

Hopkins does happily provide, with skillful indirection, a Pauline and Shakespearean base for Fancy's plight in *The Wreck*'s stanza 26, when he paraphrases the Pauline passage to which Bottom had turned:

> What by your measure is the heaven of desire,
> The treasure never eyesight got, nor was ever guessed what for the
> hearing?

Directly this is merely an expression of the heart's cheer in the coming of spring and the cuckoo's clear call, analogous to the heart's hurrah in harvest. But Hopkins, a profound meditator on the mysteries of Paul, was in a position better than Shakespeare's to know how perfectly this passage with its bottomless underthought would prepare the responsive hearer for another rare vision of a mystery that can find expression, if at all, only in the miracle of a poet's black ink.

Hopkins suggests further, at the close of stanza 27, that music must enter in to bolster and fill out the limited song of the mind, as he turns the tempest and ocean into a Wagnerian orchestra:

> Other, I gather, in measure her mind's
> Burden, in wind's burly and beat of endragoned seas.

In this too Hopkins is close to the greatest expresser of mystery in our own century, one who emerged from the same tradition and milieu in which Hopkins achieved his marvelous art, and whose magnificent words I here apply as tribute to Hopkins' sublime achievement of a century ago. This Irish voice, like Hopkins in the tradition of the prowess and pride of the ancient *poeta*, even more than Hopkins like the hearty Gaelic fashioners of the Book of Kells, prepared for his own final expression of his most rare vision with many references to Paul and to Bottom, and in the following climactic passage which I choose for an echo and a companion to the music of Hopkins, he expresses in his own magnificently musical way that most rare vision of the ultimate Word, the suprarational reality which the mind cannot code but the heart, like the hearts of Hopkins and of the nun on the wrecked *Deutschland*, can chord and cord. In his own strange, admirable way, closer than first appears to the multileveled way of Hopkins, Joyce expresses the ineffable Word in musical counterpoint that rings out from the Bottom-like close mixture and intermingling of ear and eye that transforms the tragic tones of mortal experience, so deeply intuited by Hopkins in "The shepherd's brow," into the vision that the eye, like the nun of the *Deutschland* still yearns to see again, and quickly: "The prouts who will invent a writing there ultimately is the poeta, still more learned, who discovered the raiding there originally. That's the point of eschatology our book of kills reaches for now in soandso many counterpoint words. What can't be coded can be decoded if an ear aye seize what no eye ere grieved for" (*Finnegans Wake*, 482).

Notes

1. This sonnet is quoted in full with the kind permission of Oxford University Press, copyright holders of *The Poems of Gerard Manley Hopkins*, 4th ed., ed. W. H. Gardner and Norman H. Mackenzie (Oxford, 1967).

Hopkins as Victorian Poet

The Nature of Art, Nature, and Human Nature in Hopkins's Poetry

Alison G. Sulloway*

Samuel Johnson's introduction to his English dictionary contains a bemused description of the difficulties which lexicographers encounter when they begin to define what words mean. Each definition, Johnson warned, requires another definition and then another, and each must be more precise than the last. Unfortunately, "such is the fate of hapless lexicography," that definers of words face a double jeopardy. Abstract words do not tell us enough about the specific meaning of concrete words, whereas concrete words may tell us too much, or describe what abstract words mean in ways unfaithful to the abstract meaning. Therefore, the lexicographer's task is hapless, Johnson thinks: "not only darkness, but light, impedes it; things may be not only too little, but too much known to be happily illustrated."[1]

Just as words are defined by other words, which in turn must be defined by still other words, each more precise than the last, and each risking the loss of the original abstract integrity, so also do large concepts such as Jerome Buckley's "Victorian temper" need definitions followed by others, each more precise and minute than the last, even while more and more minutiae risk the loss of a central vision. My graduate students in Victorian poetry faced just such a problem in reverse, at the very moment when I had first been asked to appear at this international conference on Hopkins as a representative Victorian poet.

When the students first encountered Hopkins's poems to his parishioners, poems such as "Felix Randall," "Brothers," "The Handsome Heart," and "The Bugler's First Communion," they sensed a distinct decrease in Hopkins's prosodic control. They pointed several times to an occasional clichéd vignette, to perfunctory metaphors as Hopkins described archetypal souls struggling for redemption, or to a disquieting tone which suggested that in some way quite beyond Hopkins's control, he was beginning to consider his parishioners as people separated from himself.

*From *Vital Candle: Victorian and Modern Bearings in Gerard Manley Hopkins*, eds. John North and Michael Moore (Waterloo, Ontario: University of Waterloo Press, 1981), 61–78. Reprinted by permission of the University of Waterloo Press.

Several students asked first whether Hopkins's spiritual exhaustion had induced in him a psychological withdrawal from his parishioners which in turn contaminated his earlier vision of art and nature as medicinally healthy. Was his withdrawal, they next wanted to know, similar to the withdrawal which he now claimed that the *deus absconditus* was forcing him to endure? If God had withdrawn his face from Hopkins, was Hopkins now unconsciously withdrawing from poetry, from nature, and from his parishioners? If so, the students finally wanted to know, was this withdrawal typical of others which characterize poets who reflect the Victorian temper? Did other Victorian poets and humanists also undergo some form of distress as they contemplated the properties, functions, and uses of art, nature, and human nature, and if so, why?

You can see that unlike Samuel Johnson, we started with concrete examples of poems which characterize the Victorian temper, and that we quickly moved to more and more abstract literary history and more and more Hopkinsian biography, as the students struggled to see similarities between Hopkins and other Victorian poets, clear as the students were upon the differences in poetic visions.

First of all, in honor of Hopkins's professional mission, we acknowledged that Hopkins's anxieties about the nature of art, nature, and human nature are distinctly Ignatian:

> Man [said Ignatius Loyola] was created to praise and reverence and serve God our Lord, and by doing so to save his soul. And the other things on the face of the earth were created for man's sake and to help in the carrying out of the end for which he was created. Hence it follows that man should make use of creatures so far as they help him to attain that end and withdraw from them as they hinder him from so doing. For that, it is necessary to make ourselves indifferent in regard to all created things in so far as it is left to the choice of our free will and there is no prohibition. . . .[2]

But Hopkins's anxieties about the proper use of nature, art, and human nature are not only quite legitimate in a Jesuit priest adopting prescribed techniques for seeking salvation. They also reflect commonplace Victorian anxieties. For the study of natural, aesthetic, social, and moral forms and their proper function is not only a Jesuit pursuit, a Platonic and Aristotelian pursuit, an Augustinian pursuit, and a Thomistic pursuit. It is intensely and peculiarly a pursuit of representative Victorian humanists such as Newman, Carlyle, Ruskin, Tennyson, and Matthew Arnold. To understand the proper uses of other creations, the examiner must first scrupulously analyze their forms and functions, since form and function dictate proper use. But the very nuances of the term "use" depend upon the degree of sophisticated modern scientific empiricism or modern pragmatism which the humanist has absorbed.

These particular humanists were post-Romantic citizens of an iron age and a utilitarian age. Most of them were Christian classicists, or post-Christian classicists, trained in university values several thousand years old; they now found themselves surrounded by pragmatists of all kinds who consistently boasted of the age's new sciences and its automatic progress. Understandably, these Victorian humanists had, in fact, absorbed far more of the age's empirical and reforming spirit than they were fully aware. They were all simultaneously blessed and cursed with the objective urges which scientists and social scientists claim to be typical only of the scientific method. In various ways, they all undertook empirical, analytical, microscopic studies of themselves, their artifacts, and their natural and social milieu with an almost missionary intensity which I believe itself represents one component of the Victorian temper. This heroic component, in utilitarians and humanists alike, I have begun to call "Victorian specificity." It represents a new empiricism from which emerged a new pragmatism or utilitarianism in many forms.

The reasons for "Victorian specificity" are varied and complex. The Victorian humanists whom I am discussing struggled to subdue the new Baconian and Macaulayan empiricism *and* the new pragmatism to humanistic requirements. They often studied the specific, minute properties, forms, and functions of art, nature or human nature as though they were humanistically and morally braced astronomers, paleontologists, geologists, bio-chemists, philologists, or social and political scientists. Inch by inch, the Pre-Raphaelite painters and poets, the essayists and the novelists recorded particular natural and human phenomena as though they were peering through a microscope or a telescope. Their intense and precise scrutiny of all created things, people, and ideas, bred in them an empiricism which became a paradoxically pragmatic morality or spirituality, or perhaps their innocent empiricism created a paradoxically spiritual or moral pragmatism. Nature, art and people, the new empiricism taught them, were to be studied for exactly what they were. But the new empiricism led to pragmatism, or utilitarianism, which said that exactly what created phenomena were, or were not, either was, or was not, of pragmatic moral use to the humanistic students of these phenomena.

Matthew Arnold was as troubled by crude Victorian pragmatism as any other Victorian humanist, precisely because it was, as he remarked over and over, not merely characteristic of the English mind, but quintessentially characteristic of his own age. Yet the new classical humanism, no less than the new pragmatism, required "the endeavour," as Arnold warned, "in all branches of knowledge, theology, philosophy, history, art, science, to see the object as in itself it really is."[3] These Victorian humanists had therefore inherited a technological obligation as well as a moral and intellectual obligation to practice Victorian specificity, "for the plain reason," as John Henry Newman insisted, "that one idea is not another idea."[4] Nor is one aspect of an artifact another aspect of that artifact, or one aspect of nature or of a particular human nature another aspect of the human nature under scrutiny.

This courageous attempt by Victorian humanists, and even by the enlightened Utilitarian, John Stuart Mill, to accommodate yet to modify Victorian pragmatism was evidently wearying to their spirits. For all their wonderfully braced vigor and their generous and varied talents, they seemed at times to have sensed themselves as creatures like Matthew Arnold's mournful traveller gazing at Chartreuse Cathedral, or as bewildered souls adrift in insoluble moral ambiguities,

> Wandering between two worlds, one dead,
> The other powerless to be born,
> With nowhere yet to rest my head,
> Like these on earth I wait forlorn.[5]

And as Arnold commented elsewhere, "the calm, the cheerfulness, the disinterested objectivity have disappeared; the dialogue of the mind with itself has commenced; modern problems have presented themselves; we hear already the doubts, we witness the discouragement of Hamlet and of Faust."[6]

The Victorian humanists' "dialogue of the mind with itself" is obviously a dialogue of minds with their society. Tennyson's *In Memoriam* (1850) considered in anguished specificity not only the beauties and dangers of a typically close Victorian male friendship, but also the beauties and dangers of art's potential narcissism, as well as the frequent failure of nature to heal grief and of science even to confront grief. Tennyson's *Idylls of the King* mournfully examines, idyll by idyll, a perennial Christian conflict, an "old imperfect tale, / New-old, and shadowing Sense at war with Soul."[7] Nature and human nature, for Tennyson's King Arthur, deserve no abstract Wordsworthian praise. The man is never far from the beast; the beast, in turn, is never far from disorderly and rampant vegetation. Art may chasten the beast in the human, but only if that moral desire resides in the artist.

Carlyle frequently celebrated nature's primitive vigor as an emanation of the divine will. Especially in essays written before "Shooting Niagara" (1867), he praised art which unconsciously displayed strenuous didactic intentions. But Carlyle's truncated form of the great chain of being created moral problems for him as he surveyed the nature and functions of art and of human nature. His heroes, as we know, are at the pinnacles of his chain of being, which he has reduced to one crude link between heroes and hero-worshippers. His humble hero-worshippers are all to be clumped together at the bottom of his chain; they are all to be modern descendents of Carlyle's Gurth the Churl. Nature's unchastened vehemences are appropriate only in the hero, and only in a modified from.

Human nature's innate narcissism is to be chastened by gruelling work; and eventually art, for Carlyle, became as suspect, for all its glories, as innately narcissistic human nature uncontrolled by the authoritarian leadership of the hero.

Ruskin also came to submit the claims of all art, nature, and human nature to his particular form of empiricism followed by moral pragmatism. Nature's beauty in all its exact specificity is medicinal, since it is the art of God who made it, just as God made human beauty. But natural and human beauties could create moral snares, and human beauty created snares both for the possessor and the onlooker. To worship nature's violence is inappropriate, since it is not a proper model for humans who seek to live by benevolent principles.

John Stuart Mill's essay called "Nature," written in the 1850s, brutally stressed that nature could be as violent, as cruel, and as whimsically indifferent to individual human needs and rights as the most hard-hearted factory or mine owner, bent upon starving or mutilating as many workers as the parliamentary commissions and as the doctrine of economic laissez faire would permit.

Newman's *Idea of a University* (1852) is more preoccupied with human nature's hunger for a liberal education and of art's role in that education, than it is with the properties and functions of nature. But Newman's radiant archetypal Oxonian Tennysons and Hallams distinctly reflect the Victorian cult of university friendships; for Newman's Carlylean hero is the mind of a liberally educated gentleman, and better yet, the liberally educated mind of one gentleman communing with others. The mind of a humanist, devoid of provincial prejudices of any kind, religious or secular, said Newman, "is almost prophetic from its knowlewdge of history; it is almost heart-searching from its knowledge of human nature; it has almost supernatural charity from its freedom from littleness and prejudice; it has almost the repose of faith, because nothing can startle it; it has almost the beauty and harmony of heavenly contemplation, so intimate is it with the eternal order of things and the music of the spheres" (Discourse VI, Section 6).

But no matter how thoroughly Newman separated the idea of a university from the idea of a monastery, or the idea of a liberally educated gentleman from the idea of a Roman Catholic priest, "for the plain reason," as he said, "that one idea is not another idea," and no matter how frequently he insisted that a liberal education has its own legitimate ends and need not apologize for those ends, nor adapt itself to other ends of other ideas, nonetheless, he eventually found himself articulating the Victorian paradox of moral utilitarianism. The ends of a liberal education, splendid as they may be, are not enough to keep the Christian faithful. But the paradox is that unless the liberal arts are taught so as to reveal their own ends, and their own ends alone, they are incapable of transcending these legitimate ends and performing their pragmatic function, which is to bring the non-Catholic to the threshold of conversion, and to allow Catholics to partake safely of the fruits of Anglican university education.

Newman is not the only Victorian humanist to describe this particular paradoxical moral pragmatism: Tennyson, Ruskin, Arnold, and of course, Hopkins himself, all said or implied that art and the liberal arts were entitled to serve their own ends primarily, as long as they served other ends ultimately. But such is the nature of this paradox, as all the Victorian humanists admitted, that any discipline which is taught, and any art which is created *primarily* for some other purpose than its own, does not achieve its own ends. Thus, only when it is created or taught for its own ends alone can it achieve utilitarian purposes such as calming the passions, civilizing the Philistines, condemning human cruelties, and leading artists and artists' patrons to espouse the moral — and perhaps even the theological — good life. For the Victorian humanists, the Horatian carrot is a carrot, and a stick is a stick, but a carrot serving its own ends becomes a moral stick serving other ends.

For these troubled humanists, nature, human nature, and the artifacts which humans created, all seem to be under some painful interdict, either literally or symbolically necessitated by the post-Edenic human predicament. The apocalyptic voice appears and reappears in their writings. It was now time, they were convinced, for English citizens of good will to repair the particularly Victorian post-Edenic damages of scientific speculation, of technological ravage, and of human greed and vulgarity which they saw all around them. It is not surprising that Victorian humanists could no longer share Wordsworth's innocent delight in nature, in humans at work and at home in the pastoral world, and in the artist's function as celebrant of nature's salvific role. Perhaps, just as the woman has notoriously been blamed for any rape she sustained, unless she resisted to the death, so nature now often seemed suspect because she could not defend herself to the death against rapacious men — because her soil was now becoming more and more eroded, her crops were often failing, the air was full of pollution, as Ruskin accurately claimed in *Storm Cloud of the Nineteenth Century* (1884), the land was crucified with industrial and commercial scars, and thousands upon thousands of impoverished English citizens were driven into ugly, unhealthy cities which were not designed to receive them or to nourish them. And so nature herself almost appeared to be morally contaminated by the humans who raped and deserted her.

As the national ravages of land and people continued apace throughout the century, corrupting both the contaminated and the contaminators, no wonder that to representative Victorian humanists, including Hopkins, the arts seemed unable to impede the pastoral and human holocaust. As Ruskin said more and more often after *Unto This Last* (1860), there is a time for art and there is a time for moral and social reforms, since the arts themselves reflect current moral and political priorities. Significantly as Ruskin and Matthew Arnold differed in their championship of social reforms, Ruskin came to share with Arnold, particularly the Arnold of "The Function of Criticism" (1864), the mournful theory that debilitated societies will produce debilitated art. For just as nature and human nature had been considerably disabled by rapacious industrialists and heartless political economists, so art, too, had been co-opted or condemned by utilitarian principles which tended to dismiss as worthless anything inimical to quantification, codification, cost-accounting, and mass production.

Hopkins was hardly more nervous about the proper uses of nature, art, and human nature than other Victorian humanists; he was merely more precise and more doctrinal in his anxieties. He too thought of art as both an end in itself and as a theological carrot leading the artist and the artist's patron to Christian faith. Art was to delight in order that it might teach. But when Hopkins described poetry *as* poetry, he was fully as anxious as Arnold was to establish in himself habits of "disinterested objectivity," that is, "to see the object as in itself it really is." Furthermore, Hopkins was fully as interested to separate poetry from its pragmatically theological function as Newman was to separate the liberal arts from theological training, "for the plain reason that one idea is not another idea." "Poetry," said the Jesuit Hopkins, "is speech framed for contemplation of the mind by the way of hearing or speech framed to be heard for its own sake and interest even over and above its interest of meaning. Some matter and meaning is essential to it but only as an element necessary to support and employ the shape which is contemplated for its own sake."[8]

Hopkins could hardly have improved his argument for poetry's technical prosodic inscape as a legitimate end in itself. But as we all know, in his letters to his friends, especially in his oddly cool yet quietly anguished letters to Richard Watson Dixon,[9] he stressed repeatedly that poetry is an amateur pursuit compared to the priestly profession, and that he feared it for himself because it stirred secular and temporal passions and ambitions in him which he thought inappropriate for a Jesuit missionary. And so, just as Matthew Arnold monitored himself in refusing to reprint his own great poem *Empedocles* because he thought that it was not morally useful (Preface to *Poems*, 1853), so Hopkins monitored his poetry because he felt it sometimes served ends and purposes unworthy of his clerical profession. And just as Arnold tried to escape the despairing mood of *Empedocles* and "Dover Beach," and in the process wrote the unreadable pseudo-classical abortion *Merope* (1858), and finally stopped writing poetry altogether, so Hopkins resolutely turned his talents to subjects suitable to a parish priest, and finally found himself unable to write with the gusto which characterizes the year or two after *The Wreck of the Deutschland* (1876). In the process of renunciation, so Ignatian and so Victorian, Hopkins endured the mental suffering also endured in various ways by Carlyle, Mill, Ruskin, Tennyson, and Arnold. Ruskin's gradual abandonment of artistic subjects seems to have begun in 1860, the year he published the last volume of *Modern Painters* and suffered critical vituperation after the publication of *Unto This Last.* Tennyson's *Idylls of the King* are of course post-Laureate, and therefore paradoxically moral and pragmatic. Splendid as the idylls often are, they contain distinct weakness of tone, diction, and perhaps even of mixed purposes, which are not apparent in "Ulysses" and *In Memoriam,* for instance. One wonders whether four of these Victorian humanists—Tennyson, Ruskin, Arnold, and Hopkins—were self-fulfilling Carlyle's prediction that serious writers will eventually come to be ashamed of creating mere art, or even talking about it, when the world's work needs to be done. Or perhaps they came to share Arnold's and Ruskin's condemnation of an age unfit for art, desperately as it needed art to cure its sickness.

Hopkins's response to nature is deliberately Ruskinian; he was a great admirer of Ruskin. In such ecstatic pastoral poems as "The Windhover" and in poems which mourn over the ravaged landscape, such as "Binsey Poplars," Hopkins perceives nature as God's art and desperately in need of human protection, just as Ruskin had before him. But as Hopkins's spirits became increasingly demoralized, nature herself came to symbolize something vaguely sinister, as though she unwillingly partook of the first parents' original sin. Here Hopkins is very close to Ruskin—and perhaps even inadvertently to Mill—in his insistence that nature is all too like rebellious and greedy men to be a reliable model for human imitation.

Hopkins's readings in Carlyle had obviously frightened him; Carlyle's untamed hero, subconsciously atuned to nature's equally untamed vigor, was clearly not of the heroic self-sacrificing mould which characterizes the *imitatio vitae Christi,* a role to which Hopkins, like Carlyle's hero-worshippers, had dedicated his life. In letters to Robert Bridges and to Dixon, Hopkins called Carlyle a moral imposter and Carlyle's writings "most inefficacious-strenuous heaven-protestations, caterwaul, and Cassandra wailings."[10] But Hopkins is a Carlylean hero-worshipper, for all his fear of Carlyle. One of Hopkins's sermons describes the love of Christ as "enthusiasm for a leader, a hero, love for a bosom friend, love for a lover" (*Sermons,* p. 48). These images reflect not only the university cult of male friendships but the Carlylean cult of hero worship, two Victorian phenomena which appear to have arisen at roughly the same time.[11] Christopher Devlin, himself a Jesuit, explains much of Hopkins's mental anguish as a temper which he inherited from "the Romantic Movement, Carlyle's 'Heroes,' and the Victorian code of ethics" (*Sermons,* p. 120). When Devlin remarks in this same passage that "undoubtedly in the nineteenth century a . . . Jansenistic spirit crept at times into Catholic spirituality," Devlin has identified the restless, heroic desire of typical Victorian humanists to make poetry, nature, religion, and even human relationships count in a spiritually utilitarian way. Although to Hopkins, as to other Victorian humanists, everything has its place and its own proper end, yet "the Victorian code of ethics" dictates that some ultimate end should invariably transcend the primary end for which art, nature, and human relationships were designed.

In no way is Hopkins more Victorian than in his assumptions about the uses of human relationships. And in no way is he more Victorian than in the way he unconsciously considered human relationships, especially those with other university men, according to the same pragmatically sacramental values with which he invested art and nature, when perceived at their best. For this subliminal and troubling connection between art, nature, and human nature is a distinct component of the Victorian temper. For example, Arnold's poems about nature, especially poems to the stars, describe nature as austere, above human turmoil, non-judgmental, and remote. He tried to make his poetry austere, non-judgmental, and remote. His friends and tutors accused him of remoteness and austerity when he was witty, yet his correspondence reveals that he could be both passionate and self-righteously judgmental. His letters to Clough, particularly, contain feints, overtures, admonitions, withdrawals, further admonitions, and then further withdrawals, as he discussed the nature of art, nature, and human nature.

Newman also encountered difficulties in his university friendships. Despite Newman's utopian attitude toward the cult of university friendship, his relationships with his friends and his university colleagues were painful in the extreme. When the friend seemed about to convert to Roman Catholicisms Newman was tender and sympathetic; when the friend wavered, Newman was harsh.[12]

Tennyson seems to have accepted the friends he made during his short tenure as a member of the delightful circle of male friends called "The Cambridge Apostles." But Arthur Henry Hallam's death seemed to have engendered in him the same nervousness about intense university friendships as Arnold suffered about Clough, as Newman suffered through his Oxonian friendships, and as Ruskin is reported to have suffered while he was at Oxford and throughout his life. Ruskin appears to have been as frightened of close male friendships as he was so notoriously frightened of marriage.[13] Carlyle bullied his friends, and they often resented his self-appointed role as moral don and pedagogue to the universe.[14] For all these Victorian humanists, withdrawal from art, or suspicion of art's moral efficacy, seemed to accompany correlative suspicions that neither nature nor human relationships were more reliably efficacious than art to heal the present human predicament.

Hopkins's ambivalent perspectives upon human relationships, especially upon male friendships, is, as we would therefore predict, all of a piece with his ambivalent perspectives upon art and nature. Hopkins, to be sure, received doctrinal permission to advance and to withdraw from all three, whenever his priestly profession required him to do so. But we all know how nervous and unhappy he was in his schoolboy friendships, how frequently he lectured Bridges and yearned to hear from Bridges, and how genuinely he cherished his friends and mourned when they did not receive the recognition he thought they deserved. His sudden passion for the visiting schoolboy, Digby Dolben, who came to Oxford to take entrance examinations, is similar in intensity, especially after Dolben's early death, to the intensity of Tennyson's passion for the dead Hallam,[15] of Hallam's for his dear familiar, William Gladstone, whom he met at Eton,[16] of Newman's for his potential converts, of Arnold's deeply ambivalent affection for Clough, and of Dr. Thomas Arnold's Rugby schoolboys for one another.[17]

Hopkins's charming apotheosis to the Oxonian friendship between his fictive Richard and Sylvester indicates how thoroughly enthralled he was by the Victorian cult of university friendships:

(ii)
But what drew shepherd Richard from his downs,
And bred acquaintance of unusèd towns?
What put taught graces on his country lip,
And brought the sense of gentle fellowship,
That many centres found in many hearts?
What taught the humanities and the round of arts?
And for the tinklings on the falls and swells
Gave the much music of our Oxford bells?

Richard now calls out to his dear familiar, whose name is "Sylvester":

(iii)
"Sylvester, come Sylvester; you may trust
Your footing now to the much-dreaded dust,
. . . Come and see.
You may quote Wordsworth, if you like, to me."

The fourth stanza describes Richard as he offers precise little Ruskinian vignettes of trees, grass, and skies, so that one sees each leaf, each cloud, each red grass-blade. In this Hopkinsian epiphany, nature and human nature are both benevolent:

A spiritual grace
Which Wordsworth would have dwelt on, about the place
Led Richard with a sweet undoing pain
To trace some traceless loss of thought again.[18]

No Oxford graduate has written more poignantly than Hopkins about the Oxonian spell which seized men with the "sweet undoing pain" of first love, and which left them with a life-long nostalgia. These "Fragments of Richard" represent a miniature *Idea of a University*. They are no less redolent of an almost post-Edenic longing for innocent days than Newman's idyllic memories of Oxford or of Matthew Arnold's various tributes to Oxford. Arnold's Preface to *Essays in Criticism* (1865) describes Oxford as a beautiful, venerable, lovely, serene city, "steeped in sentiment . . . spreading her gardens to the moonlight, and whispering from her towers the last enchantment of the Middle Age. . . ."[19] Hopkins's undergraduate response to Oxford was equally ecstatic and equally purple. To his mother, he wrote almost breathlessly, as he vainly tried to describe "all Oxford, its inhabitants and its neighbourhood," and to assure her that "everything is delightful," that the Balliol "chapel is beautiful," that the "inner quad is delicious," and that he felt, prophetically, as events were to prove, "almost too happy." These three Oxonians, Arnold, Newman and Hopkins, were merely three among hundreds who were enraptured not only by Oxford's beauty but by the strained beauty of the friendships they made there. Seventeen years later, Hopkins wrote mournfully from Liverpool, "Not to love my University would be to undo the very buttons of my being. . . ." He was writing to Alexander Baillie, another Oxonian graduate who had also tested the electric atmosphere of Balliol in Hopkins's time.[20]

It is now a commonplace that the tremendous energies of the Victorian humanists often exhausted them, so that they arranged pauses for themselves — pauses, which unlike drafts of Coca Cola, failed to refresh them. My students and I then discussed three pre-Victorian historical events which undoubtedly produced in these humanists their characteristic ambivalences toward art, nature, and human nature, however variously they may have revealed their ambivalences. Their memories of the grossly licentious Hanoverian Princes and of Princess Caroline's unsavory divorce trial provided recent examples of human nature in rebellion. The French Revolution provided another example of human nature massively revolting against social order. But I suggested that the successful revolution of thirteen of their North American colonies disturbed the humanists equally. Their profound silence on this loss to national harmony and prestige is, to me at least, highly revealing, as though they had suffered some wound to their self-esteem which they were unable to force themselves to examine. In any case, their own imperious energies may well have reminded them of three recent rebellions against domestic decorum and taste, political harmony, and imperial integrity, so that any public or private convulsions of energy came to seem dangerous to England's fragile peace.

But my students are waiting to describe exactly where, here and there, they found Hopkins's poems to be slightly vitiated by his ambivalences about nature, art, and human nature, and where they thought he transcended his ambivalences. First, these students were troubled for aesthetic reasons by such poems as "Margaret Clitheroe," "St. Thecla," and "St. Winefred's Well." They wanted to know whether most male Victorians behaved with such unconscious condescension toward women, saintly or otherwise. "Felix Randall" troubled them with its combination of slightly mawkish priestly tenderness and something casual — or was it deliberate self-monitoring? — in its colloquialisms. These lines particularly disturbed them: "Impatient, he cursed at first, but mended / Being anointed and all. . . . / Ah well, God rest him all road ever he offended!" (Poem 53). The students were aware that Hopkins's attempt to imitate Liverpool dialect was a profound compliment to his dead parishioner, but was it Hopkins at his best? There seemed to the students to be an asymmetrical vigor between the poems written, like "The Windhover": "To Christ our Lord" (Poem 36), and those written to his parishioners. When he celebrated God's presence in the world and God's gifts to the world, in his wild, exuberant meters, and when he begged his divine hero to become present to him once more, the students thought that either mood, of exhilaration or of exhaustion, had produced splendidly authentic poetry. But when Hopkins became the shepherd tending his sheep, rather than the sheep acknowledging the shepherd or looking for the shepherd, then, the students felt some psychological loss of nerve in him, as well as a loss of prosodic intensities. They felt that when Hopkins addressed Christ in joy or in anguish, his poems, whether metrically explosive or metrically smoothed out with spiritual exhaustion, as in the dark sonnets, seemed more authentic, more personal, less "strung by duty" and more "strained to beauty" than the parishioner poems ("The Loss of the Euridice," Poem 41). Yet uncomfortable as Hopkins's quite literally apocalyptic vision in "Spelt from Sibyl's Leaves" made them feel, and firmly as they seemed to reject this vision, they responded with compassionate awe to the courage of a poet-priest who was now driven to say, "Óur évening is over us; óur night whélms, whélms, ánd will end us" (Poem 61).

Nonetheless, Hopkins's apparent confusion in "Brothers" (Poem 54) between nature, art, and human nature particularly troubled my students for Hopkins himself. "Jack" the actor — the artist — is described in derogatory terms: he is "bráss-bóld," "roguish," and "Nature, framed in fault:"

> Ah, Nature, framed in fault,
> There's comfort then, there's salt;
> Nature, bad, base, and blind,
> Dearly thou canst be kind;
> There dearly thén, deárly,
> Dearly thou canst be kind.

"The Handsome Heart" and "The Bugler's First Communion" frightened my students, again, for Hopkins's own sake, above all, Hopkins's comment to Bridges about the boy-bugler: "I enclose a poem, the Bugler. I am half inclined to hope the Hero of it may be killed in Afghanistan" (Letters to Bridges, p. 92). We discussed, as we were bound to do, Victorian anxieties about sex and nineteenth-century Jesuit anxieties about sex. But when the students came to "Tom's Garland," "The Soldier," and "Harry Ploughman," they praised the explosive metrical energy of these poems, even while several of them suggested that Hopkins had been reading too much Carlyle.

The students were particularly fascinated with Hopkins's nature poems and the way he exploited Victorian specificity. Just as Rossetti's "woodspurge has a cup of three," not four, not two, but three, Hopkins microscopically examines nature, art, and human nature, feather by feather, petal by petal, line by line, color by color, and human feature by human feature. The students were immensely excited by Hopkins's adaptation of Ruskin's aerial perspective, in "Hurrahing in Harvest," where the Ruskinian wind creates "silk-sack" clouds of the upper region, "Meal-drift moulded" as they "melted across skies." The students especially admired those Ruskinian "azurous hung hills," whose blue color changes before the onlooker's eyes as the hills become "very violet sweet." Hopkins is deftly exploiting Ruskinian short-hand here, to explain that if the hills were perceived at close range, they would be green. Since they lie at a distance, the intervening air turns them blue. But another example of Ruskinian aerial perspective occurs in "Hurrahing in Harvest:" we are to understand that because the hills have turned from azure to "very violet sweet," they have momentarily been touched by the rich red setting sun, which combines with their aerial blue to create their "very violet sweet" color (Poem 38).

In poem after poem, Hopkins subjects nature to both Ruskinian specificity and to sacramental symbolism, as in "God's Grandeur," where the "black West" not only accurately describes the western skies just before dawn, but also symbolizes heretical Protestant England, still nationally unconverted to Catholicism. In the same way, "the brown brink eastward" accurately describes in Ruskinian terms the brown tinge of the horizon just before the sun rises above it, and simultaneously symbolizes Hopkins's hopes for the coming of England's conversion to Roman Catholicism (Poem 31).

The students were genuinely enchanted with one poem where Hopkins addressed the problem of art. "To what serves Mortal Beauty" touched them because Hopkins seemed to have moved authentically from music's legitimate seductions, to human beauty's legitimate seductions, to the slightly sinister "worship" of "block or barren stone," back to "heaven's sweet gift" of all created beauty, and finally to "God's better beauty, grace" (Poem 62).

The very cautiousness with which these astute and conscientious students praised Hopkins and the patience with which they analyzed his Victorian ambivalences is a tribute primarily to their own seriousness, but ultimately to Hopkins's capacity to touch people like themselves who are simultaneously "strung by duty" and "strained to beauty." They affectionately and scrupulously watched his best poems move from almost scientific specificity to theological analogy, sometimes with metrically smooth brilliance as in "St. Alphonsus Rodriguez" and sometimes in metrically riotous brilliance as in "The Windhover." They now know something about the generous, tumultuous, troubled, sad, yet buoyant times which engendered Hopkins's poems. "No wonder of it," as Hopkins joyously exclaimed in "The Windhover." "No wonder of it," they agreed, that "shéer plód makes plough down sillion / Shine," and that Hopkins's own Victorian and Ignatian "blue-bleak embers" did indeed "Fall, gall themselves," and turn to "gold-vermillion." Moreover, the students' abiding fascination with Hopkins gradually compelled them to see that his poetry, perhaps more than any other Victorian poetry, speaks not only of its age, but to serious poetry students of the next century. For they had come to see how Hopkins's poetry, in its combined Ignatian and Victorian fervor and specificity, and even in its ambivalences about art, nature, and human nature, anticipates the twentieth-century social Manichaenism, which pits the claims of objective, empirical, utilitarian science in almost total conflict with disciplines trying to protect the unquantifiable, yet equally utilitarian demands of the human spirit. Hopkins's roots in western Christianity and in western classicism would not allow him to participate wholly in that conflict. "God's better beauty" to him, was indeed "grace"; but ultimately he came to accept, even to "own" the validity of created beauty, as "Home at heart, heaven's sweet gift" to troubled humanity ("To what serves Mortal Beauty?," Poem 62).

Notes

1. Samuel Johnson, *Dictionary of the English Language*, forty-third paragraph. Standard facsimile editions contain no pagination.

2. Hopkins's translations of "First Principle and Foundation" of St. Ignatius Loyola's *Spiritual Exercises*, in *The Sermons and Devotional Writings of Gerard Manley Hopkins*, ed. Christopher Devlin, S.J. (London: Oxford University Press, 1959), p. 122.

3. Matthew Arnold, "The Function of Criticism at the Present Time," *Lectures and Essays in Criticism, The Complete Prose Works of Matthew Arnold*, III, ed. R. H. Super (Ann Arbor: The University of Michigan Press, 1962), p. 258.

4. John Henry Newman, *The Idea of a University*, Discourse V, Section 4.

5. Matthew Arnold, "Stanzas from the Grande Chartreuse," II. 85–88.

6. Matthew Arnold, "Preface" to *Poems, 1853, The Poetical Works of Matthew Arnold*, eds. C. B. Tinker and H. F. Lowry (London: Oxford University Press, 1950), xvii.

7. Alfred, Lord Tennyson, "To the Queen," Epilogue, II. 36–37, *Idylls of the King*.

8. *The Journals and Papers of Gerard Manley Hopkins*, eds. Humphry House and Graham Storey (London: Oxford University Press, 1959), p. 289. The editors have identified Hopkins's fragment, "Poetry and Verse," as notes for his rhetoric lectures: 22 September 1873 to 31 July 1874. They base their dates upon Hopkins's handwriting, watermarks, and upon Hopkins's appointment as Professor of Rhetoric at Manresa House. See preface to *Journals and Papers*, xxvii.

9. *The Correspondence of Gerard Manley Hopkins and Richard Watson Dixon*, ed. Claude Colleer Abbott (London: Oxford University Press, 1935), pp. 75, 88–89.

10. *The Letters of Gerard Manley Hopkins to Robert Bridges*, ed. Claude Colleer Abbott (London: Oxford University Press, 1935), p. 27; *Correspondence*, pp. 75, 51.

11. Carlyle clearly foreshadows his missionary vision of heroes and hero-worshippers in such early works as "Characteristics" (1831) and *Sartor Resartus* (1830–1831). But the

Victorian ethos of university friendships predates these Carlylean publications. Tennyson and Arthur Henry Hallam first met in 1828; the custom of picking one dear familiar among the "Cambridge Apostles," yet sharing paired friendships with other paired friendships, was already a delightful custom when Tennyson and Hallam arrived at Trinity College. Everybody was in love with everybody else, and particularly with somebody else. Each of the dear familiars alternated the role of Socratic or New Testament mentor and disciple, just as each member of the Apostolic Brotherhood at Cambridge played the role of mentor to brother disciples, each of whom then in turn became a mentor to the rest. See Peter Allen, *The Cambridge Apostles: The Early Years* (Cambridge: Cambridge University Press, 1978), especially the introduction and the sections on Tennyson and Hallam. The Romantic model for these intellectual friendships may well have been the fruitful friendship of two earlier Cantabrigians, Wordsworth and Coleridge, as well as the germinal "Preface" to *Lyrical Ballads*. On the cult of Romantic literary friendships, see R. C. Bald, *Literary Friendships in the Age of Wordsworth* (Cambridge: at the University Press, 1932), xviii. In Tennyson's Cambridge years, one of the commonplace debates between Cambridge and Oxford friends pitted the poetic worth of Byron against that of Wordsworth and Coleridge. Cambridge student pundits condemned Byron and praised Wordsworth or Coleridge.

12. See for example, Newman's letters to the Wilberforce brothers, particularly to Robert Wilberforce in David Newsome, *The Wilberforces and Henry Manning: The Parting of Friends* (Cambridge, Mass.: Harvard University Press, 1966).

13. Peter Quennell, *John Ruskin: The Portrait of a Prophet* (New York: Viking Press, 1949), p. 179.

14. See, for example, Charles Richard Sanders, *Carlyle's Friendships and Other Studies* (Durham: Duke University Press, 1977), pp. 206–207.

15. Nowhere is the poignant pathos of ruptured university friendships in Victorian England more hauntingly described than in Tennyson's retrospections upon the dead Hallam as he had been at Cambridge:

> And what delight can equal those
> That stir the spirit's inner deeps,
> When one that loves, but knows not, reaps
> A truth from one that loves and know?
> (*In Memoriam*, Lyric XLII).

Frances M. Brookfield, *The Cambridge "Apostles"* (New York: Charles Scribner's, 1906), pp. 124–25 and 137–39.

16. See *The Poems and Prose Remains of Arthur Clough with a Selection from His letters and a Memoir, Edited in two Volumes by His Wife* (London: MacMillan and Co., 1869), I, 21; see also *The Correspondence of Arthur Hugh Clough*, Frederick Mulhauser (Oxford: Clarendon Press, 1957), I, xvi–xviii.

17. *The Poems of Gerard Manley Hopkins*, eds. W. H. Gardner and Norman MacKenzie (London: Oxford University Press, 1967), Poem 107. All poem numbers refer to this edition.

18. Preface to *Essays in Criticism*, First Series (1865), in *Lectures and Essays in Criticism: The Complete Prose Works of Matthew Arnold*, III, ed. R. H. Super (Ann Arbor: The University of Michigan Press, 1962), pp. 289–290.

19. *Further Letters of Gerard Manley Hopkins*, ed. Claude Colleer Abbott (London: Oxford University Press, 1956), pp. 74, 79, 244, and Note K, pp. 448–449.

Gerard Manley Hopkins's Responses to the City: The "Composition of the Crowd"

William B. Thesing*

> Crowded places, I shunned them as noises too rude
> And fled to the silence of sweet solitude.
> — John Clare

In the nineteenth century the urban experience offered a perplexing challenge to many poets. How could beauty be detected or generated amidst ugly or traditionally unpoetical surroundings? How could the increasing concentrations of people in cities be viewed as a chance for the renewal of human community rather than as a threat of violent uprisings?

In addition to the often discussed tensions in Hopkins's life between the roles of poet and priest, Catholic and Englishman, he also faced directly some of the main tensions and contradictions of responding to the nineteenth-century city. Between the years 1878 and 1889, which brought assignments to such urban-industrial centers as Manchester, Liverpool, Glasgow, London, and finally Dublin, Hopkins was forced to confront the dual challenges of being a Victorian poet in a series of cities and working as a Catholic priest amongst a diverse mixture of people.

That Hopkins seems to follow a line of poets who find that the muse eludes them in urban physical surroundings is not now an especially unexpected discovery. Yet it is important to remember that Hopkins's Victorian and urban connections have only been emphasized in the last two decades. Books such as Wendell Stacy Johnson's *Gerard Manley Hopkins: The Poet as Victorian* (1968) and Alison G. Sulloway's *Gerard Manley Hopkins and the Victorian Temper* (1972) as well as several articles have insisted on studying Hopkins's solid Victorian groundings. Although G. Robert Stange's essay, "The Frightened Poets," does not discuss Hopkins's specific urban experiences, it offers valuable insights concerning the types of responses that the Victorian city evoked from poets.[1]

1

Hopkins's response to the several Victorian cities that he worked in is significant from several points of view. He condemns the noise, dirt, and ugliness of the physical surroundings in various cities. Thus, in March 1879, he complains that the charm of Oxford's landscape is being "abridged and soured and perhaps will soon be put out altogether."[2] The poems "God's Grandeur" (1877) — with its complaint that "all is seared

*From *Victorian Studies* 30, 3 (Spring 1987): 385–408. Permission to reprint this essay was kindly granted by Patrick Brantlinger, editor, *Victorian Studies*.

with trade; bleared, smeared with toil; / And wears man's smudge" — and "Binsey Poplars" (1879) — with its regret that so many beautiful trees "are all felled" — express similar sentiments.[3]

Temporarily assigned in November 1879 to Bedford Leigh, near Manchester, Hopkins finds the place to be "very gloomy." Furthermore, he writes that "Leigh is a darksome place, with pits and mills and foundries."[4] In a letter to Bridges, he describes precisely the polluting agents of a nearby Lancashire town: "I was yesterday at St. Helen's, probably the most repulsive place in Lancashire or out of the Black Country. The stench of sulphuretted hydrogen rolls in the air and films of the same gas form on railing and pavement."[5]

In January 1881 his reaction to conditions of existence in Liverpool is just as negative: "It is indeed a most unhappy and miserable spot" (*Correspondence*, p. 42). In September 1881 he writes Bridges that his transfer to Glasgow is only a slight improvement: "Things are pleasanter here than at Liverpool. Wretched place too Glasgow is, like all our great towns; still I get on better here, though bad is the best of my getting on" (*Letters to Bridges*, p. 135). On a retreat in London in December 1881, he complains of chimney soot in his room with a strain of realism that rivals the accuracy of Dickens or Gissing: "I had a worse misfortune in my own room, where the gale blew the soot all over the place and made things miserable" (*Further Letters*, p. 160). Of the buildings at Dublin's University College, he complains in an 1884 letter to Cardinal Newman that they "have fallen into a deep dilapidation" (*Further Letters*, p. 63). Or again, he writes that "Dublin is very dull" (*Further Letters*, p. 180). His assessment of the city to Bridges uses the adjectives "joyless and smoky" (*Letters to Bridges*, p. 190).

In some respects Matthew Arnold offers an instructive parallel to Hopkins in his dealings with the nineteenth-century city. Like Hopkins, he was burdened with a full schedule of work activities in various Victorian cities and he often witnessed scenes of both physical and spiritual degeneration. In 1849 Arnold set forth a key dilemma in a letter to his friend, Arthur Hugh Clough: "Reflect too, . . . how deeply *unpoetical* the age and all one's surroundings are."[6] In more instances than have been previously realized, Hopkins also bemoans the fact that urban work and poetic creation seem to be antagonistic or at best mutually exclusive. In 1878 he reflects: "My muse turned utterly sullen in the Sheffield smoke-ridden air and I had not written a line till the foundering of the Eurydice the other day" (*Letters to Bridges*, p. 48); in 1879, while working in Oxford — not strictly an industrial town, but one with an area of poverty around the Jericho canal — Hopkins complains: "I have parish work to do, am called one way and another and can find little time to write" (*Correspondence*, p. 20). In May 1880 he writes: "The parish work of Liverpool is very wearying to mind and body and leaves me nothing but odds and ends of time. There is merit in it but little Muse, and indeed twenty-six lines is the whole I have written in more than half a year, since I left Oxford" (*Correspondence*, p. 33). A January 1881 letter registers the same regret: "Liverpool is of all places the most museless. It is indeed a most unhappy and miserable spot. There is moreover no time for writing anything serious—I should say for composing it, for if it were made it might be written" (*Correspondence*, p. 42). In April 1881 he tells Bridges that only the "Muse of music" shows any faint signs of vitality in Liverpool: "Well, she is the only Muse that does not stifle in this horrible place" (*Letters to Bridges*, p. 126).

The Glasgow environment seems just as unnurturing to poetic creation. Hopkins reports to Canon Dixon: "When at Glasgow I began an ode . . . but got not far with it nor was much pleased with what I had done" (*Correspondence*, p. 76). Because of the pressing need for personal contact with destitute victims of urban poverty in Liverpool or, to a lesser degree, in Oxford, the intellectual pursuits of reading and writing became unattainable and self-indulgent luxuries to him. He reports that his parish work in Oxford "left no time, that was of any use, for reading" (*Further Letters*, p. 243), that in Liverpool he had "to put aside serious study" and "never once entered the public library" (*Correspondence*, p. 96). At Bedford Leigh he is "cut off . . . from all modern and all classical books" (*Further Letters*, p. 243). Dublin's atmosphere, too, seems antagonistic to poetic efforts: in 1885 Hopkins writes that "the Irish have little feeling for poetry and least of all for modern poetry" (*Further Letters*, p. 364). Only in London do cultural opportunities seem to be available to him: "Still I prefer London to any large town in these islands. . . . [There] are so many resources, things to go to and hear and see and do. Everything is there. No, I think that very much may be said for life in London" (*Further Letters*, pp. 292–293).

The third major category of Hopkins's response to the nineteenth-century city is from his perspective as a Tory priest who is often troubled and sometimes incensed at the moral and social degeneracy that he sees in groups of urban people, especially working-class people. Some of his letters have been frequently quoted, but some of his other observations in this vein have not drawn much critical attention. The more memorable quotations include:

> My Liverpool and Glasgow experience laid upon my mind a conviction, a truly crushing conviction, of the misery of town life to the poor and more than to the poor, of the misery of the poor in general, of the degradation even of our race, of the hollowness of this century's civilisation: it made even life a burden to me to have daily thrust upon me the things I saw (*Correspondence*, p. 97).

> What I most dislike in towns and in London in particular is the misery of the poor; the dirt, squalor, and the illshaped degraded physical

(putting aside moral) type of so many of the people, with the deeply dejecting, unbearable thought that by degrees almost all our population will become a town population and a puny unhealthy and cowardly one (*Further Letters*, p. 293).

And the drunkards go on drinking, the filthy, as the scripture says, are filthy still: human nature is so inveterate. Would that I had seen the last of it (*Letters to Bridges*, p. 110).

But one other incident recounted in Hopkins's letters is infrequently mentioned, and it also conveys the sense that, in the city, moral degeneracy is out of control. Here Hopkins expresses — after the passage of many years — his contempt for the rudeness of a group of workingmen in Liverpool. He is especially repelled by the ugly, undisciplined habit of workmen spitting on the public pavements:

Spitting in the North of England is very, very common with the lower classes: as I went up Brunswick Road (or any street) at Liverpool on a frosty morning it used to disgust me to see the pavement regularly starred with the spit of the workmen going to their work; and they do not turn aside, but spit straight before them as you approach, as a Frenchman remarked to me with abhorrence and I cd. only blush. And in general we cannot call ours a cleanly or a clean people: they are not at all the dirtiest and they know what cleanliness means, as they know the moral virtues, but they do not always practise it (*Letters to Bridges*, p. 299).

Yet at other times, Hopkins is quite complimentary of urban dwellers' resilience in the face of recalcitrant surroundings. Of Bedford Leigh residents he writes: "The place is very gloomy but our people hearty and devoted."[7] Hopkins also appreciates the resolute courage of Bedford Leigh inhabitants who work in "pits and mills and foundries" and are helpless against the fluctuating economic cycles of the Victorian Age: "Our flock are fervent, I have not seen their equal. Trade is slack but reviving" (*Further Letters*, p. 243). Of course, his most sympathetic statement concerning the plight of urban workers in capitalist England is the early and exceptional "red letter": "But it is a dreadful thing for the greatest and most necessary part of a very rich nation to live a hard life without dignity, knowledge, comforts, delight, or hopes in the midst of plenty — which plenty they make" (*Letters to Bridges*, pp. 27–28). In fact, the famous 1871 "red letter" foreshadows Hopkins's later attitudes toward any direct or violent attempt by a political group to impose the adoption of a political policy. In an abstract way he is fascinated by the promises of Marxist communism to assist in a more equal distribution of the wealth produced. His subsequent remarks to Bridges, however, reveal his inclination to see such agents of political change as uncontrolled, murderous forces of social upheaval. When Hopkins writes again on the topic to

Bridges—after a lapse of over two years—he still feels that the working classes are not being treated fairly, but he repudiates communism as a solution to the problem.

2

Once we have noted Hopkins's reactions to physical conditions of life, his conclusion that the city represents recalcitrant material opposed to the creation of poetry, and his moral repugnance over the decay of manners in city centers, it is fruitful to focus on a more specialized phenomenon of nineteenth-century urban life—crowds or groups of assembled people—in order to see what political and aesthetic challenges such scenes offered to Hopkins. The exploration of this narrower topic in turn reveals much concerning Hopkins's attitudes during his final years in Dublin (1884–89).

In the years of Hopkins's life before he came to Dublin in 1884, he shows some half-developed notions about crowds. There are really two separate strains of activity here—the manner in which he handles the aesthetic problem of how to compose crowd scenes and how he reacts politically to real crowds assembled on city streets. Thus, a special distinction should be made between Hopkins's political and aesthetic perspectives on groups of people versus his spiritual outlook which—it could be argued—allowed him as a Jesuit priest to be "composed" or assured him "composure" amidst the multitudes.

Hopkins's depictions of crowds in both his poetry and prose before 1879, the year he was first assigned to working in urban parishes, were generally happy, harmonious, and demonstrative of purposeful motion. Variants of the word "crowd," for example, appear four times in the early poem "A Vision of the Mermaids." Written in late 1862, just three months before he entered Oxford, the poem depicts a young speaker surrounded by circles of alluring sea creatures on "An isle of roses" (*Poems*, p. 8, 1. 29). Although it would be fantastic to claim any relationship between the mermaids and Victorian urban crowds, from an aesthetic point of view Hopkins's depiction of the harmonious, rounded actions of the groups working in concert is structurally significant. In this early poem Hopkins's notion of the beauty of mythological crowds in a disciplined order seems to be derived from the military metaphor and the aquatic display in Milton's *Paradise Lost* or "Lycidas." Thus, Hopkins's mermaids exhibit the disciplined movements of military troops: "I gazed unhinder'd: Mermaids six or seven, / Ris'n from the deeps to gaze on sun and heaven, / Cluster'd in troops and halo'd by the light" (*Poems*, p. 9, ll. 34–36). Their assemblage also takes on quasi-religious significance as their heads, or at least their upper bodies, seem to be appareled in a celestial light (see figure 1). Later in the same poem, the mermaids present an aquatic routine with great precision as they welcome in the springtime of the year:

1. "A Vision of the Mermaids" from *Journals and Papers of Gerard Manley Hopkins,* second edition revised by Humphry House, completed by Graham Storey. Copyright Society of Jesus 1959; published by Oxford University Press. Reprinted by permission of Oxford University Press and Society of Jesus.

> So those Mermaidens crowded to my rock,
> And thicken'd, like that drifted bloom, the flock
> Sun-flush'd, until it seem'd their father Sea
> Had gotten him a wreath of sweet Spring-broidery.
> (*Poems*, p. 10, ll. 98–101)

The wreath image that is used for describing the formation of the crowd is important: as an organic circle, the wreath represents an orderly taming of the wild and free sea creatures into a pattern of purposeful order. In the unified design of a circle, the mermaids give pleasure to the observer and submit to the male godhead figure of "their father Sea."

This same positive and orderly depiction of crowds can also be seen in another early poem, "Easter" (1866). Norman MacKenzie speaks of the "confident buoyancy" and "elation" depicted in the poem.[8] Again, elements of religion and order seem to be associated with Hopkins's artistic rendering of a group of people in this poem. A group of devout worshipers is instructed to assemble in a circle around the altar; they are reverent, but festive:

> Seek God's house in happy throng;
> Crowded let His table be;
> Mingle praises, prayer, and song,
> Singing to the Trinity.
> (*Poems*, p. 35, ll. 25–28)

Besides being assembled around the altar, there is the further unifying gesture of the harmonious blending of many different voices. Just as the three parts of the Trinity work in perfect unity, so too are the variant forms of religious expression mingled and reconciled into a single devout purpose.

A similar positive aesthetic outlook toward assembled crowds can be seen in an entry in Hopkins's journal from this same period of his Oxford undergraduate days. At an academic commemoration ceremony to award honorary degrees held on 13 June 1866 in the Sheldonian Theatre, Hopkins finds beauty and character in the "composition of the crowd."[9] The three components of beauty, character, and order come together in a pleasing and harmonious fashion as Hopkins observes the academic ritual. He looks for the line of energy that holds the disparate organism of the large crowd together. He instresses the scene by discovering the underlying principle of unity. There are a variety of assembled personages, but he discovers a unifying line of force:

> Was happily able to see composition of the crowd in the area of the theatre, all the heads looking one way thrown up by their black coats relieved only by white shirt-fronts etc: the short strokes of eyes, nose, mouth, repeated hundreds of times I believe it is which gives the visible law: looked at in any one instance it flies. I could find a sort of beauty in

this, certainly character—but in fact that is almost synonymous with finding order, anywhere. The short parallel strokes spoken of are like those something in effect on the cusp-ends of six-foils in the iron tracery of the choir gates in our chapel (*Journals*, pp. 139–140).

Here the diverse crowd repeats an ordered pattern and Hopkins appreciates the beauty. The reference to the "iron tracery" of the chapel gates also points to the terms of the order that Hopkins depicts: the gates are cold, forbidding barriers that separate the chapel from the outside world.

A more complex problem is presented in dealing with one other early poem, "The Alchemist in the City." As Norman MacKenzie points out, the alchemist-speaker's "lament that he has nothing to show for his labours reflects both the loneliness of the artist, and a personal feeling of being a misfit among the crowds. He ends with a Romantic yearning to escape to the solitude of the wilderness, no matter how bleak" (Mackenzie, p. 24). Mackenzie briefly compares the alchemist's "sense of isolation" and loneliness to that of the artist figure in Tennyson's "The Lady of Shalott"; however, this comparison is not completely valid in terms of the two entowered speakers' reactions to the crowds that they observe below in their respective villages (Mackenzie, p. 94).

Especially in the 1832 version of "The Lady of Shalott," the villagers are presented in a condescending manner and seem to exhibit qualities of rudeness (to borrow John Clare's word from the epigraph). Tennyson expresses a hostility to the masses that is common in much Victorian literature. The male peasants are "surly" and the female villagers have their minds on economic matters of supply and demand, and maybe even—given their scarlet outfits—on practicing the alluring trade of prostitution: "She sees the surly village churls, / And the red cloaks of market girls, / Pass onward from Shalott."[10] At the end of Tennyson's poem, the crowd of middle-class Philistines assembles at the wharf and these burghers or "wellfed wits" of Camelot are "puzzled more than all the rest" over the mysterious curiosity that the Lady of Shalott's life and art might possibly represent (1832 version; p. 361, ll. 175–176).

In "The Lady of Shalott," Tennyson does not make the issue of the role of the artist absolute in the village or on the island. There is some color and beauty outside the lady's tower—the glitter of sun off armor, the colorful clothes and vibrant singing of the workers in the fields. But the main point of the poem is that singers do not thrive in the region in general, whether it be in the village's community or in the tower's isolation. Unlike Tennyson, Hopkins in "The Alchemist in the City" disparages the alchemist-artist himself and not the crowds below his tower. The crowds in Hopkins's poem represent accomplishment and the expenditure of creative energy. As Jerome Bump points out, the villagers' "external world of change and motion is contrasted with the persona's still, stagnant inner world." The alchemist's "predicament" is that he is an alienated artist "isolated from the planning, building, and achieving" he sees taking place in his society.[11] The activities of the architects and workmen laboring together in an organic but structured system of society seem as natural and impressive as the change of seasons to the frustrated artist imprisoned in his lonely tower:

> My window shows the travelling clouds,
> Leaves spent, new seasons, alter'd sky,
> The making and the melting crowds:
> The whole world passes; I stand by.
>
> They do not waste their meted hours,
> But men and masters plan and build:
> I see the crowning of their towers,
> And happy promises fulfill'd.
>   (*Poems, p. 24, ll. 1–8*).

The phrase "The making and the melting crowds" (l. 3) is especially interesting given Hopkins's later presentation of groups of people. Within this observation are two paradoxical tendencies: the ability of the crowd to be "making," to gather and be creative, to be involved in harmonious employment, and the opposing force which goes toward "melting," dispersion, dissolution, and maybe even toward destruction and chaos. These potentially negative energies of crowds are not developed at this point in Hopkins's career; instead, the poem shifts focus away from the crowds to a presentation of the "powerless" incapacities of the solitary artist to find contentment in his society.

3

Between the years 1879 and 1884, Hopkins was exposed to some of the worst features and abuses to be found in nineteenth-century industrial cities. That he was morally repelled by urban crowds of workers is fairly common knowledge and was demonstrated in some of the statements quoted earlier from his letters. And yet he was often deeply moved by individual cases of poverty or hardship. In an 1880 letter to his mother, for example, he reports that in a spontaneous gesture of compassionate charity he gave away his comforter-stole to a Liverpool girl: "I blessed it and handselled it on a poor consumptive girl yesterday" (*Further Letter*, pp. 154–155). In a less well-known but fascinating case reported in detail by H. C. Sherwood, Hopkins works directly and unrelentingly as a priest to arrange a secret marriage for two of his besieged parishioners, Thomas Murphy and Mary Hennessy of Liverpool. Sherwood sees Hopkins displaying his finest qualities of "scrupulosity and compassion" as a working priest when he draws up the petition in 1881.[12]

Alfred Thomas adds to this discussion of Hopkins's individual visitings in the Liverpool district when he points out that "Hopkins never shirked his duty but carried on his priestly work in his dreadful district."[13] Thomas quotes from Hopkins's sermon "On Death" where the young curate speaks of taking Holy Communion to "filthy places . . . and worse than filthy places, dens of shame" in his role as "good shepherd going to seek the lost sheep!"[14] Of course, this Liverpool period is also significant poetically for Hopkins because he is able to draw from actual face-to-face contacts with working-class figures and turn one such experience into a fine poem about urban humanity — "Felix Randal." In his article "Hopkins's 'Felix Randal': The Man and the Poem," Alfred Thomas has convincingly demonstrated that the background of the poem is based on Hopkins's dealings with a real blacksmith named Felix Spencer in 1880. It is important to note, however, that this poem rounds to a convincing spiritual and humane harmony in strictly individualistic terms. Felix is a believable person; however, real as his basis in fact may be, he is also an idealized portrait of the Victorian Everyman in the role of happy, productive worker. Thomas admits this dimension: it was part of Hopkins's purpose that the poem would convey "the inscape of a smith at work, pride in skill which praises God, a workman's part in the commonweal, the interdependence of all mankind, and [the idea] that the true craftsman wears himself out in the service of others."[15] As a special parishioner, then, Felix the farrier is not to be taken as a typical representative of the base, "bespotted," or "downtrodden" Liverpool crowds that Hopkins fears as possibly being beyond either spiritual salvation or earthly joy.[16] Nor does Hopkins develop the point that the real Felix was a victim of pleurisy and tuberculosis at the young age of thirty-one. To what extent his unsuitable working and living conditions caused his early death is a point of investigation left unexplored in the poem. In this light Felix's exuberant spiritual transformation as captured in the closing lines "powerful amidst peers" takes on a somewhat grim irony. Thus, Thomas may not be quite accurate when he concludes that Felix's death "contains nothing for tears" (Thomas, "Hopkins's 'Felix Randal,' " p. 332).

Although between the years 1879–84 Hopkins seems to have worked best at alleviating poverty in the cities where he was sent by treating cases on an individual and direct basis, it is also true that during these years he had some direct and positive contacts with selected groups of people and even larger urban crowds. He sensed and mastered the possibilities for collective charitable action when he served as spiritual director or chaplain of his local parish's Society of St. Vincent de Paul in Liverpool. As Sjaak Zonneveld demonstrates, Hopkins took this group work seriously and the "sharp increase" in membership in 1880 "may have been partly due to the work of Hopkins."[17] The distinctions between the charitable society's membership categories are curious: on the one hand, the society's charter speaks of the great difficulty of bringing "any practical benefit to the various and numerous classes of our Catholic poor unless our means and our numbers largely increase" and on the other hand, the charter designates two distinct groups of members — "active members . . . actively at work among the poor" and "honorary members" who offered funds and prayers but did no active work and attended no meetings. The honorary members numbered twice the active members in an average year (Zonneveld, p. 111). What is striking, however, is how Catholics in general felt that the Society of St. Vincent de Paul was a vital agency to be used to ward off the demon of socialism. Zonneveld points to essays in *The Month* (August 1881) and the *Dublin Review* (April 1883) that capture this exact sentiment (Zonneveld, p. 117).

In at least three other instances between 1879–84, Hopkins is able to portray nonpolitical crowds in a favorable way. In observing assemblies of people, he can capture the line of positive energy that animates the group and admire the unity of impression or movement. One such occasion is the Corpus Christi procession through the streets of London in 1882. The scene appeals to Hopkins because it involves the ritualistic movement of religious symbolism and significance. Indeed, Hopkins offers a detailed critique of the temper of the ceremonious crowd movement: it was too slow and he would have preferred a more "brisk and joyous" pace. Still, what appeals to Hopkins is the meaning and mystery of the procession as well as the orderly, cooperative marching movement of people on urban streets (*Letters to Bridges*, pp. 148–149). In a follow-up letter Hopkins explains to Bridges the resonating significance of the cermonial march: "But the procession has more meaning and mystery than this: it represents the process of the Incarnation and the world's redemption. . . . The procession out may represent the cooperation of the angels, or of the patriarchs and prophets, the return the Church Catholic from Christ's death to the end of time" (*Letters to Bridges*, p. 149). In another letter (1882) Hopkins records the cooperative and energetic efforts of a construction crew erecting a building on the Stonyhurst College campus. The inscape of the group portrays the lively, energetic, and purposeful expenditure of human cooperative effort. He tells Bridges that the new college site is "worth seeing" because "There is always a stirring scene, contractors, builders, masons, bricklayers, carpenters, stonecutters and carvers, all on the spot" (*Letters to Bridges*, p. 151). A third favorably presented inscape of a crowd is rendered in an 1881 letter to Bridges. In a natural setting which duplicates the "heart-in-hiding" stance Hopkins took as an individual who watched in awe in "The Windhover," a group of Liverpool inhabitants gather just outside the city to witness a spectacular flock of seagulls. To overcome the shortage of food because of a deep January freeze, "throngs of people" and "the infinite flocks of seagulls" come together for a common, worthwhile purpose and act in unison to remedy a life-threatening problem: "The river was coated with dirty yellow ice from shore to shore; . . . the gulls were pampered; throngs of people were chucking them bread" (*Letters to Bridges*, p. 116). In all three of these crowd scenes – the Corpus Christi procession, the construction work, and the winter feeding — Hopkins succeeds in creating an inscape because he discovers a common line of force and positive energy.

From Febuary 1884 until his death of typhoid fever in June 1889, Hopkins served as an examiner for the Royal University and professor of Greek at University College, Dublin. P. M. Troddyn has written of the 1880s: "There was certainly a great deal of repression, and a great need for reform in Ireland then. The decade was one of the most stormy of the nineteenth century, a period of intense agitation, in particular, against the large landowners."[18] Against this larger backdrop of conflict between political factions in England and Ireland, Hopkins found it to be an increasingly complex challenge to make either artistic or political sense of a variety of crowd scenes. Inhibited by fears of social chaos and degeneration, he had difficulty focusing the elements of individualized order and distinctive beauty necessary to capture an inscape of collections of people. Yet he discussed the problems repeatedly during the turbulent 1880s.

Even within the college itself he had to confront unruly academic groups. The controversial vote and eleventh-hour stratagems that caused the "Irish row" over his appointment have been fully discussed in several articles.[19] His dual roles as examiner and teacher provided an unsettling perception of group behavior. As reported by Katharine Tynan, some students showed disrespect toward Hopkins and caused an uproar in his classroom.[20] Hopkins complained to Bridges about an unruly, "hissing" mob of students threatening to disrupt the solemnity of a college honorary degree ceremony in October 1886 (*Letters to Bridges*, p. 241).

Political rallies and even riots and demonstrations in the streets held a peculiar fascination for Hopkins during his last few years. In a remarkably candid and fluid letter to his mother dated 2 March 1885, he recreates in prose the irresistible momentum that draws his attention to a crowd gathered at a political rally in Phoenix Park, Dublin. This letter shows Hopkins's increasing preoccupation with the aesthetic and political challenge of responding to crowd scenes. His level of interest and contemplation increases as he attempts to define his reactions. He realizes quickly that his application of the stereotypical label of "monster meeting" is not an accurate response: "It was not so very monster, neither were the people excited" (*Further Letters*, p. 169). In his observation of the scene, Hopkins goes beyond an outlook prevalent in nineteenth-century poets ever since Wordsworth's labelling of the crowds assembled at St. Bartholomew's Fair as a "Parliament of Monsters" in Book VII of *The Prelude*. Yet Hopkins has two reasons for underplaying the political rally: he wants to calm his mother's fears concerning his safety in Ireland, and also to reduce the political importance (in his own mind) of the agitation.

What distresses Hopkins, however, is the apparent lack of focus to the scene. He cannot form a coherent composition of the crowd, cannot discover a single line of force or positive energy to capture an inscape because of the random competition inherent in the gathering. There are bands playing and banners fluttering simultaneously as he observes that "Boys on the skirt of the crowd made such a whistling and noise for their own amusement as must have much interfered with the hearing of the speeches." Likewise, there is a jarring juxtaposition of dress styles present: some people "were in Sunday clothes" while for others "their only suit . . . was rags" (*Further Letters*, p. 169). In the presence of a companion, Father Mallac, Hopkins turns to conversation and past history in his attempt to find a way of comprehending the "excitable" Irish before him. Fr. Mallac reports that he witnessed crowds that were unified in purpose and ordered with disciplined action in the Paris revolution of 1848 — that "there the motions of the crowd were themselves majestic and that they organized themselves as with a military instinct" (*Further Letters*, p. 170). In the next paragraph of this letter to his mother, Hopkins tries to leave the pressing scene of the Dublin crowd and turn to the intellectual abstraction of "the grief of mind" that he goes through over Irish-English politics. However, in the next paragraph he returns to his relentless analysis of the crowd's temperament because he has not settled the problem of composing it manageably in his own mind. His scrupulous rendering of its inherent and irreconcilable contradictions continues:

> I should correct what I said above about the crowd, that it was neither sad nor glad: it was, I should say, cheerful but not merry (except some drunken fellows).
> They are crying some bad news in the streets, All news is bad.
> I have no more time (*Further Letters*, p. 170).

These last two telegraphic-style paragraphs mark a curt dismissal of the problem as Hopkins gives in to a pessimistic view of public politics in the streets. He sees only dissolution and pessimism.

Donald C. Richter, in his book *Riotous Victorians*, has shown the predominant importance of demonstrations and riots amidst the "widely-held belief in the public orderliness of Victorian society." Often these disturbances were linked to the struggle for Irish national independence. Richter devotes extensive treatment to the Pall Mall Affair of 1886 and Bloody Sunday in Trafalgar Square in 1887. As Richter concludes: "Britain in the eighteeen-sixties, seventies and eighties, contrary to popular belief, was in fact a very disorderly society."[21] In fact, John Sutherland has argued that the incident of Bloody Sunday influenced Hopkins's outlook in the poem "Tom's Garland: upon the Unemployed."[22] Hopkins through his letters and through reading accounts in *The Times* kept up a sustained concern over Victorian civil disorders. A letter to A. W. M. Baillie on 11 February 1886 (just a few days after the Pall Mall demonstrations) may be cited as just one more example. Here he asks for "some on-the-spot account of the late riots, as witnessed by yourself or friends and informants, also London political gossip in general" (*Further Letters*, p. 257).

Although Hopkins was concerned with the political implications of Victorian crowds throughout his five years in Dublin, he was also preoccupied during this time period with the aesthetic challenge of how best to represent crowds in works of art. At the most fundamental level his strict conservative views regarding the proper arrangement of individuals in crowd representations may express his desire that Art serve as the supreme force of crowd control. What, then, were Hopkins's prescriptions for an inscape that would exhibit the unique line of order appropriate to an assemblage of individuals?

4

Hopkins's most extensive discussion concerning the appropriate way of composing crowd scenes is found in a letter to his brother Everard, dated 5 November 1885. The immediate occasion for the letter is Hopkins's viewing of a large (18 1/2 X 13 inches) etching by his brother that was published in the 24 October 1885 issue of the *Graphic*. The picture is entitled *Addressing the Free and Independent Electors*. From an elevated viewing stand in the upper left corner of the picture, a partially visible banner seems to proclaim the political slogan "Gladstone Forever." The scene on the floor of the hall is one of chaos: a policeman is in the process of expelling a drunkard; a determined man raises his umbrella with a threatening gesture; a man with an unkempt beard attempts to mount the speaker's podium; two women exchange concerned glances; the faces of a row of gentlemen behind a speaker's table express varying degrees of emotion, ranging from shock to indifference. On the floor chairs are arranged chaotically and one is even half-overturned (see figure 2).

Hopkins comments at great length on the subject and technique of his brother's picture and is quite specific in expressing his disappointment. He writes about his brother's failure to compose the crowd in a more orderly, dramatic moment: "As difficulties of perspective increase greatly with the scale so do those of composition. The composition will not come right of itself, it must be calculated. I see no signs of such calculation. I find it scattered and without unity, it does not look to me like a scene and one dramatic moment, the action of the persons is independent and not mutual, the groups do not seem aware of one another."[23]

After making several more specific criticisms of Everard's broadside, he offers the fascinating generalization that "Crowds have perhaps not been mastered in art yet" (Bischoff, p. 1511). Only a few good crowd scenes come to his mind. He primarily admires what he curiously labels "good simultaneous-acting crowds" such as the scene wherein Gustave Doré presents "Christ coming down the steps of the judgment hall" (Bischoff, p. 1511). He also appreciates "a fine crowd by Rembrandt" that he has seen but does not name in the letter. The reference to the Doré illustration surely refers to the successful *Doré Bible*, published in 1866

2. Everard Hopkins, *Addressing the Free and Independent Electors,* from the *Graphic,* 24 October 1885.

3. Gustave Doré, *Jesus and the Woman Taken in Adultery*, from *The Holy Bible, with Illustrations by Gustave Doré* (London: Cassell, Petter, and Galpin, 1866).

(see figure 3, for example).[24] Ira Bruce Nadel reports that most Victorian commentators praised Doré's recognizable representations of Biblical figures: "He did not romanticize place but combined new archeological knowledge with psychological realism, presenting human beings as seen by contemporary novelists or photographers. The scenes were theatrical and dramatic, however, resonating with Doré's love of *les tableaux vivants*, charades, and the theatre."[25] In his letter to Everard, Hopkins does not comment — as most Victorian art critics did — on Doré's realistic treatment of sacred stories, but instead focuses on the desirability of portraying a crowd in a position of "simultaneous" action. It takes the magnificence of a Christ-figure, a feature lacking in the ordinary Victorian political orator, to command such riveted and awestruck attention from the crowd assembled in the large hall. Christ fosters a natural and charismatic inscape: all attention is easily centered on Him as the one radiating source as He comes down the steps into the gathered assembly. It is a far greater challenge to find the principle of unity necessary for an inscape amidst a chaotic city crowd or a room full of agitated electors. It is noteworthy, too, that Hopkins makes no reference to any of Doré's illustrations from *London: A Pilgrimage* (1872). In an urban scene such as Doré depicts in *Ludgate Hill — A Block in the Street*, the only centralized focus is a somber hearse moving slowly through the traffic snarl. Although there is no record of Hopkins's reaction to this drawing, surely his opinion would have been quite negative. For, as Donald J. Gray explains the drawing, any positive features of earlier artistic compositions of London — qualities of light, space, movement, and grace — "are here suffocated in the crush of the crowd and the strong horizontal line of the viaduct and train."[26] Furthermore, as Gray points out, no one in the crowd regards the hearse, the central focus of the picture: "No one in Doré's drawing is looking at or seems to be talking to anyone else. This city is heartless as well as depressing, atomized within its crowds. . . . The figures jammed within this frame have no necessary or singular relationship to one another" (Gray, p. 51).

What specific Rembrandt painting Hopkins had in mind is difficult to determine from his brief comment in the letter to Everard.[27] If we choose paintings such as Gerrit Lundens's *Copy after the Nightwatch* or *Christ and the Woman Taken in Adultery* (figure 4), however, we can see a general principle at work. Rembrandt's crowd or group figures stand together in a significant relationship and the individuals of the group unite — due to military discipline or spiritual reverence — in a "simultaneous" action as they pay tribute or participate in a dramatic event. Art critics have pointed out Rembrandt's innovations in presenting group portraits. Of *The Night Watch* A. Bredius says: "The concept of 'marching out' makes Rembrandt's composition something of a novelty; traditionally, group portraits of the militia had shown the members either around a table or standing, full length, before or in their meeting place."[28] Other

4. Rembrandt, *Christ and the Woman Taken in Adultery*, 1644. 33" x 25 3/4."

critics have studied the influence of theatrical performances and stage movement on the work.[29] J. Bolten and H. Bolten-Rempt analyze the two crowds gathered in Rembrandt's *Christ and the Woman Taken in Adultery* and stress that "both groups show a spiritual leader with the faithful and other onlookers."[30] According to Philip Hendy, the story in the painting is "depicted with wonderful completeness. Behind, the ordinary crowd is winding up further flights of steps towards the throne of the High Priest, who in a blaze of barbaric gold is administering another form of justice."[31]

The central question embedded in these standards of artistic composition delineated by Hopkins is whether he could translate into his poems the requirements for handling crowds that he asks of painters. It is difficult to find examples of Hopkins's response to the challenge, but three poems from his Dublin years seem relevant: "Harry Ploughman," "Tom's Garland: upon the Unemployed," and "St. Alphonsus Rodriguez." But before turning to a discussion of these poems, it is useful to trace briefly the general background in which they were composed.

Hopkins was throughout his time in Ireland concerned with descriptions and representations of the Irish people in the popular press of the day. Because of these reports or political drawings and because of his own observations, he came to think and write about the Irish people in monolithic, abstract terms. In a 23 December 1885 letter to his brother Everard, Hopkins indicates the growing force of danger amidst the Irish populace: "I enclose some Irish drawings (old ones). The national papers have a coloured cartoon every week and these pictures are a power. . . . The artist is called O'Hea: he has a powerful chromo of an Irish peasant in the rebellion of 1798 at bay against an army of British redcoats and this picture like everything said or done in Ireland will go to swell the gathering and insatiable flood of hatred" (Bischoff, p. 1512). Elsewhere, Hopkins speaks apprehensively of the Irish people: "Be assured of this, that the mass of the Irish people own no allegiance to any existing law or government. . . . Their virtues do not promote civil order and it has become impossible to govern them" (*Further Letters*, p. 283).

Partly in reaction against his own stereotypical views of the Irish people, Hopkins wrote several poems in his Dublin years which attempt to present individuals pursuing purposeful work or submitting cheerfully to principles of civil or spiritual allegiance. In opposition to the "powerful chromo of an Irish peasant," Hopkins offers "Harry Ploughman," an equally powerful poem, that pictures a universally representative peasant totally devoted to his work and completely devoid of political opinion or hostile emotions. Harry represents the Irish peasantry as Hopkins would like to see them — hard at work and engaged in productive, simultaneous action. The concentration and collection of energy makes for an impressive inscape as the various parts of Harry's body work together as "one crew" (*Poems*, p. 104, l. 5). The military images further convey his subscription to a principle of allegiance:

as at a rollcall, rank
And features, in flesh, what deed he each must do—
His sinew-service where do.
He leans to it, Harry bends, look . . .

(*Poems*, p. 104, II. 9–12).

In a similar vein, "Tom's Garland" can be seen as a poem that begins as an attempt to present portraits of model urban workers who cheerfully render allegiance to king and country. Tom and sturdy Dick leave the construction site at day's end with a sense of accomplishment. Their rewards may be simple and lowly—an ingenious garland of steel nails on their boot heels, food, and shelter—but there is no reason for complaint. As Tom says,

Commonweal
Little I reck ho! lacklevel in, if all had bread:
What! Country is honour enough in all us—lordly head,
With heaven's lights high hung round, or, mother-ground
That mammocks, mighty foot.

(*Poems*, p. 103, ll. 8–12).

In the final lines of the poem, however, Hopkins offers a unique and perplexing composition of urban crowds. This dramatic moment has no equivalent in all of his poetry. Although he fails to find a line of unity to create an inscape of the dissolving image of "packs" of the "Undenizened" moving through the streets like an epidemic, he nonetheless ironically follows his criterion of presenting "simultaneous acting" crowds. What undercuts the picture he presents, of course, is the fact that the menacing crowd lacks a principle of allegiance and is thus a mob out of control. To be more precise, Hopkins ends the poem with two possible crowd options: if hunger is the motivating factor, a weary parade of despairing urban dwellers is seen—"This, by Despair, bred Hangdog dull." If, on the other hand, rage is the inspiring force behind the crowd, then the group is transmogrified into "Manwolf, worse." These dual social possibilities combine into a final, devastating image: "and their packs infest the age" (*Poems*, p. 103, l. 20). Hopkins's letter in which he explains the poem to Bridges only underscores his tendency to amass groups of passive social outcasts or agitating malcontents into a single threatening movement. In one sentence, reified troublemakers are all linked together in Hopkins's view: "And this state of things, I say, is the origin of Loafers, Tramps, Cornerboys, Roughs, Socialists and other pests of society" (*Letters to Bridges*, p. 274).

The failure to achieve an inscape at the conclusion of "Tom's Garland" probably led Hopkins to eschew any further poetic commentaries on Victorian society. His interest in presenting images of productive individuals in states of allegiance, however, did not cease. After the crowd-in-chaos image in "Tom's Garland," God is re-established as the controller of

both careers and crowds in a tightly packed image in "St. Alphonsus
Rodriguez" (1888). God directs the action and degree of challenge that
will be crowded into a devout individual's life experience:

> Yet God . . .
> Could crowd career with conquest while there went
> Those years and years by of world without event
> That in Majorca Alfonso watched the door.
>
> (*Poems*, p. 106, ll. 9, 12–14).

Alfred Thomas in his fine study *Hopkins the Jesuit* briefly mentions
that on April Fool's Day, 1873, Hopkins "delivered himself of the only
paper he is known to have read at the English Academy, 'Thoughts on
Mobs.' " He remarks that "Perhaps the day decided the subject."[32] It is
impossible to determine whether Hopkins's lost speech to the Philosophical
and Literary Society at St. Mary's Hall contained serious or comic
reflections. However, it is clear that Hopkins was fascinated with groups of
people or mythical figures, from the schoolboy "A Vision of the Mermaids," through the letters and the poetry, to the final benedictory "St.
Alphonsus Rodriguez." In these writings he distinguishes between several
types of crowds: people may be assembled for similar purposes, either
harmonious or destructive, or they may congregate randomly as their
aesthetic and ethical potentials are observed by Hopkins, the poet-priest.
Hopkins thus described other people's communal events and achievements, as well as group frustrations and disruptions of civil peace. The
composition and dynamics of crowds fascinated Hopkins over his entire
career. Because of moral, political, and aesthetic barriers, he never
developed a fully open or positive structure of response to collections of
people in his writings. Nonetheless, there are many insights to be derived
from tracing Hopkins's outlook on crowds over several decades and from
the placement of his attitudes within the larger frame of the social,
historical, and psychological experience of the Victorian City.

I am grateful to Lionel Adey, David Downes, Donald Gray, Stephen
Pulsford, Patrick Scott, and Alison Sulloway for their careful reading and
criticism of earlier versions of this paper. Several helpful suggestions for
further research were provided by Norman MacKenzie, Alfred Thomas,
and R. K. R. Thornton. Finally, I am indebted to both Richard Giles and
Norman White, the organizers of the 1984 "Hopkins in Ireland" Conference and to the American Council of Learned Societies for a travel grant
that allowed me to read an earlier version of this paper in Dublin, Ireland.
I wish to dedicate this paper to the memory of Alfred Thomas, S.J.

Notes

1. G. Robert Stange, "The Frightened Poets," in *The Victorian City: Images and
Realities*, eds. H. J. Dyos and Michael Wolff (London: Routledge and Kegan Paul, 1973), pp.

475–494. For a fuller discussion of poets and their imaginative sense of the nineteenth-century city, see William B. Thesing, *The London Muse: Victorian Poetic Responses to the City* (Athens: University of Georgia Press, 1982).

2. *The Correspondence of Gerard Manley Hopkins and Richard Watson Dixon*, ed. C. C. Abbott (New York: Oxford University Press, 1935), p. 20. Hereafter cited as *Correspondence*.

3. *The Poems of Gerard Manley Hopkins*, ed. W. H. Gardner and N. H. MacKenzie, 4th ed. (New York: Oxford University Press, 1970), pp. 66, ll. 6–7; p. 78, l. 3. Hereafter cited as *Poems*.

4. *Further Letters of Gerard Manley Hopkins*, ed. C. C. Abbott, 2d ed. (New York: Oxford University Press, 1956), p. 243. Hereafter cited as *Further Letters*.

5. *The Letters of Gerard Manley Hopkins to Robert Bridges*, ed. C. C. Abbott (New York: Oxford University Press, 1935), p. 90. Hereafter cited as *Letters to Bridges*.

6. *The Letters of Matthew Arnold to Arthur Hugh Clough*, ed. Howard Foster Lowry (New York: Oxford University Press, 1932), p. 99. See also William Sharpe, "Confronting the Unpoetical City: Arnold, Clough, and Baudelaire," *Arnoldian* 13, no. 1 (Winter 1985–86), 10–22.

7. *Correspondence*, p. 29. This phrase, "the people are hearty," is repeated in an 8 October 1879 letter to Bridges (*Letters to Bridges*, p. 90). Several weeks later, Hopkins again stresses "the charming and cheering heartiness of these Lancashire Catholics, which is so deeply comforting" (*Letters to Bridges*, p. 97).

8. Norman H. MacKenzie, *A Reader's Guide to Gerard Manley Hopkins* (Ithaca: Cornell University Press, 1981), p. 27.

9. *The Journals and Papers of Gerard Manley Hopkins*, ed. Humphry House and Graham Storey (New York: Oxford University Press, 1959), p. 139. Hereafter cited as *Journals*. For a humorous account of the diversity of the uproarious and multi-colored assembly, see *The Times*, 14 June 1866, p. 14. It is also interesting to note that *The Times* account mentions the nonpolitical nature of the gathered crowd: "A few political cries were also uttered, but no very clear indications of decided political leanings could be gathered from them" (p. 14).

10. "The Lady of Shalott," 1832 version, ll 52–54. in *The Poems of Tennyson*, ed. Christopher Ricks (London: Longmans, 1969), p. 357.

11. Jerome Bump, *Gerard Manley Hopkins* (Boston: G. K. Hall, 1982), pp. 52, 53.

12. H. C. Sherwood, "A Letter of G. M. Hopkins," *Times Literary Supplement*, 4 September 1969, p. 984.

13. Alfred Thomas, "G. M. Hopkins in Liverpool," *Times Literary Supplement*, 18 September 1969, pp. 1026–1027.

14. *The Sermons and Devotional Writings of Gerard Manley Hopkins*, ed. Christopher Devlin (New York: Oxford University Press, 1959), p. 249. See also Joseph J. Feeney's useful essay, "Hopkins' Frequent Reassignments as a Priest," *Hopkins Quarterly* 11 (Winter 1985), 101–118, which discusses the reasons for Hopkins's many relocations and mentions his ineffectiveness as a preacher before a group of parishioners: "He sometimes became confused while giving a public sermon, and he could not accurately judge the response of his audience" (p. 102).

15. Alfred Thomas, "Hopkins's 'Felix Randal': The Man and the Poem," *Times Literary Supplement*, 19 March 1971, p. 331.

16. For a fuller discussion of "Felix Randal" and Hopkins's poems about some other people, see William B. Thesing, " 'Tom's Garland' and Hopkins' Inscapes of Humanity," *Victorian Poetry* 15 (Spring 1977), 37–48.

17. Sjaak Zonneveld, "Gerard Manley Hopkins and the Society of St. Vincent de Paul in Liverpool," *Hopkins Quarterly* 9 (Fall 1982), 111.

18. P. M. Troddyn, "G. M. Hopkins: Two Unpublished Letters on Anglo-Irish Relations," *Studies: An Irish Quarterly Review* 59 (1970), 19.

19. See, for example, Norman White, "Gerard Manley Hopkins and the Irish Row," *Hopkins Quarterly* 9 (Fall 1982), 91–107; and Luisa Conti Camaiora, "Hopkins in Ireland," *Rivista di Letterature Moderne e Comparate* 31 (1978), 204–224.

20. Katharine Tynan, *Memories* (London: Eveleigh Nash, 1924), p. 156.

21. Donald C. Richter, *Riotous Victorians* (Athens: Ohio University Press, 1981), p. 163. See also chapters four and five in Patrick Brantlinger, *Bread and Circuses: Theories of Mass Culture as Social Decay* (Ithaca: Cornell University Press, 1983).

22. John Sutherland, "The Dating of 'Tom's Garland,'" *Notes and Queries* 18 (1971), 256–259.

23. Anthony Bischoff, "Hopkins's Letters to His Brother," *Times Literary Supplement,* 8 December 1972, p. 1511.

24. Doré's etching *Jesus and the Woman Taken in Adultery* seems to be a likely possibility, especially when joined in Hopkins's memory with Rembrandt's painting *Christ and the Woman Taken in Adultery.* One other reference to Doré occurs in Hopkins's writings. In a letter to his brother Arthur, dated 26 November 1888, he names no specific works, but offers an index of his familiarity with Doré: "This was Doré's weakness: he was a sketcher only; his large drawings and the engravings after his paintings (for the paintings themselves I have never seen) are the works of a sketcher sketching on a great scale." (*Further Letters*, p. 187). See John 8:3–12, for a prose account of the dramatic scene.

25. Ira B. Nadel, "Gustave Doré: English Art and London Life," in *Victorian Artists and the City: A Collection of Critical Essays,* ed. Ira B. Nadel and F. S. Schwarzbach (New York: Pergamon Press, 1980), p. 160.

26. Donald J. Gray, "Views and Sketches of London in the Nineteenth Century," in *Victorian Artists and the City,* p. 51.

27. As is the case with many paintings, our grasp of Hopkins's exact knowledge must sometimes rely on speculation until further evidence is discovered. We know, for example, that Hopkins made at least three visits to the National Gallery in London—27 June 1868, 16 February 1874, and 25 August 1874 (*Journals*, pp. 168, 241, and 257). In another context— notes on visits to the Royal Academy on 23 May and 12 June 1874—he offers a general critique of Rembrandt as "a master of scaping rather than of inscape. For vigorous rhetorical but realistic and unaffected scaping holds everything but no arch-inscape is thought of" (*Journals*, p. 245). It is useful to indicate what Rembrandts he could have seen in galleries accessible to him. The National Gallery in Trafalgar Square, London, acquired *Christ and the Woman Taken in Adultery* in 1824. The Gerrit Lundens copy of *The Militia Company of Captain Banning Cocq* (also known as *The Night Watch*) was bequeathed to the National Gallery by Rev. Thomas Halford in 1857.

28. A. Bredius, *Rembrandt: The Complete Edition of the Paintings* (New York: Phaidon, 1969), p. 584.

29. For a full discussion concerning this and many other points of composition, see E. Haverkamp-Begemann, *Rembrandt: The Nightwatch* (Princeton: Princeton University Press, 1982).

30. See J. Bolten and H. Bolten-Rempt, *The Hidden Rembrandt* (New York: Rand McNally, 1977), pp. 100–108. They also stress the realistic presentation of Christ: "Rembrandt represents Christ realistically, as a man—though a good man—standing in the midst of the people, preparing to be helpful" (p. 105). Interesting commentary on Rembrandt's problems in composing the crowd in the series of etchings *Christ Presented to the People* is also offered by Arthur M. Hind, *A Catalogue of Rembrandt's Etchings* (London: Methuen, 1923), pp. 111–112.

31. Philip Hendy, *The National Gallery, London* (London: Thames and Hudson, 1971), p. 212.

32. Alfred Thomas, *Hopkins the Jesuit: The Years of Training* (New York: Oxford University Press, 1969), pp. 121, 160.

A "Beautiful but Broken Arc"   Tom Zaniello*

> I am a Greek philosopher. . . . I shall never become a saint on my tack, no, though I lived a hundred years more. My occupations go to form such a character. I don't know how to change, and I can't make up my mind to desire to change.
>
> —Joseph Rickaby

"PROGRESSIVE SCIENCE"

Hopkins, too, was trained at Oxford to become a "Greek philosopher."[1] Perhaps, like his friend Joseph Rickaby, he couldn't change either. Like the ancient Greek philosophers, however, Hopkins, his fellow students, and later his fellow Stonyhurst Philosophers found it necessary to know science as well as philosophy. In the first place, science was news; the atomists and Darwinians saw to that. In the second place, an Oxford curriculum that included logic and the history of philosophy by definition, according to the Victorians, included science as well.

Hopkins' experience and fascination with science are a constant in his career. He remained a naturalist and amateur scientist throughout his life, as his letters to *Nature*, his journals, and his poems make clear. How he dealt with science, however, varied with his circumstances and interests. A range of attitudes towards science are apparent. At Oxford in the 1860s he saw science *as* science, a discipline with its own laws. As a priest and philosopher who returned to poetry in the 1870s, he sometimes treated science as art, the subject of poetry. And in the 1880s, even as he succeeded in publishing his own views on contemporary topics of science, he was at the same time pursuing science as a source of metaphor, science in the service of a higher calling, his philosophy and theology.

As an undergraduate Hopkins wrote two major Oxford Essays in which he demonstrated quite explicitly a sophisticated grasp of contemporary science. The first essay, "Distinguish Exactly between Deduction, Induction, Analogy, and Example," began as a routine exercise in philosophical terminology, covering material available to Oxford students in a

*From the conclusion to *Hopkins in the Age of Darwin* (Iowa City: University of Iowa Press, 1988), 130–45, 161–63.

number of commentaries, particularly those that focused on scientific method: Whewell's *History of the Inductive Sciences* (1837) and Mill's *System of Logic Ratiocinative and Inductive* (1843), for example. When Hopkins came to define "induction," he chose to illustrate a shortcut to induction called "example," in which "one or more instances are made to stand" for all possible instances. By induction, then, other instances of the same class may be assumed to resemble those instances chosen as examples. Hopkins's final paragraph cited a specific botanical example that had recently become a locus classicus in the field:

> Let us say all double roses are barren. It being impossible to reach this proposition by simple enumeration it must be formed upon a number of observed instances. But what right have we to make a proposition wider than the actual number observed? The question brings out the real nature of the inductive process and serves to put in a right light certain notions held about it in modern times. In becoming double a rose changes its generative organs into petals and we find that we are stating identical propositions: a double rose is one with an unusual number of petals: the number of petals is increased by the conversion of the stamens etc.: a rose without stamens etc. is barren.[2]

Hopkins' botanical example was actually the heart of Goethe's major contribution to early nineteenth-century science. In plant development, according to Goethe, all the parts of a flower — petals and calyx together with the sexual organs, stamen and anther — develop from the primary or primordial leaf and are all variations of the leaf. Although Goethe published "On the Metamorphosis of Plants" in 1817, a full translation by Emily M. Cox did not appear until late 1863, in the *Journal of Botany, British and Foreign*. Hopkins did have access to G. H. Lewes' popular *Life and Works of Goethe* (1855), which was in his family's library, but Lewes did not go into the botanical detail of pant morphology that was to be found only in Cox's translation:

> In those flowers whose habit is to become double, we may trace this transition through all its changes. In Roses, among perfect colored petals, others may often be seen which are contracted both in the middle and at the side. This is occasioned by a little protuberance more or less resembling a perfect anther, and in the same proportion the whole petal assumes the form of a stamen. . . .
>
> When all the stamens are changed into petals, the flower produces no seed, but if any of the stamens are developed whilst the process by which the flower becomes double is going forward, fertilization may take place.[3]

In his second essay, "The Tests of a Progressive Science," Hopkins also showed a grasp of contemporary scientific issues and an ability to place those issues in a theoretical framework. In the beginning of this short essay, Hopkins argued that one test of the development of a scientific field is whether it is inductive, that is, whether it explains "more facts": "The discovery of a new species of willow or the observation of parthenogenesis in aphids two generations longer than had before been found possible shows little progressiveness in science; on the other hand the spectral analysis by which the chemical composition of non-terrestrial masses is made out is a development of optics which cannot be called supplemental but a complete widening or alteration of its beat."[4] The second test of a progressive science is deductive, "the more exact or the more comprehensive and rational treatment of facts":

> The advance of a science in this stage is to be looked for in development of method. This means the gathering of some of its facts and laws into groups which give new starting-points and postulates. The process meant is most conspicuously seen in mathematics: thus the properties of angles given in Euclid are in trigonometry thrown together into a new conception of the angle as a measure for a wide and alien field of matter. The change of view has in fact brought within our reach facts which the prior science was too cumbrous to treat of: and this change of view is paralleled in all the sciences where we can find a link or blending between a higher and a lower.[5]

Hopkins' three examples — parthenogenesis and spectral analysis as examples of induction, a "new conception of the angle" as an example of deduction — were all topics of great interest in scientific circles during the 1850s and the 1860s.

His first example, the extended generation of aphids by nonsexual reproduction, reflected the work of Richard Owen, whose standard essay, *On Parthenogenesis* (1849), introduced the term *parthenogenesis* into English. The plant lice known as aphids, according to Owen, provided the classic example of "virgin-birth." In an authoritative manner befitting his status as the outstanding comparative anatomist of his day, he explained for the first time the facts concerning the reproductive cycle of aphids: "If the virgin progeny . . . be kept from any access to the male, each will again produce a brood of the same number of aphids: and carefully prosecuted experiments have shown that this procreation from a virgin mother will continue to the seventh, the ninth, or the eleventh generations before the spermatic virtue of the ancestral coitus has been exhausted."[6]

Additional generations of little virgin aphids did not amount to much scientific progress, in Hopkins' view. More substantial, he argued, was the spectral analysis of heavenly bodies, that is, determining the composition of their matter by analyzing the spectrum or component bands of light emitted or reflected by these bodies. Such analysis was still controversial throughout the 1860s.[7] The seminal work in spectral analysis had been accomplished in the 1850s through the collaboraton of the German scientists Gustav Kirchhoff and Robert Bunsen. Kirchhoff's landmark paper, "On the Relation between the Radiating and Absorbing Powers of Different Bodies for Light and Heat," which analyzed the chemical constitution of "the sun and fixed stars," appeared in translation in the *Philosophical Magazine* in 1860 and inaugurated a decade of controversy over the composition of the sun.[8]

Hopkins' mathematical example illustrating the "deductive" development of science is the most problematical of the three. Despite the reference to trigonometry, which Hopkins had studied, the only contemporary candidate for an "alien field of matter" is non-Euclidean geometry. This subject would certainly have provided a heady contrast to the normal Euclidean fare for Oxford undergraduates. The pangeometers, as the leading non-Euclideans were nicknamed, refused to accept Euclid's axiom on parallel lines, which states that through a given point only one line can be drawn parallel to a given line.[9] Such daring forays into a "hyperspace" where parallel lines could meet and the sum of the angles of a triangle did not have to equal 180° shook the British world of mathematics in the mid-1860s. In 1865 Arthur Cayley, Sadlerian Professor of Pure Mathematics at Cambridge University, published a modest paper in the *Philosophical Magazine*, "Note on Lobatchewsky's Imaginary Geometry," concerning one of the Russian founders of this "new," impure math. Cayley was apologetic in this very early paper on the subject, scratching his head over his lack of understanding of Lobatchewsky's proof that the sum of the angles of a triangle can, "if not in nature at least in analysis," be less than 180°.[10]

Hopkins certainly knew that trigonometry did not represent "new starting points and postulates." Only non-Euclidean geometry, with its assault on the axiom about parallel lines and its creation of spherical triangles, which did not behave as plane-surface triangles did, could be such "an alien field of matter." By the 1870s, in any case, non-Euclidean geometry had achieved general circulation and, one might add, respectability through such journals as *Nature* as well as the more broadly based *Academy*, another of Hopkins' usual reads.[11]

The Oxford Essays thus reveal an undergraduate confident in his grasp of difficult contemporary scientific problems — in brief, an understanding of science as science. Certainly Hopkins never lost this understanding. His four letters to *Nature* in the 1880s demonstrate a commendable regard for scientific observation and method. But there was another side to Hopkins and science — when he turned his science into art.

BRIGHT SUN AND BLACK BOREAS

Hopkins' poem "The Loss of the Eurydice" (1878) was his poetic response to the dramatic shipwreck of the *Eurydice*, a training ship of the Admiralty, in the English Channel just southeast of the Isle of Wight on March 24, 1878. Hopkins took both a scientific and a Catholic view of the wreck. This ship of Protestant souls was the victim of Providence in the form of such freakish weather that it foundered within minutes. A squall and snowstorm came at the ship so quickly and powerfully that it sank at once, yet one of the only two survivors testified that "the weather cleared up" almost immediately afterwards.[12]

At the time of the shipwreck, Hopkins was carrying out pastoral duties at a church in Chesterfield, in the heart of the Midlands, quite a distance from the English Channel. Yet he depicted the events with such meteorological precision that he doubtless had consulted at least one of the reports filed about the freakish weather; the weather news in the London *Times* was scanty. Because of its thoroughness the most likely candidate is W. Clement Ley's report "The Eurydice Squall," published in the April 1878 issue of *Symon's Monthly Meteorological Report*, the standard journal in its field.

Ley's document supports the precision of detail with which Hopkins describes the storm in these stanzas (5–8) from the poem:

> No Atlantic squall overwrought her
> Or rearing billow of the Biscay water:
>   Home was hard at hand
> And the blow bore from land.
>
> And you were a liar, O blue March day.
> Bright sun lanced fire in the heavenly bay;
>   But what black Boreas wrecked her? he
> Came equipped, deadly-electric,
>
> A beetling, baldbright cloud throughout England
> Riding: there did storms not mingle? and
>   Hailropes hustle and grind their
> Heavengravel? wolfsnow, worlds of it, wind there?
>
> Now Carisbrook keep goes under in gloom:
> Now it overvaults Appledurcombe;
>   Now near by Ventnor town
> It hurls, hurls off Boniface Down.[13]

The London *Times*, which Hopkins routinely read, described the squall as "a heavy bank of clouds . . . coming down from the north-west" with "a gale, accompanied by a blinding fall of snow . . . rushing from the highlands down Luccombe Chine."[14] But Ley's report contained a richer compendium of facts that more closely match Hopkins' poem. Ley believed that the squall originated in the Northumberland and Cumberland hills; with a county-by-county chart of the squall's locations on March 24, including Perry of Stonyhurst as one observer, he documented a consistent movement from the northwest and north-north-west. Hopkins was familiar with the place-names of the Isle of Wight from his sketching excursions there in the 1860s, and he presents them in stanza 7 in a northwest to southeast line, the direction of the storm as it moved from

Carisbrook Castle to the ruins of Appledurcombe House and finally to the coastal town of Ventnor at the base of Boniface Down.

Other details in stanzas 6 and 7 are corroborated by Ley's report. Ley noted that "very fine weather prevailed at 8 a.m. over nearly the whole of England" on the 24th,[15] the "blue March day" Hopkins calls a "liar." Hopkins lets the lights and darks of the "black Boreas" or north wind and the "baldbright cloud" metaphorically represent the characteristically dense, dark storm cloud with bright edges. One of Ley's Surrey observers described "an enormous black cloud like a monster balloon,"[16] while a Worcester observer described it as "resembling a white wall."[17] Ley himself, in Leicestershire, had recorded the storm "as a bank of dense white cirro-stratus" accompanied not only by hail and snow but also by violent winds and "complicated currents of air."[18]

Years later, whenever scientists took up further discussion of this remarkable meteorological event, they were always careful to praise the accuracy of Ley's analysis.[19] In the end Ley concluded that "meteorology, and not least of all, the principles of cloud observation" should "occupy a very large place in the education of seamen."[20] Certainly Hopkins would have agreed, for the moral navigation he urged upon readers of "The Loss of the Eurydice," while capable perhaps of saving "three hundred souls," would not have been able to save three hundred lives.

THE ARCHSNAKE OF THE EVOLUTIONISTS

Hopkins' prose during the early 1880s was punctuated dramatically by a number of complex images or metaphors drawn from science, in particular from natural history. When his friend Coventry Patmore stated in "Love and Poetry," an article that appeared in the St. James's Gazette in 1886, that "natural sciences are definite, because they deal with laws which are not realities but conditions of realities,"[21] Hopkins was able to agree with him. But Patmore went even further: "The greatest and perhaps the only real use of natural science is to supply similes and parables for poets and theologians."[22] Having read another article by his friend in the same newspaper, Hopkins applauded Patmore's "parable" of the carcass of a sheep found on a country lane.[12] Patmore wrote that the carcass had been "transformed into a mass of the soft, white, malodorous grubs known to anglers by the name of gentles."[24] The moral? Patmore feared that the "ordered state of England" was being transformed into the "pulsating mass of grubs" known as democracy.

However much Hopkins may have agreed with some of Patmore's reactionary politics, he expressed surprise at Patmore's absolute statements about the "real use of natural science." But in these years science did indeed come to serve Hopkins as a source of dramatic metaphors for his religious and philosophical thoughts. Thus we read of the "cleaves" of the pomegranate as selves; the serpent or the dragon as the "archsnake" or the archetypal reptilian of the evolutionists; and the "scale of being" as a scale of selves, some inclined to evil, others to Godhead.

Hopkins used the pomegranate in his meditations on St. Ignatius' *Spiritual Exercises* as a metaphor for the "infinity of possible strains of action and choice for each possible self" in this world. "God sees whole," he wrote, but "we see at best only one cleave."[26] In 1885, after his arrival in Dublin, he appended to one of his meditations this beautiful and intriguing sentence: "Of human nature the whole pomegranate fell in Adam."[27]

By the time Hopkins had devised his own audacious use of the pomegranate, that seedpod had acquired not only a Christian but also a sensual iconography. Both are no doubt related to the fruit's seediness, its "seedbed of being," in James Cotter's phrase.[28] A contemporary *Handbook of Christian Symbolism* (1865) described it thus: "The pomegranate, burst open and displaying its seeds, was accepted by early artists as the emblem of the future life, and of hope in immortality."[29] But in its sensual life the pomegranate ranged in the nineteenth century from Byron, who wrote in *Giaour* (1813) that "the young pomegranate's blossoms strew their bloom in blushes ever new," to Flaubert, who described his heroine in *Salammbô* (1886) as being "as rosy as a half-opened pomegranate."[30]

No one who has seen Rossetti's painting (1877) of Proserpine with her once-bitten pomegranate is likely to doubt its sensual associations, especially since the model was the stunning Jane Morris. Although Hopkins' affinity with some of the Pre-Raphaelites has been well documented,[31] he would not have been especially comfortable with the band of Rossetti, Morris, Burne-Jones, and Swinburne, whose conversation, as they painted the Oxford Union Debating Hall in 1857, turned to a description of Heaven as "a rose-garden full of stunners."[32] The flippancy of the Pre-Raphaelite brotherhood did not, however, keep Rossetti from attempting traditional Christian subjects. Before the image of Proserpine with her pomegranate finally emerged, Rossetti had intended to paint Jane Morris as Eve with an apple.[33]

The image of Eve brings us back to Hopkins' sentence, "Of human nature the whole pomegranate fell in Adam." That is, according to Hopkins' metaphor, the original range of choice, of our "actual" and "possible" selves, was sorely diminished with Original Sin. The compensation is of course the Incarnation or, as Hopkins wrote, the "cleave" of the "sphere of divine being" to us, the "entrance of Christ on the world."[34] It is in this context that Hopkins offered what Christopher Devlin called Hopkins' "most startling and original theological innovation."[35] Hopkins the Scotist was recycling the terms of a fifth-century heretic, Apollinaris, by distinguishing between *ensarkōsis* ("the taking of flesh") and *enanthropēsis* ("the becoming man").[36] These terms separated "the word was made flesh" and "came to dwell among us" into two orders of time, the first angelic, the second human or historic time.

Hopkins had some curious University College documentation of his

Scotist views. His old Oxford friend William Addis held a brief fellowship there in 1882. He had collaborated with one of Hopkins' current colleagues, Tom Arnold, Mrs. Humphrey Ward's father, on the *Catholic Dictionary* (third edition 1884). The *Dictionary* explained the condemnation of Apollinaris as the result of his refusal to accept that "becoming man" gave Christ a human intelligence.[37] The *Dictionary* also explained the Scotist view of the Incarnation, which Hopkins believed, that "the Word would have become man, even had there been no fall."[38]

The necessity of the Incarnation provoked another of Hopkins' striking metaphors. The satanic snake of the Garden of Eden is at once both the archetypal dragon of Revelation and, according to the evolutionists, the reptilian ancestor of all the vertebrates. In a meditation on Satan's inability to "recognize" Mary and "Christ in the flesh,"[39] which led to his refusal to serve God and his eventual Fall, Hopkins suggested that Satan was "the *kosmokratōr*, the worldwielder,"[40] who attempted to seize nature for his own purposes. Nature was nonetheless redeemed, "making it still habitable by man." Lucifer's countermaneuver made use of "the red or fiery dragon" that was the "sign that appeared in heaven," according to Revelation, chapter 12. He pulled "a third of the angels" in "his train" and "with his tail . . . swept the third part of the stars down to the earth." Hopkins concluded that as the woman is compared to the Earth in the solar system, so the dragon is to the constellation Draco, the tail of which "sweeps through 120° or a third of the sphere and which winds round the pole." P. J. Treanor, S.J., an astronomer teaching at Balliol in the 1950s, has confirmed most of Hopkins' analysis of Draco, including the possibility that the imagery of the Book of Revelation was in fact based on the position of importance that Draco held in the sky in ancient times.[41] The polestar, once the head of Draco, symbolizes Satan's attempt to establish himself with "a throne and post of vantage and so wreathing nature" in a spiral, just as his Edenic snake "wreathed himself in the Garden round the Tree of Knowledge."[42]

Hopkins carried his metaphor even further. As the "coil or spiral" is a "type of the Devil," so then is the dragon, "taken to be a reptile," a "symbol of the Devil." "So that," Hopkins argued, "if the Devil is symbolized as a snake he must be an archsnake and a dragon."[43] Dragons are almost always reptiles: "Now among the vertebrates the reptiles go near to combine the qualities of the other classes in themselves and are, I think, taken by the Evolutionists as nearest the original vertebrate stem and as the point of departure for the rest."[44] Reptiles gather "up the attributes of many creatures": they "sometimes have bat's wings," often are armored like crocodiles, sturgeons, or "lobsters and other crustacea," and display "colors like the dragonfly and other insects." This enormous variety really represents a satanic flaw. The dragon "symbolizes one who aiming at every perfection ends by being a monster, a 'fright' " — as if Satan had tried to seize the whole Chain of Being for himself.

Hopkins actually returned to the paradigm of the Great Chain of Being, refurbishing the analogy of the musical scale he had used so often in the 1860s and 1870s. As a metaphor no longer devoted strictly to inscapes or species, it came to represent for him a scale of "selves" or human "natures"[45] that is "infinite up towards the divine." The old problem that the Stonyhurst Philosophers had grappled with returned. Human nature has a "freedom of pitch" or self-determination that "is in the chooser himself and his choosing faculty."[46] God can "shift the self that lies in one to a higher, that is, better, pitch of itself; that is, to a pitch or determination of itself on the side of good." It was at this point in his meditation that Hopkins introduced the "cleaves" of the pomegranate as an additional metaphor for the "actual" and "possible" selves of human natures. With such metaphors, then, he attempted to resolve some of his most pressing theological problems.

"PAPERS, WRITINGS OR NOTEBOOKS, SKETCHES OR WHAT NOT"

In 1884 Hopkins was dispatched to Dublin to help strengthen the classics faculty of University College, whose administration had been entrusted to the Jesuits as a special project. He began a period that, although extremely difficult for him personally, brought him into a university setting of brilliant if eccentric colleagues whose scientific and theological interests complemented his own.

Nevertheless Hopkins felt out of place in Dublin. His poems attest to that feeling; bad health plagued him and Irish politics dismayed him, while more of his spectacular and quixotic exploits eventually reached legendary status within the Society. He allowed himself, so one story went, to be dragged by the heels around the lecture table by students in order to illustrate Hector's fate at Troy.[47] Others recalled that he would only lecture on material he knew would *not* be on the exams, since the extramural students were unable to attend his lectures but had to take the same exams as the attending students.[48] And, as mentioned previously, he walked out of the honorary-degree ceremony for his old friend and colleague Stephen Perry because the music played was "God Save Ireland."[49]

When his long-time Jesuit friends and colleagues donned the mask or persona of Plures to write their short biography of him for the *Dublin Review* in 1920, they were goaded to their task by what they felt were Bridges' unwarranted criticisms of Hopkins' relationship with the Society of Jesus. Bridges, they wrote, was "under the delusion . . . that Gerard caged himself in a religious prison amid the political Yahoos and clerics of Dublin like some bright plumaged songster in a bat-tenanted belfry."[50] His "terrible sonnets," as a number of his Dublin poems have come to be known, did reveal a wrestling match with his own soul: "Not, I'll not, carrion comfort, Despair, not feast on thee."[51] Plures' task was to add the perspective of Jesuit friends and colleagues "to the beautiful but broken arc" that Bridges had only begun to describe.[52] Plures saw Hopkins' final Dublin years as a "tragedy," but only because sending this "English mystic compounded of Benjamin Jowett and Duns Scotus" into Ireland was to "launch him into a further and stranger country" than if he had been sent to China.[53]

Yet Hopkins persisted in his philosophical quest for answers on his own terms. He really did resemble Joseph Rickaby, who wrote in his diary of his reluctance or perhaps inability to change. Plures said of Hopkins that "the obvious he avoided like sin."[54] Ruskin said of himself, in Fors Clavigera, that he had "the balanced union of artistic sensibility with scientific faculty, which enabled [him] to love Giotto, and learn from Galileo."[55] To remains true to such a union Ruskin may have gone insane. Hopkins' eccentric ways may have been a somewhat smaller price to pay.

When Hopkins was at Stonyhurst, a porter had noticed him staring at brightly colored objects in the path. This "eccentricity" and "simple-mindedness" soon passed into Jesuit legend as the marks of Hopkins' "whimsical genius." And perhaps this is an accurate assessment. But what of a University College professor who opened his lectures on spherical trigonometry by peeling a potato for his class and cutting it into sections? That is precisely what John Casey, Hopkins' colleague and a mathematics professor, did on the first day of classes in 1884: "We sat round him in a cluster," Father Darlington, then a University College student, reported, "and the first thing he did was to bring out of his pocket a potato with a knife, and he commenced operations by cutting it into cubes."[56] And Casey was supposedly a sophisticated mathematician!

Casey and Morgan Crofton were the mathematical stars of the University College faculty. Both men were fellows of the Royal Society, both wrote numerous scientific papers, and both were capable of intro-ducing their broader views of spiritual life into that seemingly absolute realm of numbers. Casey had the reputation of being an excellent teacher; perhaps he was simply better with a paring knife. He believed that all first-rate mathematicians were believers in God; he told Father Darlington, "If ever I came across one who was not, I knew that he was a second-rater, and I was never deceived."[57]

Crofton, when he came to sum up his ideas on probability for the ninth edition of the Encyclopedia Britannica in 1885, wrote of Newman's Grammar of Assent as he explained the differences between mathematical and "common" definitions of "certainty": "It is very difficult and often impossible, as is pointed out in the celebrated Grammar of Assent, to draw out the grounds on which the human mind in each case yields the conviction, or assent, which, according to Newman, admits of no degrees, and either is entire or is not at all."[58] Perhaps it was appropriate to quote Newman here, for philosophical if not sentimental reasons. Like Hopkins, Crofton had been received into the Church by Newman himself, albeit a decade earlier, in the 1850s. But what is of special interest is Crofton's gloss on Newman, a quotation from the astronomer Herschel that appeared in the *Edinburgh Review* (1850): "There is a sort of *leap* which most men make from a high probability to absolute assurance . . . analogous to the sudden consilience, or springing into one, of the two images seen by binocular vision, when gradually brought within a certain proximity."[59] Here again is science used as metaphor, but this time by a nationally known scientist.

Hopkins' letters from Dublin during his last years are strewn with various projects, scientific and otherwise, that he never finished. He wrote about placing "music and meter . . . on a scientific footing which will be final like the law of gravitation";[60] it was this project for which he told Bridges that he would need "new words, without which there can be no new science."[61] He wrote to Dixon about a "popular account of Light and Ether,"[62] and still later mentioned a paper called "Statistics and Free Will,"[63] surely a topic only a Galton could master, although his viewpoint would not have been Hopkins'. And while these projects continued or, more likely, faltered, he was corresponding with others about Egyptian etymology[64] and Chinese music.[65] We see a mind churning with ideas, venting theories in letter after letter.

His early death in Dublin at age forty-four was indeed tragic, the destruction of so many of his personal papers in a whirlwind cleanup of his room very sad. The unpublished letters to his parents from his brothers, Arthur and Everard, are also poignant. Everard hoped that Father Wheeler, the Jesuit in charge of household tasks in Dublin, would give Hopkins' parents "his papers — his poems among them," as well as "a little rosary" Everard sent him at Christmas.[66] Arthur wrote similarly, but with more detail: "I have only a few minutes to catch the post, but I write to remind you in case it may not have occurred to you, that before you leave Dublin it would be worth while to ask Father Wheeler for leave to look into any papers, writings or notebooks, sketches or what not that Gerard may have left. Probably they would be allowed to pass into your possession."[67] Arthur added that he believed that Gerard had "kept a Diary," and that "if there are any little Devotional Books," his wife "would much like to have one."

But Father Wheeler burned most of the papers and "what not," reserving only the poems to send to Robert Bridges. What other papers in Hopkins' hand remain from this period are either letters that he had sent or the results of the foraging expeditions of other Jesuits in his residence who wished to save something of their eccentric colleague.

But if Hopkins was whimsical, eccentric, and original in his ways, he was no more so than many of his contemporaries within the Jesuit order. We have already looked briefly at some of his colleagues in Dublin. What of his old friends and the Stonyhurst Philosophers who survived him? Henry Marchant, for example, lived out his retirement at Stonyhurst,[68] having published only two articles, one on weather reporting, the other on hypnotism. His room was filled with boxes of newspapers, magazines, books, old clothing, and bits of furniture, an arrangement that reminded the younger Jesuits there of the Roman catacombs. Still, those younger Jesuits came to him for instruction and advice because he kept up with the latest theories in physical science as well as speculations about the relationship of faith and science. He wrote but did not publish essays on the importance of radium as a paradigm of energy and the equivalence of energy and life.[69]

Two of the men who signed themselves "Plures" had distinguished careers as Catholic writers, but they too came to be regarded as eccentrics. The same young Jesuits who visited Marchant's room at Stonyhurst also attended John Rickaby's classes in ethics, where they were not "surprized when something of St. Thomas Aquinas or Suarez was illustrated by a quotation from Lewis Carroll or an old *Punch* joke." He was particularly known as a perpetrator of "atrocious puns."[70] Another Stonyhurst College student reminisced about his brother, Joseph Rickaby, known as a "brilliant, lively and eccentric man of the old school."[71]

Marchant died in 1937 at age eighty-nine, John Rickaby in 1927 at eighty, and Joseph Rickaby in 1932 at eighty-seven. Hopkins died almost forty years before his Stonyhurst friends. His poetry made the journey to the twentieth century; he did not. His contemporaries saw his life as a "beautiful but broken arc"; they based their image on many of his views and activities that have been obscured over the years. That their image, together with the figure of Hopkins in this book, should be regarded as a new portrait of Hopkins is really an accident of literary history. In fact, as I hope is obvious by now, it is really an old portrait.

Notes

1. Joseph Rickaby, diary, June 1–8, 1887, manuscript 47/8/7. archives, English Province of the Society of Jesus, Farm Street, London, England.

2. Gerard Manley Hopkins, manuscript, D.IX.1., Campion Hall, Oxford, England.

3. J. W. von Goethe, "Essay on the Metamorphosis of Plants," trans. Emily M. Cox, ed. Maxwell T. Masters, *Journal of Botany, British and Foreign* 1 (November and December 1863): 338–339.

4. Hopkins, manuscript, D.IX.2.

5. Hopkins, manuscript, D.IX.2.

6. Richard Owen, *On Parthenogenesis, Or the Successive Production of Procreating Individuals from a Single Ovum* (London: John Van Voorst, 1849), 23–24.

7. A. J. Meadows, *Science and Controversy: A Biography of Sir Norman Lockyer* (Cambridge: MIT Press, 1972), 47–51.

8. G. Kirchhoff, "On the Relation between the Radiating and Absorbing Powers of Different Bodies for Light and Heat," trans. F. Guthrie, *The Philosophical Magazine* 20 (July 1860): 20.

9. George Bruce Halsted, "Bibliography of Hyper-Space and Non-Euclidean Geome-

try," *American Journal of Mathematics* 1 (1878): passim.

10. Arthur Cayley, "Note on Lobatschewsky's *Imaginary Geometry*," *Philosophical Magazine* 29 (March 1865): 232.

11. See Hermann Ludwig Ferdinand von Helmholtz, "The Axioms of Geometry," *The Academy*, 12 Feb. 1870, 128–131, and Bernard Reimann, "On the Hypotheses Which Lie at the Bases of Geometry," trans. W. K. Clifford, *Nature*, 1 May 1873, 36–37.

12. "Loss of H. M. S. *Eurydice*, with Three Hundred Seamen," *Illustrated London News*, 30 March 1878, 298.

13. Gerard Manley Hopkins, *Poems*, 4th ed., ed. W. H. Gardner and N. H. Mackenzie (London: Oxford University Press, 1967), 72–73.

14. Norman Weyand, ed., *Immortal Diamond: Studies in Gerard Manley Hopkins*, (New York: Sheed and Ward, 1949), 382. Originally appeared in the London *Times*, 26 March 1878.

15. W. Clement Ley, "The Eurydice Squall," *Symon's Monthly Meteorological Magazine* (April 1878): 33.

16. Ibid., 34.

17. Ibid.

18. Ibid.

19. Ralph Abercromby, "On the Origin and Course of the Squall which Capsized H. M. S. 'Eurydice,' March 24th, 1878" *Quarterly Journal of the Meteorological Society* 10 (July 1884): 172.

20. W. Clement Ley, "Squalls," *Nature*, 7 June 1883, 133.

21. Coventry Patmore, *Principle in Art, Etc.*, 2d ed. (London: George Bell, 1890), 74.

22. Ibid.

23. Gerard Manley Hopkins, *Further Letters of Gerard Manley Hopkins Including His Correspondence with Coventry Patmore*, 2d ed., ed. Claude Colleer Abbott (London: Oxford University Press, 1956), 381.

24. Patmore, 217.

25. Gerard Manley Hopkins, *The Sermons and Devotional Writings of Gerard Manley Hopkins*, ed. Christopher Devlin (London: Oxford University Press, 1959), 151.

26. Ibid.

27. Ibid., 171.

28. James Finn Cotter, *Inscape* (Pittsburgh: University of Pittsburgh Press, 1972), 45.

29. W. and G. Audsley, *Handbook of Christian Symbolism* (London: Day and Son, 1865), 144.

30. The Byron and Flaubert quotations are both from the OED.

31. See Jerome Bump, *Gerard Manley Hopkins* (Boston: Twayne, 1982).

32. John Christian, *The Pre-Raphaelites in Oxford* (Oxford: Ashmolean Museum, 1974), 37.

33. Virginia Surtees, *The Paintings and Drawings of Dante Gabriel Rossetti (1828–1880): A Catalogue Raisonne* (Oxford: Clarendon Press, 1971), 131 n. 3.

34. Hopkins, *Sermons*, 171.

35. Ibid., 114.

36. Ibid., 171. See also Tom Arnold and William Addis, *A Catholic Dictionary* (1884), 6th ed. (New York: Catholic Publication Society, 1889), 437, for contemporary definitions of these terms.

37. Arnold and Addis, 39.

38. Ibid., 751.

39. Hopkins, *Sermons*, 198.

40. Ibid.

41. Ibid., 307–8.

42. Ibid., 198.

43. Ibid.

44. Ibid., 199.

45. Ibid., 146–47.

46. Ibid., 149.

47. Michael Tierney, ed., *Struggle with Fortune: A Miscellany for the Centenary of the Catholic University of Ireland, 1854–1954* (Dublin: Brone and Nolan, 1954), 32–33; Frederick Page et al., "Father Gerard Hopkins," *Dublin Review* 167 (July–Aug.–Sept. 1920): 53.

48. Eleanor Ruggles, *Gerard Manley Hopkins: A Life* (New York: Norton, 1944), 242–43; Page, 52–53.

49. G. F. Lahey, *Gerard Manley Hopkins* (London: Oxford University Press, 1930), 142; Page, 55–56.

50. Page, 47.

51. Hopkins, *Poems*, 99.

52. Page, 47.

53. Ibid., 52.

54. Ibid.

55. John Ruskin, *The Works of John Ruskin*, 35 vols., ed. E. T. Cook and A. Wedderburn (London: George Allen, 1903–1912), XXVIII: 647.

56. Fathers of the Society of Jesus, eds., *A Page of Irish History: Story of University College, Dublin, 1883–1909* (Dublin and Cork: Talbot Press, 1930), 85.

57. Ibid., 88.

58. M. W. Crofton, "Probability," *Encyclopedia Britannica*, 9th ed., (1891), 768.

59. Ibid., 768 n. 1.

60. Hopkins, *Further Letters*, 377.

61. Gerard Manley Hopkins, *The Letters of Gerard Manley Hopkins to Robert Bridges*, ed. Claude Colleer Abbott, 2d. ed. (London: Oxford University Press, 1955), 254.

62. Gerard Manley Hopkins, *The Correspondence of Gerard Manley Hopkins and Richard Watson Dixon*, ed. Claude Colleer Abbott, 2d ed. (London: Oxford University Press, 1955), 139.

63. Hopkins, *Letters to Bridges*, 292, 294.

64. See Hopkins, *Further Letters*, 257–73.

65. Clement Barraud, "Reminiscences of Father Gerard Hopkins," *Month* (July 1919): 158–59.

66. Everard Hopkins, manuscript letter, c. June 1889, Ms. Eng. Misc. a.8, fol. 82, Department of Western Manuscripts, Bodleian Library, Oxford University.

67. Arthur Hopkins, manuscript letter, 11 June 1889, Ms. Eng. Misc. a.8, fol. 82, Department of Western Manuscripts, Bodleian Library, Oxford University.

68. Denis Meadows, *Obedient Men* (London: Longmans, 1955), 160.

69. Henry Marchant, unpublished essays, "Life and Energy," "Radium and Life: A Dialogue between X and Y," and "James Clerk Maxwell . . . His Life and Character," Archives, English Province of the Society of Jesus, Farm Street, London.

70. Denis Meadows, 198.

71. McDonald Hasting, *Jesuit Child* (New York: St. Martin's Press, 1971), 411.

Hopkins and the Jesuits

The Jesuit Recognition of
Hopkins, 1889–1989

Joseph J. Feeney, S.J.*

None of his obituaries mention that Gerard Manley Hopkins was a poet. Reporting his death in Dublin on 8 June 1889, the *Nation* of Dublin saw him as a "profound classical scholar" and "discriminating art critic" who, as a professor at University College, "aimed at culture as well as the spread of the facts of philology."[1] The *Freeman's Journal* noted a "grace of character and a depth and range of knowledge which made him a special favourite with his students and his fellow professors."[2] The *Irish Times* (after misspelling his name) described him only as a "distinguished Jesuit," and in reporting his funeral the *Freeman's Journal* called him "the distinguished Jesuit and scholar."[3]

In England Hopkins's obituary appeared in the *Tablet* of 15 June 1889. Under the subtitle "Death of Rev. Gerard Hopkins, S.J.," the weekly noted his "distinguished career" at Balliol under Jowett, and memorialized him as a classicist himself and a colleague of Ireland's finest classicists. He was also celebrated for "his amiable and childlike disposition, his simple straightforward character, his considerateness for others and readiness to make allowances for all short-comings."[4] But again no mention of his poetry. Even an old school friend — Hopkins had visited him shortly before his death — memorialized him simply as "Professor of Classical Literature at the University College, Dublin, and Fellow of the Royal University of Ireland." Recalling their schooldays in an obituary for the Highgate School, this friend remembered Hopkins with clarity and affection and praised him as an extraordinary youth. He praised Hopkins's "refinement of intellect," "elegance of scholarship," and "rare power of attracting others to himself . . . and of drawing forth from those to whom he has given his confidence all that there is of the good and noble in their natures."[5] But in the course of an ample and generous obituary he, too, made no mention of Hopkins as poet.

It should be no surprise, then, that Hopkins's earliest Jesuit tributes were similarly silent about his poetry. Rather, seeing Hopkins as a person,

---

*This essay was written specifically for this volume and is published here for the first time by permission of the author.

a friend, a priest, and a Jesuit, they recalled his moral character, his academic talent, his Oxford conversion, his brilliance as a classicist, and his interest in art, music, and literature. During his life few Jesuits even thought of him as a poet; some remembered his avocation as sketching rather than writing. Yet not long after his death the Jesuits began to recognize him as a poet, published his few available poems, and in 1909 even tried — unsuccessfully — to edit his poems for publication. Well before Robert Bridges's edition of *Poems* in 1918, some English and Irish Jesuits had tried to make him better known, and in 1919 *Poems* was widely reviewed in Jesuit circles in England, Ireland, and the United States (some reviews were favorable, some not). In subsequent decades Jesuit writers unearthed bits of biography, and Jesuit scholars, though rarely initiating new approaches, kept pace with contemporary scholarship. Now, of course, as a major centennial nears, Hopkins is celebrated by Jesuits worldwide for both his poetry and his person. It is interesting — and in a way touching — to trace this pattern of gradual discovery: how his Jesuit contemporaries saw him first as friend and classicist, then as poet with attendant strangenesses, and finally as brilliant ornament to the Society of Jesus.

1889-1908: FROM FRIEND TO POET

Three days after Hopkins's death in Dublin, the Jesuits paid him their first tribute: presence at his funeral. From University College and Milltown Park, from Belvedere and Clongowes Wood, twenty-nine Jesuits (led by the Provincial of the Irish Province) assembled at the Church of Saint Francis Xavier in Upper Gardiner Street for the Office of the Dead and a Solemn High Mass of Requiem. Hopkins's mother and father were present, together with many clergymen, professors and students of University College, and other mourners; indeed, according to the *Freeman's Journal*, "the funeral cortege was of very large dimensions."[6]

The next Jesuit action, however, was less carefully considered, and resulted in the destruction of some Hopkins papers. About a week after the poet's death, Robert Bridges, Hopkins's fellow poet and friend from Oxford days, wrote to one Dublin Jesuit to ask for the return of his own letters to Hopkins. In response Thomas Wheeler, S.J., the Jesuit administrator ("Minister") who had attended Hopkins in his illness, promised to return these letters; presumably he soon forwarded them to Bridges. Over four months later (on 27 October 1889), apparently in response to a further request for Hopkins's papers, Wheeler explained to Bridges the disposition of Hopkins's papers after his death:

> F[ather] Hopkins had a presentiment that he would not recover — but I am sure he took no measure to arrange his papers, and gave no instructions about preserving or destroying them. Any suggestion to that effect would be made to me — and he never broached the subject at

all. . . . So I cannot fancy what he would have wished to be done with them. As for myself I looked in a hurried way through his papers but cannot say that I read any of them. Letters which I recognised by your writing or initials I set apart to forward. Many others I destroyed: and when I learned your wish to sift these writings in view to publication or selection I gathered them together indiscriminately and sent them to be used by you or his parents, at your discretion. From the bent of F. Gerards [sic] mind and work I should think he would have been glad to leave something permanent in literature or art, and I was much surprised to see how little he left in the way of sketches or drawings. Some of the poetry contained in the Mss. volume I read with admiration.

His conclusion was honest but unhelpful—"You see how little help I can give regarding F. Gerard's wishes"—and he then referred Bridges to a London Jesuit for possible further information.[7]

"Many others I destroyed": the destruction of any Hopkins manuscript was surely lamentable. But one of Wheeler's comments—"I should think he would have been glad to leave something permanent in literature *or art*"—indicates that, like other friends and Jesuits, he too (though he had read some poems in manuscript) had no sense of Hopkins's originality or importance *as poet.* This is confirmed by Wheeler's surprise at "how little he left in the way of *sketches or drawings.*" The burning of any Hopkins manuscript or sketch is, of course, a horror, but Wheeler's lack of knowledge makes his action at least comprehensible. And, it must be remembered, Bridges himself probably destroyed his own letters to Hopkins (they have never been located) and also most likely burned (with the approval of Hopkins's sister) what he judged a "bundle of what is practically worthless" among Hopkins's papers.[8]

Furthermore, the Jesuits still retained some Hopkins manuscripts. Despite Bridges's attempt to collect all of Hopkins's papers into his hands or those of the Hopkins family, a "great number" still remained with the Irish Jesuits or had been sent to the Jesuits in London. There was no systematic effort to collect these papers together until 1909 when Joseph Keating, S.J., in London, systematically tried to bring all the remnants together into one place.[9] This effort resulted, as will be seen, in an early and important series of essays on Hopkins.

In any case, soon after Hopkins's funeral in 1889 the Jesuits began to compose written tributes for their fellow Jesuit whom few knew as a poet. First came a short Latin epitaph, apparently anonymous but actually written by Arthur Knight, S.J., Assistant ("Socius") to the English Provincial. It stands in an official book of records, the English Province's "Register" of Jesuits, and ends a list of the major events of Hopkins's life. Written with no expectation that it would ever be read (the epitaphs seem a hobby for Knight), Hopkins's epitaph reads, "Mens illi subtilissima quae corporis fragiles vires nimis cito contrivit" ("His was a most subtle mind which too quickly wore out the fragile strength of his body").[10] This tribute, in its gentle understanding, shows a keen knowledge of Hopkins, recognizing both his devotion to Scotus (traditionally called the "*Doctor Subtilis*") and his frequent exhaustion from intellectual work. His poetry, though, again goes unmentioned.

The next Jesuit tribute, published nine months after Hopkins's death, was the English Province's formal obituary which appeared in the Province's journal, *Letters and Notices*. These obituaries, traditionally realistic and frank in their judgments, summarize a Jesuit's life and work, and evaluate him from diverse perspectives. In Hopkins's case the essay notes his talents—in drawing, singing, classics, and criticism (of both art and poetry)—and his multiple interests: music, art, archeology, architecture, literature, and religion. But most of the obituary (it runs about 2400 words) contains reflections on his character and personality; it was written by former associates and friends—two Jesuits and two laymen—and redacted by the Jesuit editor of *Letters and Notices*.

The Jesuits' recollections, reflecting the period from 1874 to about 1879–80, look on him as friend and priest, and emphasize his sensitivity, gentleness, compassion, originality, and sometimes eccentric brilliance, without any mention of his poetry. "I shall always have a grateful and affectionate remembrance of him," wrote one of these anonymous Jesuits; "what struck me most . . . was his child-like guilelessness and simplicity, his gentleness, tender-heartedness, and his loving compassion for the young, the weak, the poor, and all who were in any trouble or distress." After mentioning his devotion to purity of heart and body, his contemporary wrote, "Of his ability I need scarcely speak. He had a distinct dash of genius. His opinions of any subject in Heaven and earth were always worth listening to and always fresh and original—quaint sometimes and peculiar, but invariably with some basis for what appeared eccentric." Such sensitivity and intellectual independence caused him to suffer much, yet in "his personal holiness . . . he willingly and joyfully carried the Cross." The other Jesuit noted that "his mind was of too delicate a texture to grapple with the rougher elements of human life, but his kindness of heart and unselfishness showed themselves in a thousand ways." This man also commemorated "the high order of his intellect" and, though "of a somewhat impractical turn," its "various and often amusing extravagations . . . only added another point of attractiveness to his character." His conclusion, given the frankness of these obituaries, showed a clear affection for his deceased Jesuit brother: "The result of all was a man so loveable that we shall not soon look upon his like again." Neither the Jesuits nor the laymen made any mention of Hopkins's poetry, and, with unintended irony, one layman, a contemporary from Oxford, concluded, "If he had not been the victim of a lengthened and overwrought critical education, . . . Hopkins had all the elements of an eminent . . . literary man."[11] At the time of his death, it is clear, Hopkins's friends did not think of or remember him as a poet; indeed, only five minor poems had been published during his lifetime.[12]

Yet a few Jesuits did know some poems. The editors of the *Month* (one was an old friend of Hopkins) had read, evaluated, and rejected *The Wreck of the Deutschland* in 1876 and "The Loss of the *Eurydice*" in 1878. The community of St. Beuno's College heard "The Silver Jubilee" sung there in 1876, and in 1878 and 1883 the Jesuit authorities and (in 1883) the whole community of Stonyhurst knew about "The May Magnificat" and "The Blessed Virgin compared to the Air we Breathe."[13] Hopkins also showed some poems to two of his Jesuit contemporaries: Cyprian Splaine, S.J., had read "The Wreck" and "perhaps other poems of mine," had "shewed" the ode "to others," but ultimately "found it unreadable"; more happily, Francis Bacon, S.J., "saw all" (at least up to 1884) "and expressed a strong admiration for them which was certainly sincere."[14] In his Dublin years Hopkins wrote the sonnet "In honour of St Alphonsus Rodriguez" for publication (he planned to send it to Majorca for the new saint's first feastday), and Hopkins's friend, the journalist Matthew Russell, S.J., introduced him to the Irish poet Katharine Tynan.[15] It was Russell, too, who in 1898 first published Hopkins's "Rosa Mystica" in the *Irish Monthly* which he edited.[16] Some Jesuits, then, had known his "occasional pieces" and a few others had seen (and Bacon had deeply admired) his finer and more original pieces. Yet Hopkins, in a letter to Bridges in 1884, wrote an accurate evaluation: after enumerating the few people to whom he had shown his poems, he concluded that the poems "are therefore, one may say, unknown." Most of Hopkins's fellow Jesuits simply did not know the poems, and Hopkins thus defended the Jesuits to Bridges: "Our society cannot be blamed for not valuing what it never knew of."[17]

During this period most of Hopkins's poetic manuscripts were in the hands of his family or of his friend Robert Bridges, and only bit by bit did Bridges release them to anthologies. Eleven poems (with an introductory memoir by Bridges) appeared in 1893 in *The Poets and the Poetry of the Century* (volume 8) and five more were printed in 1895 in *Lyra Sacra: A Book of Religious Verse*; the English Jesuits also published "Ad Mariam" in 1890 and 1894 in journals of very limited circulation, and a few individual poems appeared elsewhere.[18] In 1906–07 the Jesuits, most likely stimulated by the interest created by the anthologized poems, published (for the first time) about thirty pages of extracts from Hopkins's journals, mainly about nature. Appearing in *Letters and Notices,* the notes followed a brief memoir that described Hopkins as "a man of a very original cast of mind, of very marked character, and of quaint and somewhat extravagant poetic fancy." It was often difficult "to understand the line of his thought or the play of [his] imagination," wrote the editor, and "he himself in his turn was inclined to be suspicious of and to misinterpret what was passing through the minds of others." His deep originality was manifest, but in earlier days this originality, combined with his "lengthened and overwrought critical education," sometimes "gave a character of undue strain and excess to the criticisms which he passed on the persons with whom he came in contact, as well as on the different objects he observed in nature." In death, though, he left "a grateful and affectionate remembrance."[19] This first publication of some "Journal" pages in 1906 indicates development in the Jesuits' knowledge of Hopkins: they knew a few poems, had started to collect some manuscripts, and were just beginning to recognize Hopkins as a poet and writer.

1909 to 1918: FROM THE *MONTH* ESSAYS TO *POEMS*

The first significant Jesuit recognition of Hopkins came in 1909 in a remarkable series of three essays in the *Month*. Entitled "Impressions of Father Gerard Hopkins, S.J.," they were written by Joseph Keating, S.J., an extraordinary but little-known man in Hopkins studies.[20] Even more important was Keating's attempt, some months earlier in 1909, to collect together all the Hopkins manuscripts and to edit and publish Hopkins's poems. Had he succeeded, readers would have known Hopkins's poetry almost a decade before Robert Bridges's edition of *Poems* was published in 1918.

In 1909 Keating made "the first systematic attempt to bring all the [other] remains together. . . . He searched widely and brought all that could be found into his own hands. The result of his work was the valuable series of articles in the *Month*. Since then further material . . . reached him from Dublin and other parts of Ireland."[21] Many scattered papers were thus brought together into one collection (now kept at the Jesuits' Campion Hall in Oxford).[22] But many of Hopkins's letters and poetic manuscripts were also in the hands of Bridges and of the Hopkins family.

In 1909, Keating, acting on behalf of the English Province, tried to obtain from Hopkins's family the right to publish the poems. But Bridges, prejudiced against Catholics and especially antipathetic and distrustful toward Jesuits, urged Hopkins's mother not even to tell the Jesuits that she had copies of the poems. On 7 May 1909 he wrote Mrs. Hopkins, "If [Father Keating] finds out that you have a copy of all the poems he may bother you. . . . I do not think that Gerard wd. have wished his poems to be edited by a committee of those fellows. In any case you will no doubt write me before taking any steps. I have not mentioned your name to Rev. K." In practice Bridges was to decide what the Hopkins family should do and, both determined to edit Hopkins's poems himself (as an act of friendship) and angry about what he saw as the Jesuits' lack of interest in Hopkins, he effectively prevented any Jesuit edition of the poems, thus postponing their publication until 1918.[23] Legally there was a question about precisely who owned the rights to publication,[24] but one may ask if Bridges was totally fair in discerning a Jesuit lack of interest. Bridges had seen — and was in possession of — almost all of Hopkins's poems, while few

Jesuits, except for Francis Bacon, S.J., had seen or even known about the extent and importance of his work.

In any case Keating, frustrated in his attempts to publish the poems, decided at least to prepare a series of three substantial essays on Hopkins. Appearing in the July, August, and September 1909 issues of the Jesuit journal the *Month*, the essays described Hopkins's growing reputation as a poet and referred readers to the anthologies that included his work. In a discreet sentence Keating touched on the question of a new edition — "The time has now come for Father Hopkins' poems to appear in a collected form" — and immediately added a motive that would surely have irritated Bridges — "as a distinct and valuable addition to the literary heritage of the Catholic Church."[25] Then after referring readers to a recent American essay for a literary appreciation,[26] Keating announced his own aim: to present "the personality of the man." And though Keating himself had known Hopkins, he preferred to draw his material from Hopkins's "friends' letters to him" (60) — mainly letters from H. P. Liddon, John Henry Newman, R. W. Dixon, and Coventry Patmore. While concentrating on Hopkins's conversion and his literary views, Keating noted various personality traits — courage, a spirit of sacrifice, generosity, affectionate friendship, unwillingness to publish, interest in music, tolerance of criticism (while always defending his poems), and breadth of sympathy. Keating was generous to Bridges, frequently mentioning both his friendship with Hopkins and his work in making Hopkins better known. In his last sentence Keating returned once again to the publication of Hopkins's poems, obliquely recording his disappointment at being denied permission: "In view of the impression which [the poems] made on men . . . of such ability, we venture to repeat that it would be sad if his poems were finally left to the obscurity of anthologies" (258).

In attempting to edit the poems and in writing and publishing these essays, Keating became the first Jesuit to offer a significant tribute (and perform a valuable service) to Hopkins the poet. Gracious to Bridges, Keating was even more gracious and generous to Hopkins, for "his articles," wrote a later critic, "made Hopkins known to a fairly wide Roman Catholic circle."[27]

Keating made other contributions to Hopkins studies. He confirmed Hopkins's authorship of "Ad Mariam"[28] and years later helped Humphry House in editing Hopkins's notebooks and papers. "My debts," wrote House, "are immense to Fr. Keating and Mr. Gerard Hopkins [the poet's nephew], who have made the book possible, and have also given their personal help and advice at every stage." Indeed, "the collection of . . . [Hopkins's] MSS. . . . had been made by Fr. Joseph Keating . . . [and] is the basis of this book."[29] In all this work Keating, despite his comment in the *Month* about "the literary heritage of the Catholic Church," was neither sectarian nor narrow in his approach; indeed, he came close to the status of a literary scholar and textual editor. Thus, for his important roles as collector, conservator, would-be editor, and essayist, Joseph Keating, S.J., was the first significant Jesuit — even an early hero — in Hopkins studies. And he was to do yet more.

In 1910 a brief mention of Hopkins in *Letters and Notices* named him as one of the "distinguished novices" at Roehampton.[30] More important, in 1912 the *Month* again raised the question of publication as an anonymous book reviewer asked, "What of . . . Gerard Hopkins? . . . Here is a writer emancipated from time and tradition. Here is a Prophet, a Martyr, and an Apostle who is at the same time a Poet — and which of us has the chance of reading him? Many of his poems survive in MS., are, in fact, in the careful and reverent keeping of another poet, Mr. Robert Bridges, and ultimately, we trust, are destined to see the light."[31] Then in the *Month* of June 1913 Keating rejoiced that "there seems at last some prospect" of the publication of Hopkins's poems and wrote about his careful poetic craftsmanship. Working from an early manuscript of "Rosa Mystica," Keating remarks (though without specific examples) that "besides many changes of word and phrase, there are two versions of the fifth stanza and three of the sixth." He also mentions variations between the manuscript and printed versions of "The Habit of Perfection" and "Winter with the Gulf Stream," and republishes a few stanzas of the latter to illustrate "Father Hopkins' keen sense of colour." Turning finally to a point of biography, he expresses a hope that Bridges, in amplifying his memoir of 1893, will revise the implication "that the poet was always depressed and unhappy in Dublin" for "this, I have good grounds to know, gives a quite misleading impression of Father Hopkins' Dublin career."[32] Generous as before, Keating here did pioneering work on textual variants and on biography.

In September 1915 the *Month*, under Keating's editorship, first published a "new" Hopkins poem, "Nondum." Indexed as "By the late Rev. Gerard Hopkins (?)," a footnote explains the text's provenance: "The above verses, dated 1866, were found in a second-hand classical book, lately published in Dublin. They are in the handwriting of the late Father Gerard Hopkins, S.J., and on the inner evidence of style may perhaps be attributed to his composition."[33] The *Month* printed all nine verses of the poem which, of course, is now accepted as genuine.

From 1915 until the publication of *Poems* in 1918, Hopkins received only passing comment from English Jesuits. In 1916, for example, C. C. Martindale, S.J., commented in the *Dublin Review* that "the Jesuit poet, Gerard Hopkins, . . . is, astonishingly, more pessimistic over 'the blight man was born for' even than Rimbaud."[34] But by this time Irish and American Jesuits had begun to notice and write about Hopkins. In Dublin the journal *Studies*, newly founded by the Jesuits, commented on Hopkins in a 1912 review of Katherine Brégy's *The Poets' Chantry*. The reviewer, George O'Neill, S.J., did not esteem the poems (they included "Spring," "God's Grandeur," "Thou art indeed just, Lord," "To—— [R. B.]," and part of "The Blessed Virgin compared to the Air we Breathe"), and he agreed with Brégy that "here was an essentially minor poet" with "an eccentric and literate mannerism." He questioned her association of Hopkins with the melodic Crashaw, and found Hopkins "a tiny harp indeed, and one which was very rarely handled with deftness." Hopkins "interpreted but few phrases of human experience" and the poems were "curiously cacophonous."[35] Four years later, though, the Jesuit editors of *Studies* published a warmer tribute—Joyce Kilmer's poem "Father Gerard Hopkins, S.J."—which celebrated him as an "austere, ecstatic craftsman" and effusively addressed him as "O bleeding feet, with peace and glory shod! / O happy moth, that flew into the Sun!"[36]

In the United States the Jesuit journal *America* first recognized Hopkins in early 1918, some months before the publication of *Poems*. In a bombastic and inept essay—so bad as to be comic—Aloysius J. Hogan, S.J., introduces the poet as "Gerald Stanley Hopkins" and writes that his "truly exquisite poetry" comes from a man "whose lips had been purified by the fire of true poetry, and whose soul was burning with an ardent faith." The young Hogan (he was not yet a priest) then gratuitously asserted that Hopkins's year with Newman at the Oratory School was "joyous beyond telling, for both were living again the romance of religion." Similar effusions ensue: "true Catholic poet," "marvelous spontaneity," "true poet," "true nature poet," "enchanting images that are beautifully profuse," "into his musical ear nature had whispered her sweetest harmonies." An occasional Hopkins quotation provides Hogan's sole saving grace, and near the end he offers but one criticism: "His excessive fondness for unusual words caused a certain obscurity to creep into his later poems."[37] American Jesuit criticism did not start well.

The most important Hopkins event of 1918, in any case, is the publication of *Poems of Gerard Manley Hopkins*, edited with a preface and notes by Robert Bridges. This landmark volume received wide Jesuit notice in England, Ireland, and the United States, but its reviews date from 1919 and belong to the next decade.

1919 TO 1928: EARLY REACTIONS TO *POEMS*

The first review of *Poems* appeared in the *Glasgow Herald* on 2 January,[38] and the Jesuits soon recognized the volume both in Jesuit journals and in Jesuit reviews. The first Jesuit-related review appropriately appeared in the March 1919 issue of the *Month* (edited by Joseph Keating, S.J.), written by the Anglo-American poet Louise Imogen Guiney. Published as a ten-page article rather than a mere book review, the length indicated Keating's continuing championship of Hopkins. In her review Guiney noted the poet's "almost purely Saxon" vocabulary and his "daring, originality, [and] durable texture." "Nothing is derivative," she writes, but she finds several poems—including the first part of "The Wreck of the Deutschland"—"the darkest of riddles." After commenting on

Hopkins's rhythm and diction, she ends positively: Hopkins has won "certain immortality."[39]

In the next issue (April 1919) the *Month* ran "Gerard Hopkins and Digby Dolben," a pietistic memoir of their Oxford friendship,[40] and one month later reprinted (from the *Irish Monthly* of 1898) the poem "Rosa Mystica," which Bridges had omitted from *Poems* for its "exaggerated Marianism." Here Keating again noted the poem's textual variants: "there are no less than six variants" of one couplet, and "the original MS. of the poet, which is in our hands, shows that it was only by dint of frequent change that he finally attained the perfect result."[41]

In the United States *America* reviewed *Poems* on 1 March 1919; the reviewer was Theodore Maynard, a layman, poet, biographer, and historian of minor fame. Reflecting Bridges's criticisms, he begins with Hopkins's faults — "the most densely obscure poet . . . in English" — but notes how most oddities disappear when the poem is read aloud and as a typical poem quotes "Patience, hard thing!" Most of the review deals with biography, and Maynard draws the strange conclusion that "the finest poem, to my mind, . . . was when he burnt his manuscripts upon entering the Jesuit novitiate at Roehampton."[42]

The Jesuit reviews were also diverse. In the *Tablet* Geoffrey Bliss, S.J., attacked Bridges's emphasis on oddity and obscurity, holding that "new things are apt to seem odd at first, and this poetry is a new poetry." He celebrates Hopkins's rare ability to fuse word, sound, cadence, and meaning; he discusses sprung rhythm with clarity, and affirms that alliteration "is of the very texture of Hopkins' verse." "Gerard Hopkins works his words hard," says Bliss, "but he 'pays them extra' in the revelation of what they can be made to accomplish." Pondering Hopkins's treatment of God, man, and nature ("all poets, of course, serve these shrines"), he offers a summary of Hopkins's vision that for 1919 is acute:

> For this poet it is in God's *mastery,* his creator-hood, above all, that he finds at once terror and joy. Yet he has also a most intimate sense of God's fatherly tenderness, and can speak to him with the direct simplicity of a son to an earthly father. In man it is, well, just humanity that he loves, its frailness, its beauty, the frailness of its beauty, so easily, so piteously brought to foulness and corruption. Yet this is no minor key. There is a most refreshing strength and manliness in this, the principal side of Hopkins' poetry; and his recurrent word is that the labile fairness of human things becomes immutable as diamonds if it is rendered to the Giver. In nature it was her pied raiment (his own adjective) that he loved best, her contrasts, her million-fold play of light and colour, gleam and gloom, sally and recovery.[43]

In this review Bliss shows himself an extraordinary literary critic.

Across the Irish Sea, *Studies* assigned the review to George O'Neill, S.J., a professor at University College, Dublin. Hopkins's "exquisitely refined literary sense," he writes in the June issue, "permitted him to lapse into nearly every literary fault." Influenced by Bridges's strictures, O'Neill writes of the "far-fetched phrases and queerly-assorted vocables" and of his "hard-knotted and sometimes quite insoluble syntax," providing illustrations from the poems. After adding some complimentary phrases— "unusual merits," "very genuine poetic gift," "magic of expression"—he ends this largely negative review by noting both Hopkins's "Catholic thought" and poignant "expressions of human suffering."[44]

In August 1919 another Irish Jesuit (and former colleague at University College) wrote a warmer appreciation. Matthew Russell, S.J., editor of the *Irish Monthly*, rejoiced that Hopkins's poetry "is at last beginning to receive the serious attention it merits." After a few personal memories— "his winning and very lovable character, bright and animated almost to boyishness, brought him many friends"— Russell praised the poetry which, "for all its strangeness and its tangled passages, stands out in refreshing contrast to the derivative, groove-confined verses which make up a large part of the output of modern English poets." Bridges's introduction he judges too negative and too unsympathetic to Hopkins's religious tradition, but Russell offers little analysis of Hopkins's strengths. Yet the essay offers both a personal and a poetic tribute to a Jesuit friend.[45]

Review by review, notice by notice, Hopkins's reputation gradually grew, soon bringing a short memoir written by his contemporary, Clement Barraud, S.J. Writing in the *Month*—surely by then *the* premier Hopkins journal—Barraud, who shared with Hopkins an interest in music, art, and literature, began with the ambiguous sentence, "Having had the joy of his friendship, I will jot down here a few personal reminiscences of this odd but gifted man, with whom I was in constant intercourse whilst we studied philosophy and theology together." After describing Hopkins ("a slight man, with a narrow face, prominent chin and nose, brown hair") and manner ("somewhat girlish"), he wrote that "he was a delightful companion, full of high spirits and innocent fun." His nature descriptions were admirable, thought Barraud, and his poems "full of tremendous power, yet rough and often rudely grotesque." Several nasty phrases follow, perhaps implying some personal animus: "the grotesque had an overbearing attraction for this Michael Angelo of verse," and, "Well I heard the bard himself read parts of 'The Wreck of the Deutschland,' which he was writing at the time, and could hardly understand one line of it." Barraud then ended the essay with a jaundiced accolade: "I once wrote to my friend [Hopkins] from Demerara [British Guiana], describing the Feast of Lanterns, as celebrated there by the resident Chinese. His reply was a learned disquisition on Chinese music, God save the mark! discussing its peculiar tonality, and claiming for it merits which had certainly escaped my observation. Everything bizarre had a charm for this whimsical genius. But the pure gold in his work, to use Patmore's image, more than reconciles us to the plentiful and unlovely quartz."[46] So ends Barraud's essay, arch in tone and ambiguous in attitude; was the writer perhaps jealous at this first sign of public acclamation?

After the reviews and comments of 1919, publications on Hopkins grew somewhat fewer. In 1920 the *Dublin Review* devoted twenty-nine pages to Hopkins, with nine pages of diary extracts provided by Keating.[47] In 1925 two American undergraduate journals, at the Jesuits' Boston College and Georgetown College, printed student essays on Hopkins.[48] And in 1928 the young Gerald F. Lahey, S.J., Hopkins's biographer-to-be, published "Gerard Manley Hopkins" in *America*; mostly biographical, it was at best a preparation for his book of 1930. With little literary analysis, Lahey's essay reacts defensively to Bridges's "necessarily distorted view of his life and religious ideals"; it also indicates Lahey's original research for the biography, for he writes that he had grown "to love talking with Hopkins' pupils and silver-haired contemporaries."[49]

1929 TO 1938: NEW CRITICISM,
WITH A FIRST BOOK AND OLD MEMORIES

In Hopkins studies the 1930s mark an era of both new interest and mature literary criticism. I. A. Richards's *Practical Criticism* (1929) and William Empson's *Seven Types of Ambiguity* (1930) stimulated critical interest in the poet; 1930 also brought the second (and expanded) edition of *Poems*, edited by Charles Williams. In 1931 a British critic noted "a revival of interest in Hopkins,"[50] and in 1932 came a notable defense of him in F. R. Leavis's *New Bearings in English Poetry*. Jesuit writers, both amateur and skilled, soon responded to this new tradition, but even before the New Critics took up the cause, a Canadian Jesuit was at work on the first book fully devoted to Hopkins.

Published in 1930 (four years before the author was ordained a priest), G. F. Lahey's *Gerard Manley Hopkins* drew on Keating's work,[51] and on Lahey's own research and interviews; however, he rarely mentioned New Criticism (108). In what he called "this little study" (147 pages of text, with excessive quotations) the author combined biography and criticism; beginning with Hopkins's early love of beauty, he stressed "the evolution of his character [which] is peculiarly fascinating" (vii, 3), and then treated Hopkins's friendships (with Newman, Patmore, and Dixon), his craft (mainly rhythm), and his poetic art. The forty pages on Hopkins's poetry comment on his prosody (sprung rhythm, rhythmic variety), his obscurity (tmesis, omitted pronouns, word-order), and some similarities to other poets. Recognizing Hopkins's originality, Lahey briefly analyzes "The Windhover" (102–4, 116–17) but scants most other poems. Like Keating, Lahey treats Bridges generously: "The staunch love and the highest literary appreciation of [Hopkins] . . . prevented Dr. Bridges from flooding an unappreciating and uncomprehending literary public with the rays of so original a source of pure poetry, so that he bided his time and with careful discrimination slowly educated his future readers with selections given to anthologies" (16). Even Bridges's prejudice against Catholicism is muted by affirming Bridges's friendship and by noting that the editor's "mind has been led into regions which, perhaps, are beyond the scope of any critic no matter how great" (17). Lahey can disagree with other critics — as on the burning of Patmore's "Sponsa Dei" (66–68) — but he is more an enthusiast than an analyst. His conclusion is valid, though wordy: Hopkins's "peculiar interest comes from the perennial source of surprises which meet any reader however well-informed; his peculiar greatness lies in the amazing union of intellectual profundity with great emotional intensity and imaginative power, under the control of a highly developed faculty of expression and structural perfection" (88).

Lahey sometimes uses an original detail or two — at the Oratory School Hopkins caught frogs and newts for classroom use (47) — but he generally summarizes anonymous sources. Footnotes are rare (in the fashion of the era), but Lahey also makes errors of fact: a wrong birthdate for Hopkins (1, 148), misattribution of one poem and of the "star of Balliol" accolade (30–32, 139), and misstatement of his post at Mount St. Mary's (140). Some statements are misleading (Hopkins's theology course is called "successful" [132]),[52] and Lahey wrongly writes that Hopkins's pain in Dublin "did not in any degree eclipse his peace and happiness" (140). Some assertions rest on questionable evidence, as when he called Hopkins a mystic "on the bleak heights of spiritual night with his God" (142–43). Nevertheless, this groundbreaking study, though defensive and even mistaken, was valuable and original for its time.[53]

More interesting today than Lahey's book are some of his research notes. This material, deposited in 1986 in the Jesuit archives in London, offers new insights into Hopkins's life and personality. In one document the well-known and wise Joseph Rickaby, S.J., a classmate of Hopkins, writes of their days together at St. Beuno's: "I was a great friend of Gerard. We went long walks together [sic], and conversed intimately. Being a genius, he was a difficult man to describe. He was highly original, even whimsical, and said and did odd things. But he was an excellent Religious and thorough Catholic. He was perhaps the most popular man in the house. Superiors and equals, everybody liked him. We laughed at him a good deal, but he took it good-humouredly, and joined in the amusement." "Though a poet and peculiar," continues Rickaby, "he was anything but silly. He had a good solid judgment, and was accounted the best moral theologian in the class. In speculative theology he was a strong Scotist" — a quality that led to Hopkins's "failure" in his third-year theology examination. Towards the end of his letter Rickaby offers a general evaluation: "I cannot say he was a success either as a teacher or a missioner [parish-priest]. He was too whimsical, and too tender-hearted towards the miseries of the poor. His place would have been at Oxford, had Campion

Hall been then started. . . . He would have been a great success, and made a name in the University, for he was still remembered at Balliol. But he was too delicate a mind for a good deal of the rough work that we have to do in the Society." Recalling Hopkins's unhappiness in Dublin, Rickaby concludes, "He died before his time, for as I knew him, he was robust and strong."[54]

Other letters add to the portrait. H. Lucas, S.J., remembers Hopkins as "a little 'odd,' " reserved, and "a very able and spiritual man."[55] Joseph Darlington, S.J., an associate in Dublin, recalls the poet in Ireland: his appearance was "ethereal" and rather "girl-like" and his conversation was "of *simple* things." Interested "in collecting Irish sayings of the poor class," Hopkins "was always full of fun and simple jokes."[56] He was "original and quaint," Darlington writes in another letter, and "everybody loved him." While denying (too defensively) that Hopkins was unhappy in Ireland, he remarks that the poet "had no sympathy with any persons who did not think England the greatest people and best in the world."[57] In later letters Darlington also affirms the depth of Hopkins's spiritual life.[58]

Other unpublished Lahey documents add more details. An interview with a former Dublin student records that the poet was "a v[ery] good religious" who was "devout and absorbed" while saying Mass (though showing "some peculiarities") but "suffered a good deal — due to temperament." In his first year (1884–85) he was depressed during meals, did not enjoy food, and was silent at recreation "because [the] talk [was] local and outside his knowledge"; to overcome this his "superiors introduced him to good people and important people to recreate him."[59] In a later unpublished essay Lahey concludes that Hopkins "did suffer all his life from the rough edges of many he met, and, though always a popular companion, sedulously guarded a well of deep reserve about himself."[60] Other Dublin memories appeared in the Jesuit-edited *A Page of Irish History* (1930), an early history of University College, Dublin, which notes Hopkins's "highly wrought temperament" and "many trials" in Ireland.[61]

Lahey's book was of mixed quality; similarly mixed are the essays in *Blandyke Papers* (1930–55), written by young Jesuit students of philosophy at Stonyhurst and Heythrop Colleges.[62] Notable are two early essays by Christopher Devlin, S.J., later a major Hopkins scholar; published in 1930 and 1931, they deal with Hopkins's poetry and with Scotus's theory of knowledge. This latter essay prepared Devlin for his more important and scholarly essay on "Hopkins and Duns Scotus" in the special Hopkins issue of *New Verse* (April 1935). In the same year Devlin wrote in *Blackfriars* on "The Ignatian Inspiration of Gerard Hopkins."[63]

During the thirties the Jesuits, stimulated by Hopkins's growing popularity, expanded their interest in the poet. In Washington the Jesuits' Georgetown University brought forth in 1931–32 a short-lived Gerard Manley Hopkins Poetry Society (complete with a journal called *Measure*).[64] Elsewhere, while such writers as Dylan Thomas, Ezra Pound,

W. H. Auden, C. Day Lewis, Louis MacNeice, Edwin Muir, Herbert Read, F. R. Leavis, R. P. Blackmur, and M. D. Zabel discussed Hopkins in essays and reviews, Jesuits wrote about him in such journals as the *Archivum Historicum Societatis Iesu, Commonweal,* the *Irish Ecclesiastical Record,* the *Month, America,* and *Thought.*[65] One essay of 1932 well summarizes the Jesuits' response: "Somewhat . . . to the surprise . . . of the English Province of the Society of Jesus, the general public are being told by the best critics of the day and by the chief important national reviews that a Jesuit, who died over forty years ago, named Gerard Manley Hopkins, must be regarded as one of England's great poets."[66]

More Jesuit essays developed from the publication of Hopkins's prose: *The Letters of Gerard Manley Hopkins to Robert Bridges* (1935, ed. C. C. Abbott), *The Correspondence of Gerard Manley Hopkins and Richard Watson Dixon* (1935, ed. C. C. Abbott), *The Note-Books and Papers of Gerard Manley Hopkins* (1937, ed. H. House), and *Further Letters of Gerard Manley Hopkins* (1938, ed. C. C. Abbott). In the *Month* Joseph Keating, S.J., praised Abbott's editions of the letters to Bridges and Dixon, and published the autograph of "Rosa Mystica" with Hopkins's authorial changes. But he also argued that Bridges, Dixon, *and* Abbott, since they were not Catholics, could understand neither Hopkins's poetry nor his dedication to God: "To picture the poet as tossed and strained by anxiety as to whether he was not absolutely right in subordinating his high natural gifts to the supernatural purposes of his priestly life, is to ascribe to him an ignorance of spiritual conditions that would shame the veriest beginner." Keating does recognize the sympathy and good will of Bridges, Dixon, and Abbott—though he is rankled by Bridges's dislike of "medievalism" ("*i.e.,* Catholicism," writes Keating) — and this essay is more defensive than those of earlier years.[67]

Across the Atlantic defensiveness also prevails, as in an essay of J. J. Daly, S.J., in *Thought:* "Certain writers . . . agreed that, whatever its merits, [the Society of Jesus] could not produce a great poet. And then suddenly Gerard Manley Hopkins was sprung upon them by leading literary critics as a major poet of the nineteenth century." Yet, he continues,

> the Jesuits . . . were not allowed to enjoy a triumph over the prophets. . . . Why did they receive the young poet into their Society? . . . Why did they allow him to bury his genius in the pursuit of their strange spiritual ideals? Why for so many years did they subject him to the common discipline and burden him with occupations of a dray-horse kind? Why did they never accord him the recognition he deserved? And so on, and so on. . . . Thus we arrive at an interesting conclusion. If the Jesuits produce no poet, they are scorned. And, if they produce a poet, they are scorned. You would think Hopkins was a Jesuit asset: he turns out to be a Jesuit liability.[68]

Even granted the anti-Catholic prejudice of the 1930s and the inability of some writers to reconcile priest and poet, such defensiveness was unfortunate. But in the 1930s Jesuit scholarship on Hopkins also came of age — Christopher Devlin is a notable example — and in 1936 two longtime Jesuit critics maintained an admirable perspective as they questioned whether Hopkins was a "major" or "great" poet. Joseph Keating, S.J., concluded that "the meagreness of his output would debar him from being recognized as a major poet," and Geoffrey Bliss, S.J., thought that "Hopkins will be 'great' for all time to poets, as Donne and Crashaw are, but not perhaps to the general bulk of men. I've an idea, too, that a considerable mass of output greater than Hopkins' is necessary for the attainment of the status of *a great poet*."[69] Such careful judgments show that Jesuits can admire and yet judge objectively, and thenceforth a number of Jesuits stand among the finest Hopkins scholars.

1939 TO 1988: MATURE SCHOLARSHIP AND REFLECTION

The last fifty years manifest a mature and objective scholarship among Jesuits, and show an easier confidence in both Hopkins and in his religious traditions as Catholic and as Jesuit. The Jesuit scholarship of these years is fairly well known to both scholars and lovers of Hopkins, and a brief treatment suffices, ordered first under authors (by birthdate) and then under some broader categories.

In 1939 Martin D'Arcy, S. J., published a balanced essay on Hopkins's personality and on his interconnection of body, mood, and spirit.[70] Similarly Christopher Devlin, S.J., building on his early work on Hopkins as a Scotist, matured into the painstaking and careful editor of Hopkins's *Sermons and Devotional Writings* (1939).[71] In the late 1940s Anthony Bischoff, S.J., discovered unknown Hopkins manuscripts, collected invaluable material for a biography, and in 1947 unearthed in Dublin a copy of Hopkins's will, resolving a longstanding legal question about copyright.[72] From a different language tradition the Dutch Jesuit W. A. M. Peters, S.J., in *Gerard Manley Hopkins: A Critical Essay towards the Understanding of His Poetry* (1948), argued that Hopkins's style grew out of both his worldview and his theory of poetry; years later Peters again returned to the poet in *Gerard Manley Hopkins: A tribute* (1984).[73]

In 1949 a young Walter Ong, S.J., published a well received essay on Hopkins's sprung rhythm; nearly forty years later, drawing on contemporary theories of language and literature, he published an equally well received study of Hopkins's view of self: *Hopkins, the Self, and God* (1986).[74] A fellow American, Robert Boyle, S.J., stressed Hopkins's literary dimensions in various reviews and essays, and devoted his book *Metaphor in Hopkins* (1961) to the poet's close linking of metaphor (and rhythm) with God.[75] An unusually prolific Jesuit scholar was the Englishman Alfred Thomas, S.J., cofounder (with Tom Dunne and Norman White) of

The Hopkins Society in 1969. He edited most of the issues of the *Hopkins Research Bulletin* (an annual, 1970–76), helped arrange The Hopkins Society's Annual Lecture and Annual Sermon, and collected funds for the Hopkins Memorial in Westminster Abbey's Poets' Corner; his essays appear in diverse journals and he is best known for his positivist biography *Hopkins the Jesuit: The Years of Training* (1969).[76] Finally, Peter Milward, S.J., an Englishman teaching in Japan's Sophia University, stimulated Hopkins studies in Japan; he is best known for his textual commentary in *Landscape and Inscape: Vision and Inspiration in Hopkins' Poetry* (1975) and he edited *Readings of* The Wreck (1976) for the centenary of *The Wreck of the Deutschland*.[77]

Besides these major scholars other Jesuit items merit a note. Several places are dedicated to Hopkins: preeminently the Hopkins-manuscript room at Oxford's Campion Hall, but also the Hopkins Room (and Collection) at Spokane's Gonzaga University, Hopkins House at Boston College, and Hopkins Hall, the residence for Jesuit graduate students at the University of Chicago. Two Hopkins centennials also deserve notice. In 1944 the centennial of Hopkins's birth was marked by *Immortal Diamond: Studies in Gerard Manley Hopkins*, a book of uneven essays, all by Jesuits, edited by Norman Weyand, S.J. (wartime conditions delayed publication until 1949).[78] The centennial was also commemorated—on time despite the war—by Jesuits and others in England, Ireland, New Zealand, and the United States.[79]

In 1975 came the centennial of "The Wreck of the Deutschland"; it was celebrated not only by the Milward collection but also by a special issue of the *Month* devoted to the poem. There the Jesuit editors, in a most gracious and graceful apology, made amends for their hundred-year-old mistake: "Few periodicals live long enough to regret a major literary blunder a century old. But there it is. One hundred years have passed by since Hopkins submitted his greatest poem to the Editor of the *Month* and had it rejected. And it has to be admitted, as we bite on the bullet, that one unwise blunder has gained for the *Month* more notoriety than all the distinguished articles it has wisely published." But, continue the Editors, "confession . . . is good for the soul, and we are glad to be still around in this centenary year, prepared to make a clean breast of our misdeeds, delighted to join whole-heartedly in the celebration of a poem which is perhaps destined to survive all the journals and periodicals that are household names today."[80]

1989: THE CENTENNIAL

As 1989 nears, Jesuits and their institutions in the English-speaking world look to commemorate Hopkins on the centenary of his death. His native Province plans commemorations at Oxford, St. Beuno's, and London. Oxford's Campion Hall will devote the 1988–89 D'Arcy Lectures to Hopkins; offered to the university at large during the Michaelmas term 1988, these prestigious lectures will be given by Norman H. MacKenzie, dean of Hopkins scholars and the series' first non-Jesuit lecturer. Furthermore the Bodleian Library, the world's premier repository of Hopkins manuscripts, will present a Hopkins exhibition during the summer of 1989, at the initiative of the Master of Campion Hall.[81] At St. Beuno's the Rock Chapel will be restored by the Province, and in May 1989 St. Beuno's will host the Welsh Academy as it devotes its annual conference to the centennial. In June Paul Edwards, S.J., will lecture there to the North Wales Arts Association; in late summer St. Beuno's will host the village of Tremeirchion for tea; and at the end of September the Jesuits of St. Beuno's will work with the North Wales Music Festival as it presents, in the nearby small cathedral city of St. Asaph, a Hopkins exhibition and a commemoration of him in word and music.[82] In London, finally, the *Month* will devote part of its own 125th-anniversary issue in 1989 to an essay, by Jerome Bump, on its varied amends to Hopkins after its 1876 rejection of *The Wreck of the Deutschland*.[83]

In Dublin the Irish Jesuits propose to hold a small exhibition of Hopkins material from the Province archives; these holdings include the manuscripts of the poems "St. Thecla" and "In Theclam Virginem." They hope also to beautify his burial-place in Glasnevin Cemetery and, with University College, Dublin, to sponsor a Mass in University Church followed by a wreath-laying and poetry-reading at Hopkins's grave.[84] Japan, too, will have its part: in 1989 Peter Milward, S.J., of Tokyo's Sophia University, will guide a Japanese study group through Hopkins sites in England, Ireland, Scotland, and Wales.[85] And from Rome the annual Jesuit *Year Book*, published for a worldwide audience, will commemorate Hopkins in its 1989 edition.[86]

The United States, for its part, will have Jesuit-related celebrations, many involving Jesuits as contributors; I record here only those which at the time of writing have passed from hope to plan. Symposia on Hopkins are scheduled at Georgetown University (as part of its Bicentennial celebration, with a concert of Hopkins-related music), and at Canisius College and Loyola University of Chicago. Special lectures are planned at Saint Joseph's University, Loyola College in Maryland, Xavier University, and Creighton University (including its Honors Lecture in spring, 1989); students will take Hopkins courses or seminars at Saint Joseph's, Loyola of Maryland (with Peter Milward, S.J., of Japan, as visiting professor), and Loyola Marymount University. At Marquette University the journal *Renascence* will publish a special issue on Hopkins, and Gonzaga University will mount a special exhibition from its Crosby Library's well-known Hopkins Collection.

Hopkins will also be memorialized in art, drama, and academic spectacle. Loyola of Chicago will present Peter Gale's one-man play *"Hopkins!"*; a new one-man play, *Immortal Diamond*, written by William

Van Etten Casey, S.J., takes the stage at Boston College and the College of the Holy Cross (several other productions are also likely). Two universities—Loyola Marymount and Santa Clara—look to the art of Michael Tang, S.J., for their celebrations; in his "Hopkins Series," Tang, fascinated by Hopkins's "spiritual/sensual" evocations of nature and his "linguistic rhythms," has tried to recreate Hopkins's innovations in a three-dimensional art, using (as his correlative innovations) "appropriate foreign materials: plexiglass, wood, glitter, branches" together with the traditional pigment.[87] Among the Jesuit celebrations, finally, one event will offer a gracious academic tribute: in the spring of 1989 Saint Joseph's University will confer an honorary doctorate on the Hopkins scholar and text-editor Norman H. MacKenzie.[88]

In this Jesuit context one other celebration merits note—an exhibition on Hopkins and his influence, running from June through September 1989 at the Harry Ransom Humanities Research Center of the University of Texas at Austin. For this exhibition twenty-seven Jesuits have so far contributed information or promised material; Jesuits have also promised original paintings, collages, photographs, slides, essays, books, music, film and a play. By the end of October 1987, the curator, Carl Sutton, had gathered over 1500 individual items from all six inhabited continents; with its focus on Hopkins's influence after his death, this exhibition will thus eloquently justify its title, *Hopkins Lives*.[89]

After about twenty-one Jesuit years in life and one hundred years in death, Hopkins lives also in the minds and memories of Jesuits. A sensitive man, in his Jesuit life Hopkins loved greatly, rejoiced greatly, and suffered greatly. After his death he was remembered as holy and eccentric, funny and pained, a faithful friend, a quintessential Englishman, a champion of the young and the poor. Then bit by bit Jesuit memories transmuted him from friend to poet, and with varied motives and diverse talents Jesuits began to compose memoirs, biographies, and literary criticism. Some liked his poetry, some did not. Some wrote to counter religious prejudice, some manifested it. Some were defensive, believing that only Jesuits could understand Hopkins; others trusted the facts of his life and work. In 1909 one fine Jesuit tried to edit his poems and proclaim his genius, and decades later several Jesuits became world-recognized Hopkins scholars. And gradually Jesuits came so to know and esteem his poems that Hopkins-phrases have entered their everyday vocabulary in book titles, conversations, sermons, lectures, parodies, jokes, and prayers. Hopkins has by now affected Jesuit language and consciousness, and has provided words that with rare accuracy and flamelike power express the Jesuit view of the world.

It was thus curiously appropriate that in 1970 a Jesuit Superior General celebrated Hopkins in the same London pulpit where the poet (according to an old story) had once stood and in all seriousness talked comic-wonderfully of the church-as-cow feeding the world with the milk of seven sacraments.[90] In that Farm Street pulpit Pedro Arrupe, S.J., publicly praised the Victorian poet and publicly ratified that world-affirming "vision which was shared by your English Jesuit poet, Gerard Manley Hopkins, who saw the glory and grandeur of God flashing out from the created world."[91] Among Jesuits surely, after one century, Hopkins is yet well recognized, Hopkins is yet alive.

Notes

1. Anon., *Nation* (15 June 1889), 8. For my data on the obituaries I rely on the research collection of the late Alfred Thomas, S.J., now in the British Province Archives, London.

2. Anon., "Death of the Rev. Gerard Hopkins, S.J., M.A., F.R.U.I.," *Freeman's Journal* (10 June 1889), 5. "F.R.U.I." means "Fellow of the Royal University of Ireland"; the Royal University was only a group of examiners. Classes were offered by University College, Dublin, on whose faculty Hopkins served.

3. Anon., "The Late Rev. Gerald [*sic*] Hopkins, S.J., F.R.U.I.," *Irish Times* (12 June 1889), 3; Anon., "Funeral of the Rev. Gerard Hopkins S.J., F.R.U.I.," *Freeman's Journal* (12 June 1889), 6.

4. Anon., "Death of Rev. Gerard Hopkins, S.J.," *Tablet* 73 (15 June 1889):936.

5. Anon., "Obituary. Gerard Manley Hopkins," *Cholmeleian* 16 (1889):179.

6. *Freeman's Journal,* (12 June 1889), 6.

7. Quoted in Graham Storey, "Preface," in *The Journals and Papers of Gerard Manley Hopkins*, ed. Humphry House (London: Oxford University Press, 1959), x–xi. The Jesuit in London would have been Arthur Knight, S.J., who as assistant to the English Provincial would have charge of such matters; this same Fr. Knight wrote the Latin epitaph mentioned below.

8. Claude Colleer Abbott, "Preface," in *The Letters of Gerard Manley Hopkins to Robert Bridges*, ed. C. C. Abbott (London: Oxford University Press, 1955), vi; Storey, "Preface," xii–xiii. Hopkins's sisters also burnt, unread, one diary on which Hopkins had written, "*Please do not open this*" (Storey, "Preface," xiv).

9. Storey, "Preface," xv.

10. "Prov. Angl. S.J. Register," ms. in the British Province Archives, London, p. 378; translation mine. The author was Arthur Knight, S.J., assistant to the Provincial; see my "Gerard Manley Hopkins, His Jesuit Contemporaries, and the Epitaph Master: Notes on Arthur Knight, S.J.," (London) *Letters and Notices* (henceforth *LLNN*) 85 (1983):285–96.

11. Anon., "Father Gerard Hopkins," in my "Hopkins' Earliest Memorial: The Jesuit Obituary of 1890." *Hopkins Quarterly* 8 (1981):54–56.

12. Tom Dunne, *Gerard Manley Hopkins: A Comprehensive Bibliography* (Oxford: Clarendon Press, 1976), 3–6; I treat "A Trio of Triolets" as one poem.

13. *The Poems of Gerard Manley Hopkins*, ed. W. H. Gardner and N. H. MacKenzie (Oxford: Oxford University Press, 1970), 254, 283; Norman H. MacKenzie, *A Reader's Guide to Gerard Manley Hopkins* (Ithaca: Cornell University Press, 1981), 27, 28, 59–60, 101, 157. On the editor of the *Month* (Henry Coleridge, S.J.) as Hopkins's "oldest friend in the Society," see *Further Letters of Gerard Manley Hopkins*, ed. C. C. Abbott (London: Oxford University Press, 1956), 138.

14. *Letters to Bridges*, 196–97. Splaine was a classmate of Hopkins and was also with him at Stonyhurst from 1882 to 1884; he was remembered for his gentleness, kindness, sensitive nature, and skill in moral theology—traits he shared with Hopkins; see his obituary, Anon., "Father Cyprian Splaine," *LLNN* 21 (1891–92): 515–16. Bacon, like Hopkins a

convert from Anglicanism, was with him during one year of Novitiate at Roehampton (1868–69), one year of philosophy at Stonyhurst (1870–71), and one year of theology at St. Beuno's (1874–75); see his obituary, Anon., "Father Francis Edward Bacon," *LLNN* 38 (1923):247–54. Bacon's papers were unfortunately destroyed during World War II (Norman H. MacKenzie, "The Lost Autograph of *The Wreck of the Deutschland* and Its First Readers," *Hopkins Quarterly* 3 [1976]:109–10).

15. *Letters to Bridges*, 292–93; Matthew Russell, S.J., "Poets I Have Known, No. 5. — Katharine Tynan," *Irish Monthly* 31 (1903):259–61; Katharine Tynan, "Father Matthew Russell, S.J.: Dearest of Friends,," *Irish Monthly* 40 (1912):555.

16. *Irish Monthly* 26 (1898):234–35; on Russell's editorship, see the note to "Rosa Mystica" in the *Month* 133 (1919):339.

17. *Letters to Bridges*, 196–97.

18. The journals were *Blandyke Papers* and *Stonyhurst Magazine;* see Dunne, *Bibliography*, 6–11, and MacKenzie, *Reader's Guide*, 27. Dunne lists the poems in the anthologies.

19. "The Diary of a Devoted Student of Nature," ed. J. G. MacLeod, *LLNN* 28 (1905–6):390–91. MacLeod was with Hopkins at Roehampton, 1873–74; see his obituary, Anon., "Father John George MacLeod," *LLNN* 32 (1913–14):568–70.

20. For a brief memoir of Keating (1865–1939) see his obituary, Anon., "Fr. Joseph Keating," *LLNN* 54 (1939):135–46, 176–78; longtime editor of the *Month* (assistant, 1907–1912; editor, 1912–39), he was kind, humorous, a lover of poetry, and committed to social justice for the poor.

21. Humphry House, "Preface," in *The Note-Books and Papers of Gerard Manley Hopkins*, ed. Humphry House (London: Oxford University Press, 1937), xii–xiii. Regarding 1908, see the date of the O'Donohoe letter (xiv).

22. Storey, "Preface," xv.

23. Jean-Georges Ritz, *Robert Bridges and Gerard Hopkins, 1863–1889: A Literary Friendship* (London: Oxford University Press, 1960), 160–63, esp. 160 n. A briefer treatment appears in Ritz's *Le Poète Gérard Manley Hopkins, S.J., 1844–1889: L'Homme et l'Oeuvre* (Paris: Didier, 1963), 25–26.

24. See Storey, "Preface," xi; and Ritz, *Le Poète*, 26; in *Robert Bridges and Gerard Hopkins* Ritz notes that Hopkins's Jesuit will, dated 1878, was registered in the High Court of Justice, Dublin, on 13 July 1889 (162 n).

25. Joseph Keating, S.J., "Impressions of Father Gerard Hopkins, S.J.," *Month* 114 (1909):59–60. Further references in the text.

26. Katherine Brégy, "Gerard Hopkins: An Epitaph and an Appreciation," *Catholic World*, 88 (1908–09):433–47, reprinted with few changes in her *The Poets' Chantry* (St. Louis: Herder, 1912), 70–88. For this book, Fr. Keating provided her a photograph of Hopkins (p. 81).

27. Ritz, *Robert Bridges and Gerard Hopkins*, 161 n.

28. *Poems*, 253; MacKenzie, *Reader's Guide*, 27.

29. House, "Preface," xi, xiii, xxxv.

30. Anon., "Manresa House, Roehampton," *LLNN* 30 (1909–10):391, 468.

31. Joseph Keating, S.J., "Catholic Poets," review of *The Poets' Chantry*, by Katherine Brégy, *Month* 120 (1912):439.

32. Joseph Keating, S.J., "The Poetry of Father Gerard Hopkins, S.J.," *Month* 121 (1913):643–44.

33. "Nondum," *Month* 126 (1915):246–47. For evidence that Keating was editor of the *Month* and thus presumably of the poem, see pp. iii, iv, 123, 416.

34. C. C. Martindale, S.J., "Anthologia Laureata," review of *The Spirit of Man*, edited by Robert Bridges, *Dublin Review* 158 (1916):261.

35. George O'Neill, S.J., "A Poet's Chantry," review of Katherine Brégy's *The Poets' Chantry*, *Studies* (Dublin) 1 (1912):736–37.

36. Joyce Kilmer, "Father Gerard Hopkins, S.J.," (Dublin) *Studies* 5 (1916):106.

37. Aloysius J. Hogan, S.J., "Father Hopkins' Poetry," *America* 18 (1918):477–78. According to the 1918 Catalogue of the Maryland-New York Province, Hogan (b. 1891) was then teaching at Boston College.

38. For the reviews see Dunne, *Bibliography*, 14–18, and Elgin W. Mellown, "The Reception of Gerard Manley Hopkins' Poems, 1919–1930," *Modern Philology* 63 (1965):38–51.

39. Louise Imogen Guiney, "Gerard Hopkins: A Recovered Poet," *Month* 133 (1919):205–14. Keating's editorship is clear from [Contents] and 13.

40. E. M. Harting, "Gerard Hopkins and Digby Dolben," *Month* 133 (1919):285–89.

41. "Rosa Mystica," *Month* 133 (1919):339–40.

42. Theodore Maynard, "The Solitary of Song," *America* 20 (1918–19):533–34.

43. Anon., "Gerard Hopkins' Poems," *Tablet* 133 (5 April 1919):420, 422. For the identity of the reviewer see Dunne, *Bibliography*, 16–17. After Bliss's death in 1952 his obituary noted, "He should have written more about G. M. Hopkins; he could have done" (L. Boase, "Father Geoffrey Bliss," in *Our Dead: Memoirs of the English Jesuits Who Died between January, 1949 and December, 1953* [London: Manresa, 1954–56], 340).

44. George O'Neill, S.J., "Poetry," *Studies* (Dublin) 8 (1919):331–35. In a footnote O'Neill graciously adds, "Irish readers may be reminded of Fr. Hopkins' connection with the Royal University of Ireland, during many years, as Fellow and Examiner" (332). Later that year he expanded the review into a chapter of *Essays on Poetry* (Dublin: Talbot, 1919) which has more biography, more examples, and a more sympathetic judgment of the poetry (117–38).

45. Matthew Russell, S.J., "Father Gerard Hopkins, S.J., and His Poetry," *Irish Monthly* 47 (1919):441–48.

46. C[lement] B[arraud, S.J.], "Reminiscences of Father Gerard Hopkins," *Month* 134 (1919):158–59. For him as classmate in theology (Barraud being in the "Short Course"), see *Catalogus Provinciae Angliae S.J.* (Roehampton: Manresa Press, 1875), 11, 12; (1876), 11, 12; (1877), 11, 12; on Barraud's life and interests see his obituary, Anon., "Fr. Clement Barraud," *LLNN* 41 (1926):242–43, 313–15.

47. Frederick Page *et al.*, "Father Gerard Hopkins," *Dublin Review*, 167 (1920):40–66.

48. Dunne, *Bibliography*, 172.

49. Gerald F. Lahey, S.J., *America* 39 (1928):619–20.

50. "K. R. W.," in the *Liverpool Post*, quoted in Dunne, *Bibliography*, 22. For early Hopkins criticism, see Maurice Charney, "A Bibliographical Study of Hopkins Criticism, 1918–1949," *Thought* 25 (1950):297–326.

51. House, "Preface," xi; G. F. Lahey, S.J., *Gerard Manley Hopkins* (1930; rpt. New York: Octagon, 1970), viii; further Lahey references in the text. In 1931 Lahey completed one of the earliest dissertations on Hopkins, for a Fordham M.A. (Dunne, *Bibliography*, 261).

52. On his examination "failure" see my "Hopkins' 'Failure' in Theology: Some New Archival Data and a Reevaluation," *Hopkins Quarterly* [forthcoming].

53. For reviews of Lahey, see Dunne, *Bibliography*, 53–54; see also John Pick, "In Memoriam: The Revd. Gerald F. Lahey, S.J.," *Hopkins Research Bulletin*, no. 1 (1970):22–24.

54. Letter of Joseph Rickaby, S.J., to G. F. Lahey, S.J., dated "29.ii.27"(?), in Lahey Papers (1/4/5/1), British Province Archives, London. I thank Rev. Francis Edwards, S.J., former Archivist, for his hospitality and for permission to publish.

55. Letter of H. Lucas, S.J., to G. F. Lahey, S.J., 19 April 1928, in Lahey Papers, Brit. Prov. Archives.

56. Letter of Joseph Darlington, S.J., to G. F. Lahey, S.J., 13 July 1928, in Lahey Papers, Brit. Prov. Archives.

57. Darlington to Lahey, 19 November 1928, in Lahey Papers, Brit. Prov. Archives.

58. Darlington to Lahey, 5 October 1930, 26 October 1930, 15 November 1930, in Lahey Papers, Brit. Prov. Archives.

59. Interview of Martin Maher, S.J., by G. F. Lahey, S.J., Dublin, undated, in Lahey Papers, Brit. Prov. Archives.

60. "Notes on Gerard Manley Hopkins, S.J.," typescript, June 1932, in Lahey Papers, Brit. Prov. Archives, p. 7.

61. Fathers of the Society of Jesus, *A Page of Irish History: Story of University College, Dublin, 1883–1909* (Dublin: Talbot, 1930), 106.

62. For an annotated bibliography of this material see my "The *Blandyke Papers:* An Addition to the Bibliography of Essays on Hopkins," *Hopkins Quarterly* 9 (1983):127–32.

63. Christopher Devlin, S.J., "Hopkins and Duns Scotus," *New Verse* no. 14 (1935):12–15; "The Ignatian Inspiration of Gerard Hopkins," *Blackfriars* 16 (1935):887–900.

64. Anthony Bischoff, S.J., "The First Hopkins Society?," *Hopkins Research Bulletin* No. 1 (1970):15.

65. Dunne, *Bibliography*, 56–57, 174–90.

66. Martin C. D'Arcy, S.I., "Gerard Manley Hopkins, S.I.," *Archivum Historicum Societatis Iesu* 1 (1932):118–22.

67. Joseph Keating, S.J., "Priest and Poet: Gerard Manley Hopkins in His Letters," *Month* 165 (1935):125–36. Keating is defensive in "Fr. Gerard Hopkins and *The Spiritual Exercises*" (*Month* 166 [1935]:268–70) but more relaxed in a review of H. House's edition of *The Note-Books and Papers* (*Month* 169 [1937]:175–76).

68. J. J. Daly, S.J., "Father Hopkins and the Society of Jesus," *Thought* 13 (1938):9.

69. Joseph Keating, S.J., and Geoffrey Bliss, S.J., in letters to Maurice Leahy, quoted in his "A Priest-Poet: Father Gerard Manley Hopkins, S.J.," *Irish Ecclesiastical Record* 47 (1936):363.

70. Martin D'Arcy, S.J., "Gerard Manley Hopkins," in *Great Catholics*, ed. Claude Williamson, O.S.C. (New York: Macmillan, 1939), 358–66.

71. *The Sermons and Devotional Writings of Gerard Manley Hopkins*, ed. Christopher Devlin, S.J. (London: Oxford University Press, 1959). See also Madeleine Devlin, *Christopher Devlin* (London: Macmillan, 1970); the Devlin citations in Dunne, *Bibliography;* and his obituary in *LLNN* 67 (1962):59–69.

72. D. Anthony Bischoff, "The Manuscripts of Gerard Manley Hopkins," *Thought* 26 (1951):551–80; see also the Bischoff citations in Dunne, *Bibliography*, and Storey, "Preface," xv.

73. W. A. M. Peters, S.J., *Gerard Manley Hopkins: A Critical Essay towards the Understanding of His Poetry* (London: Oxford University Press, 1948), xv–xvi; *Gerard Manley Hopkins: A Tribute* (Chicago: Loyola University Press, 1984); see also the Peters citations in Dunne, *Bibliography*.

74. Walter Ong, S.J., "Hopkins' Sprung Rhythm and the Life of English Poetry," in *Immortal Diamond*, ed. Norman Weyand, S.J. (New York: Sheed and Ward, 1949), 93–174; *Hopkins, the Self, and God* (Toronto: University of Toronto Press, 1986); see also the Ong citations in Dunne, *Bibliography*.

75. Robert Boyle, S.J., *Metaphor in Hopkins* (Chapel Hill: University of North Carolina Press, 1961), xi–xxiv; see also the Boyle citations in Dunne, *Bibliography*.

76. Anon., "The Hopkins Society," *Hopkins Research Bulletin* no. 1 (1970):25; see also *HRB* no. 6 (1975):27, 30; no. 7 (1976):19–29, and the Thomas citations in Dunne, *Bibliography*.

77. Peter Milward, S.J., and Raymond Schoder, S.J., *Landscape and Inscape: Vision and Inspiration in Hopkins's Poetry* (Grand Rapids, Mich.: Eerdmans, 1975); Peter Milward, S.J., ed. *Readings of* The Wreck: *Essays in Commemoration of the Centenary of G. M. Hopkins'* The Wreck of the Deutschland (Chicago: Loyola University Press, 1976); see also the Milward citations in Dunne, *Bibliography*.

78. *Immortal Diamond: Studies in Gerard Manley Hopkins*, ed. Norman Weyard, S.J. (1949; rpt. New York: Octagon, 1979), ix.

79. Dunne, *Bibliography*, 141, 198–206.

80. Anon., "Felicity and Perfection," *Month* 136, n.s. 8 (1975):339.

81. Letter of Philip Endean, S.J., to author, 24 February 1988.

82. Telephone interview with Gerald McLoughlin, S.J., 2 March 1988.

83. Interview with John McDade, S.J., London, 14 July 1987; letter of Kevin Fox, S.J., to author, 22 February 1988.

84. Letter to John Humphrys, S.J., to author, 2 March 1988.

85. Letter of Peter Milward, S.J., to author, 17 February 1988.

86. Letter of John J. O'Callahan, S.J., to author, 16 February 1988.

87. Michael Tang, "Hopkins Series," from the exhibition "The Inner Core," Laband Art Gallery, Loyola Marymount University, 16 September–17 October 1987.

88. Information on commemorations kindly furnished by each institution's president (or designated representative) in letters to author, 21 January–14 March 1988.

89. Letters of Carl Sutton to author, 1 November 1987 and 12 February 1988.

90. For the story, see Bernard Bergonzi, *Gerard Manley Hopkins* (New York: Collier, 1977), 95.

91. Pedro Arrope, S.J., "Homily Preached by Fr General at Farm Street Church, London . . . ," *LLNN* 75 (1970):117–19.

INDEX

Notes on Contributors

Robert Boyle, S.J., is Professor emeritus at Marquette University in Milwaukee. He is the author of *Metaphor in Hopkins* (1961), *James Joyce's Pauline Vision* (1978), and "Hopkins, Brutus and Dante," (*Victorian Poetry*, Spring 1986) as well as a contributor to *Immortal Diamond* (1949) and *The New Catholic Encyclopedia* (1967).

Jerome Bump is professor of English at the University of Texas, Austin. He is coeditor of *Texas Studies in Literature and Language*; author of *Gerard Manley Hopkins* (1982) and of essays on Hopkins in *ELH, JEGP, Renascence, Victorian Poetry, Hopkins Quarterly*; and a contributor to several anthologies and other journals. Professor Bump is the annual reviewer of Hopkins scholarship for *Victorian Poetry*, and he has delivered papers on Hopkins at the Modern Language Association and numerous other conferences.

David A. Downes is a senior professor of English at California State University, Chico. He is the author of *Gerard Manley Hopkins: A Study of his Ignatian Spirit* (1959) and *Victorian Portraits: Hopkins and Pater* (1965). He has contributed centenary essays on Hopkins to *Studies in the Literary Imagination* (Spring, 1988) and *Gerard Manley Hopkins 1844–1889: New Essays* (Edwin Mellon, 1989), and he has just finished *The Ignation Personality of Gerard Manley Hopkins* (forthcoming, 1989).

Joseph J. Feeney, S.J., is professor of English at St. Joseph's University in Philadelphia and in 1986–87 held the Jesuit chair at Georgetown University. He has published on Hopkins in the *Hopkins Quarterly, Thought*, the *Victorian Institute Journal, America, Renascence, Theological Studies*, the *Month*, and *Victorian Studies*. He has also contributed other essays to anthologies and journals in the United States, England, and Germany and has lectured on Hopkins in England, Ireland, and the United States.

Richard Giles completed his doctorate at the University of Toronto while he functioned for more than a decade as the editor of the *Hopkins Quarterly* and, later, as the coordinator of the *International Hopkins Association*, posts he still holds. He is the author of numerous articles and notes on Anglo-Saxon poetry, Donne, Marvell, Meredith, Patmore, Plath, and Hopkins. Dr. Giles is a teaching master at Mohawk College, Hamilton, Ontario.

Paul Mariani is a distinguished university professor at the University of Massachusetts, Amherst. He is the author of *A Commentary on the Complete Poems of Gerard Manley Hopkins* (1970) and *A Usable Past: Essays on Modern and Contemporary Poetry* (1984), as well as biographies of William Carlos Williams and John Berryman.

Rachel Salmon has published essays on Hopkins and Henry James and on critical theories. At present, she is working on a book on Midrashic hermeneutics both as an interpretive model and as specific theological discourse that engages the problems of paradox. Dr. Salmon teaches English and American literature and literary theory in the English Department of Bar-Ilan University, Israel.

Alison G. Sulloway, the volume editor, retired as the Senior Victorian from Virginia Polytechnic Institute. She is the author of *Gerard Manley Hopkins and the Victorian Temper* (1973), *Jane Austen and the Province of Womanhood* (1989), and numerous essays in anthologies, journals and conference proceedings on Hopkins and Austen. She has contributed five centenary essays on Hopkins in the United States and abroad.

William B. Thesing is associate chairman and professor of English at the University of South Carolina in Columbia. He is the author of *The London Muse: Victorian Poetic Responses to the City* (1982), coauthor of *English Prose and Criticism, 1900–1950* (1983) and of *Conversations with Carolina Poets* (1986), and editor of *Victorian Prose Writers Before 1867* (1987) and of *Victorian Prose Writers after 1867* (1987).

Norman White is lecturer in Modern English Literature at University College, Dublin. Dr. White was formerly Leverhulme fellow at the University of Liverpool and honorary fellow at the Institute for Advanced Study in the Humanities at the University of Edinburgh. He has published more than fifty articles on Hopkins, and he is close to completing a biography of Hopkins commissioned by the Oxford University Press.

Tom Zaniello is professor of English at Northern Kentucky University. He is the author of *Hopkins in the Age of Darwin* (1988), *Explorations in Reading and Writing* (1987) and *Cinematic Perspectives* (forthcoming from Mayfield Publishing Company, Mountain View, Calif., in 1990).